The Columbus Stocking Strangler

ALSO BY WILLIAM RAWLINGS

The Lazard Legacy (2003)

The Rutherford Cipher (2004)

The Tate Revenge (2005)

Crossword (2006)

The Mile High Club (2009)

PUBLISHED BY MERCER UNIVERSITY PRESS

A Killing on Ring Jaw Bluff (2013)

The Second Coming of the Invisible Empire (2016)

The Strange Journey of the Confederate Constitution (2017)

The Girl with Kaleidoscope Eyes (2019)

Six Inches Deeper (2020)

Lighthouses of the Georgia Coast (2021)

The Columbus

Stocking Strangler

William Rawlings

MERCER UNIVERSITY PRESS
Macon, Georgia

MUP/ P670

© 2022 by Mercer University Press
Published by Mercer University Press
1501 Mercer University Drive
Macon, Georgia 31207
All rights reserved

26 25 24 23 22   5 4 3 2 1

Books published by Mercer University Press are printed on acid-free paper
that meets the requirements of the American National Standard for
Information Sciences—Permanence of Paper for Printed Library Materials.

Printed and bound in the United States.

This book is set in ADOBE CASLON PRO.

Cover/jacket design by Burt&Burt.

ISBN   Paperback 978-0-88146-891-5
ISBN   eBook   978-0-88146-843-4
Cataloging-in-Publication Data is available from the Library of Congress

To the Memory of

Jaclyn Weldon White

1948–2021

MERCER UNIVERSITY PRESS

Endowed by

TOM WATSON BROWN

and

THE WATSON-BROWN FOUNDATION, INC.

CONTENTS

Part I

The Murders

Prologue

"One Maniac Is Changing the Town of Columbus"

From the *Charleston News and Courier*, February 5, 1978:

One maniac can make a difference. There is a maniac here, somewhere, who has made Bill Parker richer and Margaret Stevens lonelier. He has made whites suspicious of blacks and blacks angry at whites. He has cost Columbus thousands of dollars and its policemen hundreds of hours of sleep. He has driven the crime rate up and the people behind locked doors. Singlehandedly, the man known as the Columbus Stocking Strangler has altered the lifestyle of this southern Georgia city.

In the last four months, five elderly women have been strangled in their homes by an intruder who sexually assaulted them. The five deaths drove the 1977 murder rate up 16 percent. And they caused a far larger proportion of the city's 175,000 residents to nail windows shut, arm themselves and install new locks.

Bill Parker is one of the few who has profited from this. He owns the locksmith shop nearest the neighborhood where the slayings have occurred. In just two months, Parker and his brother installed 7,000 deadbolt locks and sold thousands of sets of burglar bars and cans of Mace. One of his biggest customers was Margaret Stevens, 71, a retired teacher. Not only are the windows of her brick ranch home barred, but she has pins inserted in the windows to secure them. A new, glassless front door was installed, and a burglar alarm system, and floodlights, and $300 worth of deadbolt locks.

She was lucky. She did most of this before the night the Strangler came. He tried the basement window, but couldn't open it. He cut through the screens on her back porch, but failed to open the sliding glass door. He tried a living room window and then left—leaving a profusion of footprints in the mud of her backyard. That was in September, on a Friday. On Monday, he came back and slew her next-door neighbor, Jean Dimenstien, 71.

The thing that still bothers her—the reason she hasn't opened her door to a soul in three months—is that Dimenstien had been just as prepared as she. Her floodlights were on, the telephone handy, the neighbors alerted, and there were new burglar-proof locks on her doors. So the Strangler, in the glare of the floodlights on her carport, merely removed the kitchen door from its hinges and murdered her in her bed.

At 71, Stevens carries Mace with her to the supermarket. When she comes home at night, she has someone search the house before she enters, "even the closets and the shower." Since the advent of the Strangler, life has become unpleasant for a lot of people in Columbus. Perhaps Los Angeles, with its Hillside Strangler, or Boston, which had its notorious Strangler some years ago, are better able to adjust to the knowledge that a maniac is on the loose. Columbus is not so laid back.... Now, Columbus is like other urban areas—uptight.

Gun sales at the numerous pawn shops have doubled. For a time after one of the attacks, people nearby took to sitting in their front yards in the evening with loaded guns. One suspected prowler was grabbed and severely beaten by residents before police could arrive. An elderly lady put a shotgun blast through her bathroom window—and shot a shadow dead. Two lives have been lost in accidents related to security precautions taken against the Strangler, according to Muscogee County Coroner Donald Kilgore. One woman was killed in an accident involving a pistol she had obtained, and another woman died when she was unable to escape her burning house because of the special, complex locks she had installed.

Then there is the effect on race relations. Blacks make up more than a third of the population here, and their leaders say that tensions have not been as bad since the near-riot conditions of 1971. All the victims have been white, and there seems to be a widespread assumption that the Strangler is black. Blacks complain of being stopped and questioned frequently by police, who concede only that they are frequently stopping and questioning everyone.

Georgia Gov. George Busbee had described the situation as a "reign of terror," and Columbus Police Commander H. W. Boone speaks of "a fear that has gripped the entire community." The strangulations have centered on a neighborhood called Wynnton, a pleasant area with plentiful shade trees and rambling old brick homes...[1]

The killings would continue.

Chapter 1

A Settlement on the Frontier

The city of Columbus, Georgia, is unique for many reasons, not the least among them being the fact that the land on which it was founded was acquired by treachery and paid for in blood. At the end of the American Revolution, Georgia was the least populous of the newly created states. Her vast lands stretched from the Atlantic seacoast in the east to the Mississippi River in the west, fertile ground for settlers seeking their fortunes in the new republic. As reliable cross-country roads were few, initial settlement of the state took place near the seacoast and along the waterways of the Savannah and Ogeechee Rivers. Ignoring claims of ownership by both the Spanish monarchy and Native American tribes, syndicates of speculators were able to purchase from the state millions of acres of virgin forest in what is today the states of Alabama and Mississippi, paying only pennies an acre, courtesy of a corrupt state legislature. This debacle, which came to be known as the Great Yazoo Fraud, would force Georgia to cede her western lands to the federal government in 1802, setting the Chattahoochee River as the lower part of the state's western boundary.

During the latter years of the eighteenth century and well into the nineteenth, Georgia's settlements spread from east to west along either side of the geologic Fall Line, the remnant of the ancient seashore that in recent ages has marked the division between the rolling hills of the Piedmont and the flat expanses of the coastal plain. It was here, the furthermost point of unobstructed upstream navigation on the state's rivers, that Georgia's earliest inland cities were founded. These lands were also among the most attractive to settlers, as the climate and soil were ideal for the production of cotton, the prime source of the state's wealth after Eli Whitney's invention of the cotton gin in the 1790s. Hence, the path of settlement was marked by a series of Fall Line towns and cities. Augusta on the Savannah River was established in 1736. Louisville on the Ogeechee River was incorporated in 1786 as Georgia's first permanent capital. A planned settlement, it was laid out to resemble Philadelphia, at the time the nation's capital and another Fall Line city far to the north. As the state's center of population moved westward, less than two decades later the capital city moved westward as well, to Milledgeville on the falls of the

Oconee River. Further west, the town of Macon was established in 1823, its broad streets named after the trees of the local forest and carefully laid out in a rectangular fashion facing the Ocmulgee River.

Each incremental westward expansion was made possible by land cessions from Native American tribes: from the Savannah to the Ogeechee Rivers in 1763 and 1776, from the Ogeechee to the Oconee in 1790, and from the Oconee to the Ocmulgee in 1802 and 1805. The Indian tribes, however, found themselves increasingly forced from their traditional lands, their way of life threatened by wave after wave of white settlers. In 1821, representatives of the Creek and United States governments signed the first Treaty of Indian Springs, ceding some four million acres between the Flint and Ocmulgee Rivers to the United States in exchange for a total of two hundred thousand dollars to be paid over fourteen years. The Creek National Council, having little or no influence on the treaty's terms and angered by the continued loss of their territory, swore that no further land cessions would be made. Those violating this decree would face punishment by death.

Under pressure from state and federal governments, a group of Creek chiefs signed a second Treaty of Indian Springs in February 1825, ceding millions of additional acres between the Flint and Chattahoochee Rivers to the United States. The treaty was negotiated on behalf of the Indians by William McIntosh, son of a union between a Scottish frontiersman and a Creek mother. Noting that McIntosh did not have the right to speak for the tribes, the Creek National Council declared him a traitor and decreed that he be executed. Just before dawn on April 30, 1825, "nearly four hundred Creek warriors" surrounded McIntosh's home. The house was set ablaze. As McIntosh fled to escape the flames, he was killed.[2] McIntosh died a gruesome death. One historian noted that his body "was pierced with more than a hundred bullets, and when he at last fell he was dragged into the yard, where he was scalped, stabbed to the heart, and his tongue cut out. His scalp was taken by his murderers to their chief village and a ceremonial dance performed around it."[3] Even though the federal government repudiated the treaty, other treaties soon followed that effectively transferred the lands to the state of Georgia, thus opening them for settlement by whites and the forced removal of many Indian tribes.

The validity and morality of the 1825 Treaty of Indian Springs aside, less than four months after its signing, the Georgia legislature established Muscogee County out of the land ceded by the agreement. In 1827, the state called for the establishment of a trading post in the region of the

Indian settlement of Coweta Town, near the highest point of navigation on the Chattahoochee River.* In 1828, a site for the new city, to be named Columbus, was chosen on the east bank of the river near the series of rocky shoals that mark the Fall Line. It was to be the last state-planned city in Georgia, laid out in a twelve-hundred-acre rectangle along the river, measuring thirteen blocks from north to south and nine blocks from east to west. Beyond the Chattahoochee to the west was the as-yet-untamed frontier, home to Indian tribes and often outlaws beyond the reach of federal authority.

The new city grew rapidly, a place for those seeking a new home and a jumping-off point for those headed west to seek their fortunes. Mirabeau Lamar, originally from Louisville, Georgia, founded Columbus's first newspaper, the *Enquirer*, in 1828. Ever restless, he would leave in 1835 to fight in the Texas Revolution and later become the second president of the Republic of Texas. James Fannin passed through in late 1835, seeking volunteers to join the Georgia Battalion in the fight for Texan independence. In what would become known as the Goliad Massacre, most were brutally murdered in March 1836 after being captured by Mexican troops. The ready availability of water power from the Chattahoochee fostered the construction of mills to process timber, weave textiles, and forge iron. The noted landscape architect Frederick Law Olmsted visited Columbus in 1853, pronouncing it "the largest manufacturing city south of Richmond, Virginia."[4] By 1860, on the cusp of the Civil War, Columbus was the fourth most populous city in the state, with a population of 9,621, including 3,547 slaves. In what had been wilderness a mere three decades earlier, a thriving center of commerce now existed, its mills and markets funding the elegant mansions of the well-to-do. Two-and-a-half miles east of Columbus's riverfront, the agricultural village of Wynnton had sprung up around the plantation of William Wynn. In 1860, it was the sixteenth largest town in the state, with a population of 557 whites and 912 slaves. More than a century later, having been swallowed by the growth of Columbus, Wynnton would become the epicenter of the Stocking Strangler's murders.

During the Civil War, the mills and factories of Columbus became major sources of matériel for the Confederate cause. Textile mills produced uniforms, while other companies manufactured swords, pistols, and

---

* Coweta Town was on the west bank of the Chattahoochee, just south of present day Phenix City, Alabama.

rifles. The Columbus Iron Works, founded in 1853, began fabricating cannon and mortars, and later armor for the ironclad *CSS Muscogee*. As the city was far out of Gen. William Sherman's path of destruction, it survived the war intact until mid-April 1865. In what was one of the last battles of the conflict, Maj. Gen. James Wilson's Union troops, fresh from their victories in Selma and Montgomery, attacked the badly outnumbered Confederate defenders after dark on the night of April 16th.[†] By the next morning, Columbus was under federal control. Wilson ordered anything that could aid the Confederate war effort be demolished, resulting in the burning of mills and factories, the destruction of the port facilities, and the sinking of the *CSS Muscogee*.

Many of the destroyed mills and factories were rebuilt promptly after the war. The latter third of the nineteenth century brought a return of prosperity to the city, especially with expansion and new construction of textile mills. As the economy expanded, so did the city. In 1887, a steam-powered trolley line was built eastward to the village of Wynnton, ushering in development of the growing city's suburbs.[‡]

To the west, directly across the Chattahoochee in Alabama, the villages of Girard and Brownville had grown up, bedroom communities for many who worked in Columbus. In 1897, the merged towns were rechristened by the Alabama legislature as Phenix City. During the Great Depression, Phenix City went bankrupt, having accumulated more than a million dollars in debt. To meet their financial obligations, city authorities turned to licensing fees collected from illegal gambling, saloons, and prostitution, making the city a popular destination for soldiers stationed at Fort Benning. By the 1940s, Phenix City was under the control of organized crime bosses. In response, a grassroots effort to clean up the city arose, resulting in the 1955 assassination of Alabama's newly elected attorney general, who had helped lead the campaign. Later that year a local grand jury indicted more than seven hundred people, finally putting an end to the decades-long reign of corruption and criminality.

In the years between 1860 and 1900, Columbus's population grew steadily but relatively slowly. The twentieth century brought rapid growth,

---

[†] The Battle of Columbus is also known as the Battle of Girard since much of the action took place in Girard (now Phenix City), Alabama, directly across the river. Word of Lee's surrender at Appomattox had not reached Columbus at the time of the engagement.

[‡] Wynnton would formally become part of the city of Columbus in 1925.

with the population more than tripling between 1900 and 1940, and nearly tripling again to 155,000 by 1970. A major factor was the 1918 creation of Camp Benning, a new military base located south of the city. Named for Brig. Gen. Henry L. Benning, a Columbus resident and officer in the Confederate army, in 1922 the base was made a permanent installation and renamed Fort Benning.

While many of the city's residents shared in its growing wealth, there were many who did not. During the Jim Crow era and until the 1970s and beyond, blacks, who made up nearly half the population of Columbus and Muscogee County, were relegated to the role of second-class citizens, facing discrimination in almost all facets of daily life, including employment, housing, education, political freedom, and income. In the textile mills, for example, the workforce was almost uniformly white. Blacks, if employed in the mills at all, were limited to menial, low-skill, and low-paying jobs. Housing in the subsidized "mill villages" was reserved for whites only. Until recent years, the same sharp dichotomy extended to Columbus's housing patterns in general.

A black physician, Dr. Thomas H. Brewer, was one of the pioneers of the civil rights movement in Columbus and an outspoken advocate for the cause. He was one of the founders of the local chapter of the NAACP.[§] His support in mounting a legal challenge to all-white Democratic primary elections was vital in opening the voting process to African Americans. He was instrumental in the integration of the Columbus police force with the 1951 hiring of four black officers "to patrol the downtown black neighborhoods."[5] On February 18, 1956, the sixty-one-year-old Dr. Brewer was shot and killed by Lucio Flowers, a white man and owner of the F&B department store "in the downtown Negro business section."[6] Both men had been acquainted for some time; the building that housed the department store was also the location of Dr. Brewer's medical office. Some days prior to the shooting, both had observed the arrest by the police of a badly intoxicated black man. Brewer thought the officers used excessive and unnecessary force. Flowers disagreed and refused to make a formal statement on the issue, leading Brewer to "threaten to get" him, according to newspaper reports.[7] On the evening of February 18th, Dr. Brewer confronted Flowers in the department store office. Though initial reports said there were no direct witnesses, Flowers testified that he shot Brewer seven times with a .25 caliber automatic pistol as he feared Brewer was about to

---

[§] National Association for the Advancement of Colored People.

shoot him first. An unfired .32 caliber pistol was found in Brewer's coat pocket. Flowers was arrested and held without bond. Prior to a Superior Court grand jury hearing two weeks later, the prosecutor "told newsmen...that a witness saw the 61-year-old Brewer reach into a pocket just before the 54-year-old merchant opened fire." The jury refused to indict Flowers, leading to his release.

Brewer's death made national news, including front-page coverage in the *New York Times*. While both local and national NAACP figures said the murder was unrelated to the organization's activities, many remained convinced that Brewer was killed for his outspoken quest for social and political justice. The killing led to an exodus from Columbus of a number of black professionals. Almost exactly one year later, national headlines read "Gunman Freed in Negro's Slaying Lured to Death," and "Georgia Man Shot, Killed: Event Avenges Death of Negro."[8] On February 11, 1957, Flowers was found shot to death in the alcove of a "Negro movie theater" just across the street from his department store. In her history of Columbus, Virginia Causey recounts that Flowers died

> from gunshots to the head, a handkerchief in his mouth and two pistols by his side, both fired. His death was ruled a suicide, though the puzzle pieces did not fit. His clothes were ripped, his pockets turned out, and his head bruised. The pistols were wiped clean of fingerprints. A rumor swept the white community that one of the black police officers killed Flowers, and the Klan paraded down First Avenue in his commemoration. The black community, which believed Brewer was assassinated, contended the police later killed Flowers to cover up his role in the plot.[9]

While some progress was made, the city of Columbus was slow to change its ways. By 1970, for example, there were more black police officers, but they were refused membership in the Fraternal Order of Police and suffered discrimination in professional advancement. During the summer of 1971, the city exploded in a series of mass demonstrations precipitated in part by the shooting of an unarmed twenty-year-old black man who attempted to flee after crashing his car through a series of roadblocks. Between June and September, a total of 161 arson-set fires, many aimed at white-owned businesses, caused more than a million dollars in damage. There were multiple reports of snipers and cutting of the water hoses of the firemen who attempted to control the blazes.[10] Though the immediate situation gradually improved, suspicion between the races remained.

Whites accused blacks of crimes; blacks were certain that their race alone made them objects of police harassment. These attitudes would become a major issue during the reign of terror caused by the Stocking Strangler.

Chapter 2

Crime Wave

At approximately 11:20 A.M. on Sunday morning, September 11, 1977, Columbus police received a call from the Columbus Rescue Squad in reference to a possible assault at 2703 Hood Street in East Wynnton. This part of Wynnton was a predominately white neighborhood of neat but modest homes dating from the 1940s. Many of the residents were older retirees, including a number of widows. The original call to the rescue squad had been placed at the request of Ms. Elizabeth Bell, a seventy-year-old neighbor of Ms. Gertrude Miller, who had earlier walked over to Miller's home to catch a ride to the 11:00 mass at Holy Family Church. Both women were widows and friends; Ms. Bell often helped as an unpaid volunteer at the kindergarten that Ms. Miller, age sixty-four, had operated at her home for more than three decades. To her surprise, she found the side door to the house standing open. No one answered her call. Venturing further inside, she found Ms. Miller in her bedroom on the floor slumped against the bathroom door, dazed and incoherent, "covered with blood," and mumbling only the words "beat, beat." On the arrival of the police, the victim was taken by ambulance to St. Francis Hospital, her condition described as "critical," her prognosis as "guarded."

Shortly after her arrival at the hospital, Ms. Miller was able to give a brief statement to police officers. Though still stunned due to her injuries, she was able to tell the detectives that shortly after midnight, she was awakened by an intruder, a black man, in her bedroom. He tied her up, beat her about the head with a board or plank, and raped her. She was bleeding from her left ear; medical evaluation revealed a skull fracture. A gynecologic exam done two days later found presumptive evidence of forceable intercourse.

The attack on Gertrude Miller, though brutal and shocking, was not a unique event. In fact, violent crime had become an all-too-common occurrence in Columbus. Armed robberies, rape, and murder had been and continued to be a seemingly insoluble dilemma. The problem of crime was not a new one, and for the people of Columbus the issue seemed inextricably intertwined with race. An article in the *Columbus Enquirer* more than twenty months earlier noted that in December 1975 and early January

1976, about sixty percent of the armed robberies had been committed by blacks, with the other forty percent by whites.[11] Gary Parker, president of the Columbus College Black Student Union was quoted as saying, "It's being projected that if you're young and black you're a criminal." Stating that the robberies and two associated killings were "not a racial thing," Parker continued, "It's not a vicious attack by blacks on whites.... It's the have-nots after the haves." Bandits "rob places where the money is," he explained.

Only weeks before the attack on Ms. Miller, the *Enquirer* noted that "at least two dozen slayings of a non-domestic nature" had occurred in the Columbus-Phenix City area over the preceding twenty months.[12] The details of the crimes, each briefly listed by the newspaper, were horrific: a sixteen-year-old boy shot to death by shotgun-wielding bandits as he lay on the floor during the robbery of a small restaurant; a fifty-three-year-old businessman "gunned down" as he walked home from his fiancée's house; a Columbus police officer shot and killed "after stopping a vehicle suspected of involvement in an armed robbery minutes earlier"; a twenty-three-year-old woman "kidnapped, raped, robbed and shot to death near her Columbus home"; and numerous others.

The preceding day, the *Ledger*, the sister paper of the *Enquirer*, had featured an article titled "Slayings Create Climate of Fear."[13]* In the last ten months, "four young Columbus women [had] been slain after being sexually assaulted by an assailant they apparently didn't know." Two other women were killed during robberies. The crime wave, which had started in the summer of 1976, seemed to show no sign of abatement. "One twenty-one-year-old woman who grew up in Columbus remembers when she and her girlfriends stayed out late on summer nights, carefree and unconcerned that lurking in the darkness might be a rapist or killer," the reporter wrote. "No more. Now the woman has asked her father to come over to her apartment and put bars on her windows and a chain lock on the door. When she's alone in her apartment at night, she puts a chair in front of the door." Despite their best efforts, the police seemed powerless

---

* In the late 1970s, Columbus had two daily papers, the morning *Columbus Enquirer*, founded in 1828, and the afternoon *Columbus Ledger*, founded in 1886. In 1930, they came under the same ownership, thereafter continuing the separate morning and afternoon editions but publishing combined *Ledger-Enquirer* weekend editions. In 1988, the two papers merged into a single daily edition, the *Columbus Ledger-Enquirer*.

to stop the lawless attacks on innocent citizens. In an attempt to assist law enforcement, local CBers[†] organized a program to report potential crime to the police on a specific radio channel. Georgia Power asked the 250 employees of its Columbus district office to be "eyes" for the local police while on duty.[14]

While Gertrude Miller was being treated in the intensive care unit of St. Francis Hospital, detectives and crime scene technicians were searching her home for clues, removing a number of items for further analysis. Among them were a one-piece bra and girdle and a pair of pantyhose, both heavily blood-stained, that police assumed were used to bind the victim. A second pair of pantyhose rolled up in a ball appeared to have been used as a gag. The assailant seemed to have entered the house through a bedroom window. Latent fingerprints were lifted from the window sill and the bedroom door. Meanwhile, other detectives spent the day of the crime and the following two days canvassing the neighborhood, seeking any clue or sighting of suspicious individuals who might be suspects. A four-and-a-half-inch-wide wooden board measuring more than two feet in length was found in the yard. It was thought to be the weapon used to assault Ms. Miller.

By Friday, September 15th, Ms. Miller had improved enough to talk with detectives from her bed in the intensive care unit. Even with her skull fracture and other injuries, she was lucid and able to give a more detailed account of her ordeal. She said she had gone to sleep just after midnight but woke up shortly thereafter to find a black male standing in her bedroom. As she asked him what he was doing there, he struck her in the head with a board and then began tying her hands with pantyhose that he had taken from her dresser before she woke up. He then removed her clothing and assaulted her. Afterwards, he turned on the bedside lamp briefly, allowing her a good look at him before he turned it off and left the house. Beyond this point she seemed to remember little other than the fact that he struck her with the board at least once more, after which she apparently lost consciousness, not awakening until the following morning. It was the impression of investigators that her assailant may have left her for dead.

[†] "CBers" refers to users of citizens band radios, a widely used two-way radio system open to the general public. First available in the late 1940s, CB radios were especially popular in the 1970s and featured prominently in such movies as *Smokey and the Bandit*. With the introduction of cell phones, CB radios fell out of general use.

Miller was able to give an overall description of the man who raped her, a black male between five feet, eleven inches and six feet in height, with a neatly cut afro an inch to an inch and a half in length. She recalled that he had no facial hair and was able to give a detailed description of the clothes he was wearing. Though she said she had never seen the man before, she was certain that she could identify him if she saw him again.

Police commander James B. Hicks told a reporter that the attack on Ms. Miller was "the fifth rape or attempted rape in a little over a month," and the fourth occurring on the east side of Columbus, all of which had been committed in the victims' homes.[15] It appeared to be, quite simply, another incident in the ongoing crime wave that was sweeping the city.

Chapter 3

Six Days Later, Seven Blocks Away

On Friday morning, September 16, 1977, Ms. Mary Willis Jackson did not come to work. Ms. Jackson, known familiarly to everyone as "Ferne," was the director of education for the Columbus Health Department. Fifty-nine years old and widowed for four years, she had been a tireless advocate for good health practices for the preceding twenty-six years and a highly respected member of the community. Her secretary was off for the day, and Ms. Jackson had not mentioned to anyone that she planned to be away from the office. When she hadn't arrived at the health department by 10:00, two coworkers, concerned for her well-being, rode over to her house to check on her. Ms. Jackson lived at 2505 17th Street in a comfortable one-story ranch house set well back from the street. Her car was not in the driveway, no one answered the doorbell, and both the front and back doors to the house were securely locked. It was assumed that she had an appointment somewhere and that she would return to the office before the end of the day. When nothing had been heard from her by four o'clock, Ms. Jackson's colleagues notified the police.

Ann Schwan, Ms. Jackson's stepdaughter, met the police at her house. One of the officers gained entry through a living room window. He found Ms. Jackson's body in her bedroom, covered by a pink sheet and obviously deceased for a number of hours. According to the police report, she "was lying on her back in her bed with a woman's nylon stocking tied around her neck. The bed was very disarranged and the room had apparently been ransacked. Contents from Ms. Jackson's purse were lying on the floor, dresser drawers were pulled open with some of the contents on the floor. A jewelry box sitting on the dresser was open with the contents disarranged in it." Her body, nude from the waist down, was identified by her stepdaughter shortly after 5:00 P.M.

The victim's car, a brown 1975 Mercury Montego, was missing. Police put out an all-points bulletin at approximately 5:10 P.M. About two and a half hours later, patrol units found the car parked on a side street a few blocks away—and only about two blocks from the home of Ms. Gertrude Miller. A resident of the neighborhood said he saw a lone black male park the car there about 8:30 A.M. that morning, but could not provide a further description of the driver.

Local and Georgia state crime lab technicians gathered evidence at the crime scene. The killer appeared to have entered the house through a sliding glass door that opened onto a patio off the living room. Pry marks were found on the door; several latent fingerprints were collected there, together with others from the bedroom area. Among the items of evidence gathered were a ladies' nylon stocking wrapped three times around Ms. Jackson's neck and a number of hair samples found on and near the body. These items and others were sent to the crime lab for further analysis.

Interviews with neighbors produced little useful information. There were "numerous" reports of prowlers late at night. Two women said their doorbells were rung about 2:00 A.M. on the night Ms. Jackson was killed. That same night, the home of Muscogee County Coroner Donald Kilgore's mother was burglarized, and a television was stolen. The night before her murder, Ms. Jackson had attended church at St. Luke Methodist with her best friend, Lucy Mangham. After the service, Ms. Mangham drove her home and waited until Ms. Jackson was safely inside the house before leaving. Another close acquaintance, Ann Barton, said that she formerly lived in Ms. Jackson's neighborhood but had moved out to a condominium four years earlier "because she was afraid that what eventually happened to her friend would happen to her."[16] "Why does this happen to people who do so much good for so many people all these years?" Ms. Barton asked. "I feel horrified. This is the worst thing that can happen to someone. And she was a great contributor to human services."[17]

The autopsy report detailed the trauma suffered by the victim. There was a "massive contusion" of the left face and forehead and hemorrhage in the left eye. There were other contusions and abrasions on the legs, arms, and chest, the latter accompanying a fracture of the sternum.* "Massive perineal trauma" was noted with multiple vaginal lacerations and contusions consistent with sexual assault. The cause of death was listed as strangulation from the stocking, which had been wrapped tightly around the neck three times, then fixed in place with multiple knots. The report's summary also noted, "At the site there are strands of hair distinctly different from the hair of the victim. The hair strands are glistening black and

---

* "Contusion" is a medical term for bruise, usually caused by a blow or direct impact. "Sternum" is the anatomic term for the breastbone. In other words, Ms. Jackson had been severely beaten before her death.

coiled into ringlets and waves." These were sent to the crime lab for iden-tification. The lab's report, received ten days later, estimated the time of death to be between 1:00 and 2:00 A.M. on September 16th. There was evidence of seminal fluid in a specimen collected from the victim's vagina, but no spermatozoa were identified. Some of the hairs found on and around the body revealed "characteristics which are consistent with Ne-groid hair."

The reactions from Ms. Jackson's friends, fellow workers, and the community at large were ones of shock, sorrow, anger, and outrage. Edi-torials in the city's papers spoke of her losing her life "in a senseless and terrible manner, seemingly a victim of the random violence that stalks our society."[18] Her work in the field of public health was nationally recognized. Later in the fall she was to have been presented the National Health Ed-ucator of the Year award by the American Public Health Association.

The similarities between the assault on Gertrude Miller and the as-sault and murder of Ferne Jackson had not escaped police notice. Deputy Commander James Hicks stated that the authorities "have no physical ev-idence to link the cases beyond locality." Although the police had ques-tioned several men, Hicks refused to reveal other information or "say whether or not a suspect [had] been identified."[19]

Chapter 4

We've Got a Maniac

On Saturday night September 24th, Jean Dimenstien went out to dinner with two older ladies, both close friends, at Morrison's Cafeteria in the Cross Country Shopping Center near her house in east Wynnton. Dimenstien, seventy-one, was the retired co-owner of Fred and Jean's department store. Unmarried, she had lived in her "spacious brick home" at 3027 21st Street for twenty-three years, and in Columbus for thirty-five.* One of the friends later told a reporter for the *Ledger*, "We'd been fussing at her for staying at home all alone. Last night Jean said, 'I've about decided to sell my house and move into a condominium.'" After dinner the three went back to Dimenstien's house and chatted for a while. They left at about 9:30 P.M., their host "calling to them that she'd see one of them the next day when she'd visit over coffee and a snack."[20] Except for her killer, they were the last persons to see Jean Dimenstien alive.

Ms. Dimenstien had ample reason to be afraid. The night before, there had been an attempt to break into the house of her friend and next-door neighbor, Ms. Margaret Stevens. The intruder (or intruders) managed to get inside a screen porch but were stopped by a locked sliding glass door. It was, in fact, Ms. Stevens's husband who called the police on Sunday morning when he noted that Dimenstien's car was missing, the lights were on in her house, and the carport entry door removed from its hinges.

Police responded promptly. The first item noted was that the carport door had been opened by removing the hinge pins and taking it out of the door frame. The house had been "ransacked." Dimenstien's lifeless body was found lying on its back, a brown nylon stocking wrapped tightly around the neck. Her rabbi, Theodore Feldman, identified the body. Ms. Stevens explained, "We guessed the inevitable when we saw the door leaned up like that. She was one of the dearest friends we had for a long time. When we saw what was there, we just called the police. We didn't go in."[21]

Initial investigation of the crime scene found Dimenstien's face and head covered with a pink pillowcase and her body covered with a sheet.

---

* The name of 21st Street was later changed to Cross Country Hill Street. The house numbering remained the same.

She appeared to have been beaten and sexually assaulted. An autopsy done later in the day revealed "massive" bruising of the face and eyes, as well as of her breast and left knee. There was "extensive trauma and hemorrhage" in the vaginal and perineal area consistent with sexual assault, confirmed by spermatozoa found in vaginal fluid. The cause of death, strangulation, was evidenced by a fracture of the hyoid bone and "triple ligature marks" around the neck.[†] Time of death was estimated to be around midnight Saturday night.

As in the case of Ferne Jackson, Dimenstien's car, a 1975 white, two-door Chevrolet Malibu, was missing. Police discovered it less than an hour later parked on King Street. The location was only about a block from where Jackson's car had been found on the morning following her murder. And, like Jackson's vehicle, both cars had been "wiped clean" of fingerprints. No witnesses had observed the car being parked, only that it had appeared on the street curbside overnight.

The headline of the *Ledger* on Monday morning, September 26th, proclaimed in bold font, "Sex Killer Strikes 2nd Time," the lead sentence reading, "The second elderly Columbus woman in nine days was found molested and strangled in her home Sunday, and authorities believe a sadistic fiend is on the loose who finishes his grisly work by killing his victims." In interviews with Police Chief Curtis McClung, Columbus mayor Jack Mickle, and Coroner Donald Kilgore, the *Ledger's* writer, Carl Cannon, painted a grim picture. All three men expressed their certainty that both Jackson and Dimenstien were murdered by the same person. Describing the alleged killer as "an out-of-the-ordinary criminal," Chief McClung announced that he was cancelling all days off for policeman, both patrol officers and detectives, "while the massive investigation continues." Administrative police officers were being reassigned to patrol work instead of headquarters. Mayor Mickle, interviewed in front of Dimenstien's house after being called out of church on Sunday morning following the discovery of her body, was described as "ashen-faced." "'I hope we get this guy—we gotta get this guy,'" Mickle beseeched in a quiet husky

---

[†] The hyoid is a small horseshoe-shaped bone found in the anterior neck below the mandible and above the so-called "Adam's apple." It is frequently broken during traumatic strangulation.

voice. In contrast to McClung's assessment of the killer, "the mayor was more blunt, saying, 'We've got a maniac.'"‡

Coroner Kilgore, who was rapidly earning resentment from law enforcement for what many considered his overt willingness to share too many details of the cases, opined that "he believed some sort of inflexible object was used to violate the women." In the same sensationalistic vein, Kilgore speculated that "a pillow found over their faces was used to muffle their horrified screams while being tortured sexually before death. 'The motive is torture...and murder.'"[22] Kilgore went on to reveal that in both cases, the victims were wearing diamond jewelry at the time of their deaths, which the killer ignored. In a separate interview with a reporter from the *Enquirer*, Kilgore commented on the similarities between the Jackson and Dimenstien murders: "If you took a television picture and replayed it, that would be about how similar these killings were. The fellow that did them needs to be caught bad. He just wants to hurt."[23]

In a Monday morning news conference, Mayor Mickle called for a "calm and alert citizenry," asserting, "The guilty people will be caught and removed from our society if we all cooperate in the effort." He announced a reward of $6,000 for information leading to an arrest in either case. $1,000 of the reward was offered by Georgia governor George Busbee, and the remaining $5,000 by the City of Columbus. The amount would soon be increased to $11,000 based on the promise of an additional $5,000 from an anonymous Columbus citizen. Meanwhile, Columbus police were pushing back at Coroner Kilgore's comments on the case, stating that while there were similarities, they had not yet determined that the same person committed both slayings. "Kilgore has been investigating homicides for a few months but we've been at it a little longer," one unnamed detective was quoted as saying.[24]

A sense of apprehension and uncertainty gripped the citizens of Columbus. A headline in the *Ledger* read, "Guns, Guard Dogs Sought by Fearful Residents."[25] Pawnshops and sporting-goods dealers in Columbus

---

‡ In a letter to the editor published in the *Ledger* two days later, a female reader who described herself as "a student of journalism and communication" chastised Carl Cannon for his "unnecessarily explicit" reporting in this article. Noting that "the sick creature [i.e., the killer] will be the only one to gain from having his deed exposed to the public in print," she ended her note by stating, "It is my opinion that this type of sensationalism has no place in your newspaper." (*Columbus (GA) Ledger,* 28 September 1977.)

and Phenix City reported a spike in inquiries about firearms for personal protection, especially from women. The director of the city animal pound said "women are calling about dogs who will bark and alert them to intruders, and men are asking about 'mean' dogs."

Law enforcement officials described their hunt for the killer as "intense," at the same time expressing the concern that "the killer knows a great deal about police investigation procedure." Authorities were said to be "trying to develop a description to pass around, but are proceeding carefully for fear a description could possibly hinder as well as hurt the search.... The police say they believe the killer may be anything from a perverted detective novel bug to an ex-cop."[26] There had been no matches for the fingerprints lifted from the scenes of the Jackson or Dimenstien murders. The one piece of possible evidence police possessed was a composite drawing of a shoeprint left at the Dimenstien house. It appeared to be an Adidas tennis shoe, size 10½, a design that had been sold at only one store in the Atlanta area. The bad news was that the design was not copyrighted, so any other shoe manufacturer could copy or produce a variation of it. Images of the design were given to patrolmen with the instruction, "If you stop a suspicious looking suspect with this type of shoeprint bring him to the detective division."

The *Ledger's* Carl Cannon interviewed five local psychologists and psychiatrists for their opinions as to the motivations of the killer, reported under the headline, "Killer Vents His Bottled Up Hatred." All "talked of the killer's obvious hostility toward women, citing conflicts with his mother or grandmother as the most likely cause. All said he'd been subject to traumatic pressure, not of his own making....What emerged was a picture of a secretly enraged person, completely anti-social, who went over the brink one day and began acting out the tremendous hatred bottled up inside and began striking back. He probably never knew the victims...but this killer is responding to subconscious feelings, and he doesn't care who his victims are, the five said."[27]

With the intense speculation as to the possible identity of the killer, the inevitable question of race arose. Though authorities had not officially said they were searching for a black man, there was a widespread belief that the killer was a person of color, based in part on the numerous rumors that flowed among Columbus's citizens. A "citizens news conference" called by Mayor Mickle was held on Wednesday, September 28th, in the Columbus city council chambers. An editorial in the *Enquirer* two days later articulated the essence of the message those participating in the meeting hoped to convey: "The atmosphere of fear generated by the violent crimes should not be allowed to inflame racial emotions and undermine community black-white relations." Stating that the killer might be black or white, "whatever his race, it should be remembered that he did not commit these crimes because of the color of his skin." He was, in the words of African American mayor pro tem A. J. McClung, "a sick man," commenting as well "that the police have not mentioned race." "The killer is," the editorial continued, "the enemy of all citizens, black and white. Police officers, black and white, are working together to solve the crimes."[28,29]

In less than three weeks, the city of Columbus had been plunged into a sense of ill-defined uneasiness. The routines of daily life were now less certain, the fear of the unknown hovering like a dark cloud on the horizon. In the words of one unmarried forty-seven-year-old working woman, "I'm not a scary person, but I'm frightened. There's just a pervasive feeling—a miasma of fear over the community."[30]

Chapter 5

A Suspect

The possibility that a single individual murdered both Ferne Jackson and Jean Dimenstien was a cause of major concern to the Columbus police. On October 1st, Ronnie Jones, director of the Robbery/Homicide Squad, issued an interoffice memo titled "Particulars on Jackson and Dimenstien Murders," which listed a number of common characteristics of the two crimes: Both victims were "elderly" white females (age fifty-nine and seventy-one, respectively). Both had lived alone for some time. Both had been out to dinner with friends on the evenings before their deaths. The bedrooms of both women had been "ransacked" and both pocketbooks emptied. Both victims' vehicles were stolen and later found parked in the same general vicinity in a nearby neighborhood. Other than the cars, nothing of major value was stolen from the residences. Both had been beaten about the left side of the face and eye, "apparently with a blunt instrument." Both were found "lying in bed on their back practically nude with sleeping apparel pushed around their neck and chest." "Both had received vaginal damage according to medical reports from some instrument being entered into the vagina."

The two murders, plus the earlier assault on Gertrude Miller, spawned a growing sense of fear among the city's residents. On October 2nd, under the headline "Trail to Killer Growing Cold," a reporter for the *Ledger* wrote, "Each prowler and mysterious noise takes on a new importance as unfounded rumors spread of other women being accosted. Last week," the article continued, "an elderly Hilton Arms Apartment resident fired shots at a fleeing prowler who had returned for a second look in her rear door. And Thursday night, a band of young men from the Forrest Road area ran down a prowler and roughed him up before calling police." Detective Commander Herman Boone urged patience, promising to continue the investigation "until every lead is exhausted." Sounding exasperated, Boone urged people to "take note of the [$11,000] reward."[31]

That same morning brought what appeared to be a break in the case. At approximately 9:55 A.M., police were called to 535 Annette Avenue in the southern part of the Wynnton district, where an unconscious black female, appearing to be in her fifties, had been found lying between two abandoned houses. Alive, but with shallow respiration and a weak pulse, she appeared to have been badly beaten about the face. Her pants "had been pulled down below her knees," suggesting that she had been raped. The victim was later identified as Beatrice Brier, who was said to have a girlfriend-boyfriend relationship with a man named Jerome "Duck" Livas.[*] An earlier tip from a police informant suggested that a black man named "Jerome" might be connected with the Jackson and Dimenstien murders. Livas, a twenty-five-year-old black male, was arrested later that night. He was initially charged with the assault on Brier, but was also considered a suspect in the earlier murders of the two women.

Once in police custody, Livas readily admitted that he beat and raped Brier, justifying this by saying that he had seen her with another man. Livas, who would later be described in the press as "mentally slow and illiterate,"[†] was then questioned about possible involvement in the attack on Gertrude Miller and the murders of Ferne Jackson and Jean Dimenstien. During several hours following his arrest, he gave investigators a remarkably detailed description of his alleged entry into each of the women's homes, and how he assaulted and raped them. Driving around the neighborhoods where the attacks occurred, he was said to have pointed out the houses of the victims and provided details that were not generally public knowledge. According to the police report of Livas's interview, he had been informed of his Miranda rights[‡] and gave his statements freely and without the presence of an attorney. The police report of Livas's questioning noted,

> [The detectives] returned Livas to the detective office and asked if he would give a written statement concerning what he had just showed and told the detectives, and he said he would. It was

---

[*] Brier died as a result of her injuries on October 8th.

[†] Multiple news reports used this and/or similar terms to describe Livas.

[‡] "Miranda rights" refer to a potential defendant's rights against self-incrimination and the availability of legal counsel based on the Fifth Amendment of the US Constitution. A typical "Miranda warning" given by authorities might be, *"You have the right to remain silent. Anything you say can be used against you in court. You have the right to talk to a lawyer for advice before we ask you any questions. You have the right to have a lawyer with you during questioning. If you cannot afford a lawyer, one will be appointed for you before any questioning if you wish. If you decide to answer questions now without a lawyer present, you have the right to stop answering at any time."* The name derives from the 1966 US Supreme Court case *Miranda vs. Arizona.*

decided that the statement given by Livas would be taped and a tape recorder was obtained and placed in the interview room. Livas became nervous with the presence of the tape recorder and it became obvious that it was not going to be able to be taped. The recorder was removed. The only portion of the interview that was taped in any extent was the reading of the rights and the complete statement after it had been taken. In giving the statement, Livas became very vague and could not recall some of the details he had been able to recall out on the street and no pressure was placed on him in an attempt to make him recall these details. The statement was taken just as Livas gave it.[32]

There were problems with Livas's "confession." He was reported to have said, for example, that he went with a female friend to Gertrude Miller's house on the night he beat and raped her. The friend denied being with him. He said he had disposed of the keys to Jackson's and Dimenstien's stolen vehicles in the sewer, but neither set could be found. Importantly, the written documentation of Livas's statements was based on the memory of the detectives. While he may have signed an acknowledgment of his statement, he was illiterate and could not have read it. An interview with Livas's fellow employees at his workplace produced the assessment "that Livas is afraid of people." Most critical, however, is the fact that he recanted his statements the following day.

On Monday morning, October 3rd, Columbus mayor Jack Mickle set off a "flurry of interest" by an off-hand remark he made about "a suspect" during an interview on the *Rozelle Show*, a local television program. Stating that the police had "a suspect," but refusing to go into detail, Mickle said "he was referring to a twenty-five-year-old man booked Sunday for beating and raping a fifty-five-year-old woman who was identified as his former girlfriend." Police Chief Curtis McClung and Director Ronnie Jones expressed surprise at Mickle's remark, referring vaguely to other possible suspects and saying no one had been formally charged with the Jackson and Dimenstien murders.[33] Unnamed police sources revealed Livas's name, describing him as a "construction worker" and stating that he had confessed to both the Jackson and Dimenstien killings and then recanted his confession. Refusing to confirm or deny the rumors, Chief McClung said, "Even if he did confess, we couldn't go just on his say-so. We couldn't ride just with that. When you get a case like this you have all kinds of kooks coming out of the woodwork."[34]

With public sentiment running high and law enforcement under pressure to apprehend the murderer, the Columbus police decided to take credit for the arrest of a potential suspect in the Jackson and Dimenstien cases. Speaking to a Kiwanis Club meeting on Wednesday, October 11th, Deputy Commander J. B. Hicks reminded his audience that Columbus was not "the sleepy mill town it once was," having transitioned to "a sprawling urban area replete with violent crime." "It's a terrible shame to live in a country as great as America when the morality has dropped so low that a woman isn't safe," Hicks said. "Something is wrong and we don't know what it is." Offering a bit of reassurance in referring to the recent murders, he also said, "We have a suspect. I believe there's a good possibility we might have our man."[35,36]

Though the man in police custody, Jerome Livas, was in fact a suspect, at that point he was nothing more. Before he could be tried on any charges, the evidence against him in the Jackson and Dimenstien murders would need to be presented to the local district attorney, who in turn would make the decision to refer the case to a grand jury. Only if the grand jury agreed that the evidence warranted a trial could the case against Livas proceed. Police Chief McClung had scheduled a press conference, at which time he planned to publicly discuss Livas's arrest, and with it the unspoken implication that the cases had been solved. On the morning prior to his presentation, McClung requested a meeting with Chattahoochee Judicial Circuit district attorney E. Mullins Whisnant, who, accompanied by Assistant District Attorney William J. Smith, met with McClung at police headquarters. After discussing the evidence with McClung, Whisnant advised him not to proceed with the press conference, pointing out that more investigation needed to be done and since Livas was being held anyway on charges of murdering Beatrice Brier, he no longer represented a potential threat to public safety. McClung politely disagreed, saying his plans had been made.

On Friday, October 14th, Assistant Police Chief C. B. Faison read a statement to reporters: "Jerome Livas is being held by the department as a suspect in the murders of Ms. Ferne Jackson and Ms. Jean Dimenstien. All evidence by the department is being turned over to the district attorney's office for presentation to the grand jury and indictment." At the same time, police disclosed that a previously unpublicized stakeout designed to catch the killer was being discontinued after the arrest of Livas.

Police said sheriff's deputies, backed by a beefed-up patrol force, stayed the night at the homes of elderly and single women—people they believed to be possible targets of the killer of Ferne Jackson and Jean Dimenstien. The stakeout, which involved nearly fifty officers staying in as many homes, lasted from September 28th to October 4th.... "The city was living in fear, especially the older people," said an officer who helped hatch the plan. "This did a lot to calm people down."[37]

The intense police scrutiny evidently had other positive effects. The number of residential burglaries decreased significantly, though some still occurred. One such crime happened on the night of October 7th. A burglar broke into the residence of Ms. Callye J. East and Ms. Nellie Sanderson at 1427 Eberhart Avenue in the Wynnton sector. The two were elderly sisters, age eighty-five and seventy-eight respectively, who had moved in together after the deaths of their husbands. Perhaps unknown to the intruder was the unusual fact that Ms. Sanderson had house guests that night, her son Henry R. Sanderson and his wife, from Dadeville, Alabama. The burglar apparently slipped silently into the bedroom of the sleeping couple, found Mr. Sanderson's keys, and stole his car, a 1975 Toyota. It was recovered the following morning approximately two miles away at 610 Mill Road, shortly after Sanderson reported the theft. The only thing of significance that appeared to be missing was Mr. Sanderson's pistol, which had been left under the driver's seat, a .22 caliber blue-steel Ruger automatic, serial number 13-70073. A police report was duly completed, and with no other obvious leads, filed with the dozens of other such crimes reported that week.

With the good news, the city of Columbus seemed to breathe a collective sigh of relief. An October 18th editorial in the *Enquirer* under the headline "Fear Subsiding" summed up the changing mood:

Just a few weeks ago—after two older women were found strangled and sexually assaulted in their homes—Columbus citizens were gripped by fear for the personal safety of themselves and their families. Today that fear is subsiding. People are less apprehensive about staying alone in a residence at night. No longer do they jump at the slightest sound, sure it's a prowler or worse about to break in on them. The reasons for this calmer attitude are not hard to find. The most important reason is simply that there has not been another sex assault-slaying in the last three weeks. Equally significant is the fact that police officials believe they have solved the two widely publicized cases.[38]

Now that the problem appeared to be solved, life in Columbus would soon return to some semblance of normal. That mistaken sense of security would be shattered three days later on the afternoon of Friday, October 21st.

Chapter 6

Ten Days Shy of Ninety

At about 2:50, on the afternoon of October 21, 1977, Paul G. Scheible dropped by his mother's house at 1941 Dimon Street in the Wynnton area of the city. Scheible, age sixty-six, was a retired army colonel. His mother, eighty-nine-year-old Florence Scheible, lived alone in a small apartment on a quiet Wynnton residential street. Widowed since 1964, and despite poor hearing and vision, Ms. Scheible had managed to live independently, though she had recently been released from a rehabilitation facility where she was recovering from a broken hip. It was Col. Scheible's habit to check on his mother daily, either by phone or in person. He knocked on the door but received no answer. Finding it unlocked, he let himself in and called his mother's name. Again, there was no response. Sensing that "something was wrong," he left without looking further and drove home to pick up his wife. They returned shortly and began checking the house, only to find Ms. Scheible in the bedroom "covered up with bed clothing." Col. Scheible's wife "picked the pillow up by the corner and then dropped the pillow back in place." Her mother-in-law appeared to be dead. After calling the police, she and her husband waited outside for their arrival.[39] Police and the rescue squad arrived within minutes and confirmed Ms. Scheible's death. The coroner, Donald Kilgore, and detectives from the Robbery/Homicide division were contacted.

News reports the next day confirmed that Ms. Scheible was "killed and sexually assaulted in much the same manner as Ferne Jackson and Jean Dimenstien." The coroner left no doubt as to the exact manner of her death by revealing to reporters that "she was strangled by a stocking wrapped around her neck twice.... 'She was killed in her bed and he used a pillow [over the woman's face],' Kilgore said."[40] Nothing appeared to have been taken from her apartment.

Investigators tried to reconstruct the events of the hours before Scheible's death. A woman delivering phone books in the neighborhood saw "an elderly woman using a walker to hold on to while she tried to rake her yard." The tenant who lived in the apartment below the victim said she had heard someone stirring about upstairs around 10:00 A.M. Both commented that Ms. Scheible seemed to be nearly deaf. Her son told police, "She could only see people as blurs and would get confused as to who she was looking at." The neighborhood postman, Gene Clark, said he came by to deliver her mail about 11:35 A.M., but found her door closed. That was unusual, he said, as she would normally leave the door open waiting for him. Because of her poor vision, he was in the habit of reading her mail to her. Other neighbors confirmed that Ms. Scheible often left her door open during the day. Though her apartment was only a few yards from the street, "it was obscured by a large tree in front and bushes to the side." Also, a long narrow alleyway that led to a parking area behind the house offered a potentially secluded route for a would-be intruder. The alley led to Cherokee Avenue and Lakebottom Park, a large streamside green space.* With impairment of her sight and vision, and in the habit of leaving her front door open, investigators surmised that it would have been easy for Ms. Scheible's killer to gain access to her apartment without her knowledge. "Anyone could have come in on her," a neighbor said when interviewed. "She didn't see all that well and she'd always be out in her yard on nice days like today."[41]

Both local and state crime scene technicians processed the crime scene, yielding several pieces of evidence. A report from the local branch of the state crime laboratory identified a single hair "removed from inside the victim's legs" as having "Negroid characteristics." "Chemical examination" of stains on her bedding, clothing, and sheets "suggest[ed] the presence of seminal fluid. No spermatozoa [were] identified microscopically."[42] A shoeprint from the hardwood floor of the victim's bedroom would later be matched with a shoeprint found at the Dimenstien residence.

An autopsy of the body performed on the afternoon of the 21st by the Muscogee County medical examiner, Dr. Joe Webber, estimated the time of death as between noon and 1:00 P.M. The cause of death was confirmed as strangulation caused by a nylon stocking wrapped around the victim's neck. The hyoid bone was fractured. In addition, Ms. Scheible appeared to have been severely beaten. Her neck was fractured, a possible fatal injury in and of itself.† There was otherwise bleeding and bruising

---

* Lakebottom Park (or Lake Bottom Park) was once the site of a shallow man-made lake, hence the name. It is also known as Weracoba Park.

† Ms. Scheible suffered a "fracture-dislocation of C-1 on C-2," usually produced by forcible hyperextension of the neck. Such fractures most commonly result from motor vehicle accidents or falls in elderly adults. This type of injury is

around the face and head, in addition to trauma to the vaginal area consistent with "some type of penetration."

A canvass of the area generated no other useful information. The names of several men who had done yard work or similar jobs yielded no suspects. The police received reports and took statements from several neighbors which, perhaps influenced by the arrest of Jerome Livas, seemed to focus on unknown black males: A black man in his late twenties or early thirties had been seen a week or so earlier jogging on Dimon Street. Two days prior to Scheible's murder, a black man came by a woman's house seeking work. At about 8:30 or 8:45 P.M. on the night before the murder, a sixteen-year-old girl driving down Dimon Street with her aunt saw a black man walking on the sidewalk. She described him as having a "medium afro" and about five feet, eleven inches in height. "We thought it unusual for a black male to be in the area that time of night." she told police. On the day of the murder, a woman described a black man "in his twenties, about six feet tall and slender," walking along the street a block or two from Scheible's house. In a city plagued by a wave of murders, the fact that only three houses separated the Scheible residence from the home of Callye East and Nellie Sanderson, the site of the burglary two weeks earlier, did not seem of significance at the time.

With a third elderly woman now murdered in a manner that suggested the possibility that all three were killed by the same person, the Columbus police were faced with a dilemma. Jerome Livas, the person they had labeled as the "prime suspect" could not have killed Ms. Scheible; he was in jail. District Attorney Whisnant, believing that the evidence against Livas in the Jackson and Dimenstien killings was relatively weak, had not presented his case to a grand jury. On Monday, October 24th, Whisnant announced that he did not plan to do so. An editorial the next day in the *Enquirer* pointedly addressed the problem:

> The death of Mrs. Florence Scheible, eighty-nine, was a double shock—not merely because it involved the brutal and senseless taking of a life but because it indicated that the killer was still at large. Confronted with a third slaying after a lull of three and a half weeks, police could choose between two possible conclusions, neither of them attractive:

---

sometimes referred to as a "hangman's fracture" as judicial hanging can result in this pattern of damage.

Their suspect did not commit the assault-slayings.

A second killer was at work.

There was no indication which of these theories police were inclined to believe. Meanwhile top police officials—acting swiftly and responsibly in an unusual situation—geared up for another all-out effort to solve the murders and to protect citizens fearful for their own safety.[43]

Extra patrols were being added in the Wynnton district. All days off for detectives were cancelled.

The calm that appeared to be returning to Columbus after Livas's arrest had now been shattered. As two reporters for the *Ledger* wrote,

> The near-identical slayings of three elderly women has [*sic*] alarmed Columbus residents finding 'suspects' almost daily. In their homes. Breaking through their windows. Knocking on their doors. Stalking their streets. Noises people would have once ignored by going back to sleep now bring men out of their houses with shotguns. Strange behavior by prowlers which once would have been attributed to a man drunk, drugged, or just weird [now] terrifies women. Burglars are now considered to be in houses for murder, not for valuables.

A couple who had just purchased their house from an eighty-year-old-widow who lived alone were terrified when an unknown man rang their doorbell just before midnight. Hearing a noise at his front door, a man who lived a few blocks away from the homes of Ferne Jackson and Jean Dimenstien rushed out of his house "brandishing a cocked and loaded gun" only to confront a tame possum that had escaped several days earlier from the home of a little girl in the neighborhood.[44]

If Ms. Scheible had lived only ten more days, she would have celebrated her ninetieth birthday.

Chapter 7

Number Four

Martha Thurmond was fearful of what might happen. A sixty-nine-year-old widow and retired schoolteacher, she lived alone at 2614 Marion Street, a pleasant neighborhood of winding streets and small but well-built houses, most dating from the 1940s. The area was located just south of Wynnton Road in the general vicinity of where three other older women had been murdered over the preceding weeks. Following the murder of Florence Scheible on October 21st, Ms. Thurmond and a friend had driven by the crime scene, only about six-tenths of a mile away. For her protection, she had "installed burglar bars on her windows, nailed them shut and installed dead bolt locks on her doors, neighbors said."[45] Her son, William Thurmond, with his wife and son, drove down from Atlanta to spend the weekend with her after the Scheible killing, departing for home about 3:30 on Monday afternoon, October 24th. A friend urged her to go back to Atlanta with him, but she refused. Ms. Thurmond no doubt felt she was as prepared as anyone could be. In addition to the locks and burglar bars, she had purchased a can of Mace to protect herself. That evening, a relative spoke with her about 9:30 P.M. to confirm that Ms. Thurmond was still planning to come to her house the next day to sit with an aged parent for a few hours.

On Tuesday morning, the 25th, Ms. Thurmond missed her appointment. The relative, a niece by marriage, called her house but no one answered. Concerned, she contacted Irene Darden, an elderly friend of Ms. Thurmond's who lived nearby. Ms. Darden walked over to the Thurmond residence where she discovered the front door open, its lock broken. She called the police, who arrived shortly after 12:30 in the afternoon. On entering the house, the officer discovered Ms. Thurmond's lifeless body "covered with bed sheets and covers," a nylon stocking wrapped tightly around her neck.

Despite a steady rain, a crowd soon gathered in the street in front of the Thurmond home. A neighbor and friend of the victim, speaking to a reporter for the *Enquirer*, said "she and Mrs. Thurmond took precautions to secure their homes. 'We nailed our windows shut. We put extra locks on the doors—you know, deadbolt locks, like the police said...we even inspected each other's houses to make sure there was nothing we'd over-looked.'"[46] Mayor Jack Mickle, protected by a borrowed yellow raincoat, was among the crowd, together with the police chief and "seemingly every high-ranking officer on the force." Chief McClung refused to answer most questions, saying only that "foul play was suspected."[47] The coroner, Don-ald Kilgore, usually willing to disclose details, was scarcely more forthcom-ing. "We're not going to give out any more information," he said. "We're going to try another way this time with the idea that the killer might be standing out in the crowd laughing at us...and we don't want to release everything."[48] In that regard, "an officer questioned those standing watch across the street. 'What's your name and how did you find out about this?' he wanted to know. Another officer was photographing the groups who had gathered."[49] The frustration felt by the police was readily evident. "'We've just got to stop him,' one officer said. Another high-ranking of-ficer said grimly, 'This bastard must be an animal.'"[50] In a note of cruel irony, a dozen friends had planned to gather with Ms. Thurmond on the evening of her death to help her celebrate her seventieth birthday.

Examination of Ms. Thurmond's body at the city morgue confirmed the cause of death as strangulation due to a nylon stocking wrapped twice around her neck and secured with a knot. Like the other victims of the Strangler, she had been savagely beaten. There was evidence of a blow to the left rear of her head and both sides of her face. Possible fingernail or tooth marks were found on the left side of the neck. A "large bruise" at the vaginal entrance was presumptive evidence of sexual assault. Coroner Kil-gore estimated the time of death as between 1:00 and 4:00 A.M. on Octo-ber 25th.

A report of evidence analysis from the state crime laboratory docu-mented "the presence of seminal fluid" on the victim's bedding and in vag-inal swabs. Spermatozoa were identified microscopically. As with previous victims, two strands of hair recovered from the bed area displayed "Ne-groid characteristics" but could not be matched with samples collected from the Jackson and Dimenstien murders.[51]

It seemed evident that Ms. Thurmond's killer entered her house through the front door. She had recently had three dead bolt locks in-stalled, but the job was done incorrectly. The backing plate, to which the lock mechanism was attached, had been placed on the outside of the entry doors, allowing an intruder to simply unscrew the lock mounting. After inspecting the house, her son told police that a pump shotgun seemed to be missing, as well as a small amount of cash. Ms. Thurmond's car had not been taken, but all four tires had been punctured by "a small object, believed to be a screwdriver."

As in the case of the other killings, interviews with neighbors produced some possible leads, none of which turned out to be productive. All seemed well when her relative had spoken with Ms. Thurmond at about 9:30 P.M. the night before her death. Another neighbor had observed that the lights in the Thurmond house were on at about 10:30 P.M. Several other neighbors reported dogs barking unusually loudly at about 11:15 P.M. And although the event had occurred nearly a week earlier, perhaps the most compelling clue to a possible suspect was given by Irene Darden, who had originally discovered Ms. Thurmond's front door forced entry.

On October 19th, two days prior to the Scheible murder, Ms. Darden, a widowed, seventy-five-year-old white lady who lived diagonally across the street from Ms. Thurmond, attended Wednesday evening services at St. Luke Methodist Church. She had just arrived home between 8:30 and 9:00 P.M. when she heard a noise at her back door. Peering out, she saw a shadowy figure jump from the back porch and run toward the street. She rushed to the front door, trying to catch a glimpse of the would-be intruder as he fled. To her shock, she discovered that her front door screen had been cut in two places, the screws removed from the bottom hinge, and the lock on the screen door opened. Apparently unable to open the main front door, the burglar was in the process of trying to enter from the back when she surprised him. When asked by the police to describe the man, she said,

> He was a small person. I would say a little over five feet. He had black and kinkie [sic] hair. His hair was neat. He had on a light tan jacket. It looked like leather to me. The coat came down below the waist.... I don't know how old he was, but I feel that he was young in the way he jumped off the porch and ran out of the yard. I feel sure that it was a black person because of his hair. I did not notice his shoes, but I feel like he had on tennis shoes because he did not make any noise when he jumped off the steps. I think he was a light complexed [sic] black.[52]

In search of how or why the murderer chose his victims, one of the city detectives noted that the 1977 edition of the Columbus City Directory listed the name, address, and marital status of each of the four murder victims, as well as that of Gertrude Miller, who at this point in the investigation was assumed to be the Strangler's first victim, though she survived.

At the time, businesses commonly used city and business directories as marketing tools. It was not unreasonable to consider the possibility that the Strangler had chosen his victims from this source.*

With four victims whose deaths appeared to follow the same general pattern, the press and citizens alike began referring to the murderer as the "Stocking Strangler." Police, frustrated by the long hours demanded of them and their seeming inability to capture the elusive killer, were under constant and increasing pressure to do more. Criticism from Don Kilgore, the county coroner, did not help matters. He first heard of Ms. Thurmond's murder when a reporter from the *Ledger* called him on the afternoon of the 25th to ask for an interview. More than an hour had elapsed between the arrival of the police at the victim's house and when Kilgore was contacted. Stating "the police leaders are unhappy that news reports on the multiple deaths have come from his office," Kilgore said, "I don't like it. I don't know what the problem is. They don't want me telling the press nothing. They can run the police department. They're not going to run the coroner's office." Stressing his perceived importance in death investigations, Kilgore said, "I told them I was going to run the coroner's office according to the laws of Georgia, and the hell with them."[53]

In an effort to reassure the public, the following day Police Chief McClung released a letter addressed "To the Citizens of Columbus." Giving his assurance of the police department's "deep concern for your personal safety and well-being," he noted that the personnel of the Columbus Police Department and the Muscogee County Sheriff's Department were "working diligently around the clock conducting the largest investigative and preventative program ever initiated in this community." Both departments were fully utilizing the services of the Georgia Bureau of Investigation (GBI) and State Crime Laboratory, as well as "working in concert with the Federal Bureau of Investigation" and other independent technical services. He confirmed to reporters that a "psychological profile of the killer" had been developed for police, and that he'd "talked informally to a former FBI agent and expert on the subject of sex criminals." An emergency hotline established by the police was "inundated" with hundreds of tips on its first day of availability.[54] The reward for information leading to

---

* The Columbus City Directory was published by R. L. Polk and Company of Richmond, Virginia. The Polk Company, was founded in 1870 to publish business and city directories. It remained an independent corporate entity until 2013 when it was purchased by IHS, Inc., for $1.4 billion.

the arrest and conviction of the killer had been increased to $15,000, a third of which was offered by the state of Georgia. "The reign of terror in Columbus must be stopped in its tracks—and I'm offering these rewards as the maximum allowable under the law," Gov. George Busbee said.[55]

McClung's reassurance may have helped calm some, but as long as the Strangler remained at large, citizens—especially women—were taking no chances. Pawnbrokers and gun-shop owners reported elderly women buying pistols. Hardware-store dealers confirmed a run on door locks and dead bolts. Some older women chose to temporarily relocate, staying with relatives or moving out of town. With Halloween only a few days away, Mayor Mickle suggested that trick-or-treating be cancelled or cut back, "concerned that a trigger-happy, frightened Columbus resident might shoot a child."[56] A letter to the editor of the *Ledger* suggested prayer as the solution. "You have tried everything except the one solution, and that is Jesus.... If you want this killer, we will pray him out of hiding and into confession.... God will force this killer to give himself up before another innocent life is taken."[57] Perhaps in response, more than a hundred people, many of them elderly women, attended a special prayer service at the Wynnton United Methodist Church on Friday evening, October 28th.

The fear that permeated the city spawned a number of reported instances of women, both young and old, receiving threatening notes or phone calls. An elderly widow living on Wynnton Road reported to police that she had received calls from a man claiming to be the killer and telling her she would be "next on the list." In another incident, police arrested seventeen-year-old Longelle Jones, who called a twenty-seven-year-old woman and told her, "I want you to know I'm the person who killed four women and I call all my victims before I kill them." His case was bound over for grand jury presentation.

The Sunday, November 6th, edition of the *Ledger-Enquirer* carried an update on the investigation, in the process mentioning that police "have quietly circulated a composite drawing of the rapist they believe may be the Stocking Strangler who has sexually slain four elderly women in the last seven weeks." The drawing, that of a young black male in his early twenties, was based on a description given by Gertrude Miller (though the paper did not reveal her name). Carl Cannon, the reporter, noted "further details of the drawing are not being published because they might harm the investigation."[58] The revelation of a police sketch upset authorities. Chief McClung said information about the "composite drawing was not an official release by the police department," although he did not deny the accuracy of the report. Mayor Mickle, calling the release "unfortunate," objected to the article "because it said police believed the stocking killer to be black." "He thought the article might instigate a form of 'harassment' for blacks because the sketch was of a black man and citizens might now feel suspicious of blacks."[59,60] In what appeared to be an unfortunate choice of words, in announcing a program to curb crimes against the elderly, Georgia governor George Busbee stated, "We've got to take immediate action to prevent future atrocities like those in Columbus from transforming sunset years into black nightmares."[61]

Even though Jerome Livas, the man originally thought to be the Strangler, could not have murdered the last two victims, Police Chief McClung refused to publicly discount him as a suspect. Privately, police officials were willing to admit he was not, and Livas's attorney had been so informed. The sole piece of evidence against him was his confessions, but—in the words of reporter Carl Cannon—Livas was "mentally slow, intimidated by authority and easily led into saying things." Cannon took matters into his own hands. In an article published in the Sunday, November 20th, edition of the *Ledger-Enquirer*, Cannon wrote, "The belief that Livas would admit to virtually anything was bolstered last week when Livas signed a jailhouse confession for the Ledger that he killed Presidents John F. Kennedy and William McKinley. Livas also 'confessed' that he was present when Charles Manson killed actress Sharon Tate in Hollywood and that he knew when the Lindbergh baby was to be kidnapped in the 1930s." Asked why he "wouldn't publicly discount [Livas] as a suspect even after two other women were strangled in nearly the same way, McClung said, 'You can't come out and exonerate people. What if people had come forward later and said he did it, and we had (already exonerated him)?'"[62]

Chapter 8

Close to the Vest

Though several weeks had passed without another incident attributed to the Strangler, the citizens of Columbus remained wary of what the future might hold. The arrest of Jerome Livas as a possible suspect had, for a few brief days, appeared to be a glimmer of hope beaming through dark skies of fear. Now, nothing was certain. The Livas affair had damaged the credibility of law enforcement. Columbus police, hoping to avoid another similar misstep, had in turn adopted a policy of keeping their plans confidential. While highly visible patrols had a certain deterrent value, too much public knowledge of the exact nature of their efforts might paradoxically assist a killer determined to avoid them. With two more murders occurring four days apart, a renewed and intensified plan was needed.

The greater Wynnton district of the city, an area roughly two miles by two miles in size, would be divided into twelve "beats," each to be intensively patrolled by a team of officers. Some would be highly visible, others less so: to the north, Edgewood Road and the Country Club of Columbus marked the boundary of the patrol area; to the east, the Cross Country Plaza shopping center and Auburn Avenue; to the south, Buena Vista Road; and to the west 13th and 14th Avenues. Officers in marked vehicles would be responsible for patrolling each beat, working in three overlapping shifts of nine hours each. An October 25, 1977, interoffice memo from Deputy Commander J. B. Hicks outlined the schedules for detectives: Thirteen were assigned to follow up on leads on the murder cases. Two were assigned to interview suspects. Twenty-one were to patrol the Wynnton district in unmarked cars, supplementing other officers in marked patrol cars. The vice squad was given patrol duty from 6:00 P.M. to 2:00 A.M. Six additional officers were assigned to answer calls not related to the murders.[63]

Officers on patrol, either overtly or covertly, were advised to stop and question any person or persons deemed to be in the least way suspicious. Those stopped were usually asked their purpose in the area and requested to show some form of identification. Records of the encounters were recorded on "Field Interview Cards," to be kept for future reference. They would eventually number in the thousands.

The patrol teams were supplemented by additional staff who answered the special phone lines from 8:00 A.M. to midnight daily. Questions, concerns, and information provided by callers were recorded on paper, to be followed up as appropriate. A very small sampling of the hundreds of such messages recorded in the first week after the Thurmond murder is representative of the type of information and feedback gleaned from this source:

- A woman named Judy offered to share a spare bedroom with an elderly citizen.
- A lady who formerly lived down the street from Ms. Thurmond called to give the name of an insurance agent she described as "very unstable" who had been "heard to say all old people should be eliminated."
- There were numerous reports of "suspicious" vehicles of various types.
- A student majoring in criminal justice at a local college suggested that the killer might be a woman, and asked if the police had considered using women on stake-outs.
- A man from Phenix City reported that "several years ago a man from Lanett [Alabama] was arrested for kicking and assaulting his wife." He advised the operator to see if the man was in prison.
- Several calls reported door-to-door salesmen of such things as insurance and encyclopedias as possible suspects.
- George, an ex-military policeman, suggested necrophilia.
- A caller who refused to give his name wanted to know if all of the victims were insured by one particular company. If so, he stated that "he might have some info."
- Several women reported threatening calls, most saying they had been told they would be killed next, or were on the Strangler's list.
- A woman who had been keeping a "chart of the area" called to advise police that the next murder would take place in the Springdale Drive/Oak Avenue area, just south of the country club.

• A man who worked at Bibb Mills found an inscription written on the wall in the men's room: "The next lady will be killed on Wednesday."

• A woman called to say that the locations of four murders, when plotted on a city map, formed a "cross bones and skull symbol." She believed the killings were the work of "a Satanic cult."

For the most part, the call lines provided a wealth of useless information, the sheer volume of which made recognition of valuable clues all the more difficult. At the same time, however, their availability provided a way for a concerned public to contact the police.

The "psychological profile of the killer" that Chief Curtis McClung had alluded to was based on an October 27th visit to the FBI Academy in Quantico, Virginia, by police department director Ronnie Jones and another official. After spending some four hours with three agents, one of whom was a "sex crime expert," they were able to develop a speculative profile of the killer. If their assessment were correct, the Strangler would be a black male between sixteen and twenty-one years of age, a high school graduate. At a younger age, he was a possible bed-wetter, fire-starter, or animal-torturer. He is cunning, with no anxiety, remorse or guilt. He lives near the crime scene area, is "sexually inadequate" and a "pathological liar." In terms of background, he "may have been raised by his grandparents, or did not have a mother for a long time. He may have been raised by an older person who was dominating to him." In summary, the profile described the Strangler as "a psychopath with inadequate tendencies. He's hostile and aggressive, but intelligent. He is a braggard [sic], likes publicity. He is challenging the police. He will continue to kill until such time as he is...caught. In all probability it will take evidence to get a conviction. He will not be a talkative person."[64]*

The controversial police sketch displaying a proposed image of the Strangler as a black man was drawn during and after an October 29th hypnosis session with Gertrude Miller, now considered the killer's one surviving victim. Ms. Miller was interviewed at the Columbus Police Department headquarters in the hope that under hypnosis she would be able to give a more accurate description of her attacker. The details of the session

---

* Although endorsed by the FBI and widely used, the subjective nature and actual value of "criminal profiling" has been questioned by many experts.

were recorded and later transcribed. The hypnotist was Dr. Stewart Wiggins, a PhD psychologist and member of the faculty of the Medical College of Georgia (MCG) in Augusta.[†] In addition to Wiggins and Miller, several police officials and a sketch artist were present. Under light hypnosis, Ms. Miller was again able to recall the events of her ordeal. While the artist was able to produce a sketch, on a practical basis no new information was gained from the session. Other than the fact that her attacker was a younger black male, the transcript suggests that Miller and the artist could not agree on the details of his appearance.

Although mostly behind-the-scenes, the intense police surveillance did have some results in identifying possible suspects. For example, at approximately 11:45 P.M. on October 29th, two patrolmen stopped a "suspicious looking vehicle," a 1976 yellow Pontiac Firebird, "cruising" the Peacock Avenue area only a few blocks from the Scheible and Thurmond residences. Two men, both "Iranian by birth," were questioned and arrested after a search of their car revealed "an assortment of burglar tools." Both were photographed, fingerprinted, and had "pubic and public hair" samples collected. No connection to the murders was established. On another occasion, police department detectives traveled to the Chatham County Correctional Institute in Savannah to interview an inmate who had written the department claiming knowledge of a possible suspect. The prisoner related a detailed but fanciful tale of catching a ride with a red-headed man with "large ears that stuck out far from the head" who displayed a perverse interest in having sex with "old women." Prison officials, including the warden, told the investigators that the prisoner was "a con artist" who had produced bogus information before.

[†] Dr. Wiggins had been recommended by the Georgia Bureau of Investigation, which he had assisted on several occasions in attempts to elicit through hypnotism more detailed memories from witnesses or victims of crime. He was an associate professor of psychiatry at MCG and held the same academic rank in psychology at Augusta College. In late 1979, Wiggins was called to Americus, Georgia, to interview witnesses in death of Leigh Bell, a fifteen-year-old cheerleader who had been raped and murdered. In a bizarre series of events, Wiggins apparently suffered a paranoid episode while there and attempted to shoot one of the Sumter County deputies. These strange events are recorded in greater detail in a five-part series published in the *Americus (GA) Times-Recorder* between June 5 and July 2, 2019. Wiggins died by suicide on November 8, 1981. His obituary listed him as being retired, referring to his academic career in past tense.

In late October, a janitor for the Muscogee County School District, a black man named Frank Brookins, spoke to police about his nineteen-year-old son, James, who had been identified as someone who "roamed the Columbus Square-Wynnton area on foot."‡ The boy "will not stay at home," the father told police. "He roams the streets at night." Police questioned the father based on the psychological profile they had established earlier: Had James "ever wet the bed, set fires or tortured animals"? (He wet the bed when he was "real small.") Is he "cunning"? (No.) Does he "show fear"? (No.) Is he "remorse[ful]"? (No.) Does he "show guilt"? (No.) Does he "like older women"? ("Not that I know.") Is he "intelligent"?[65] ("Yes he is.") In many ways, the police interview was that of a hard-working father frustrated at his teenaged son's lack of focus and ambition. While police files contain numerous examples of dead-end leads, this one seemed different. The investigators decided to look more closely at James Brookins as a potential suspect.

Despite all the effort, despite the intense police patrols, the hotlines, and the urgent desire of everyone to bring the killer to justice, as of the end of October 1977, apprehension of the culprit was no closer than it had been when he committed his first known attack nearly two months earlier. On October 30th, Constance Johnson, a staff writer for the *Ledger*, penned a column titled, "Columbus Will Never Be the Same."

> Somewhere in Columbus, someone with a hideously distorted mind is watching, with weird satisfaction, the character of a city change. Fear has become the constant if resented companion for thousands of Columbus citizens, men as well as women. Because of the bizarre rituals in each of the four slayings, women naturally feel more fearful. They are the potential victims. For few if any doubt that the demented stalker, acting alone or with others, is plotting a fifth strike, perhaps more. Along with fear there is anger and defiance among the women of Columbus, attitudes that the mayor, law enforcement leaders and policemen, being men, may not fully understand. Some of this anger is directed at them. Justified or not, the mayor and police have invited it by failing to call in Georgia Bureau of Investigation agents and expert criminal investigators weeks ago. "They are on an ego trip," said one woman. "They don't want to acknowledge that

---

‡ Frank and James Brookins are pseudonyms.

someone else might know more than they do." Another said she considered the police department's anxiousness to name a suspect in the first two murder cases a desperate effort to ease public pressure.... "I'm mad," said one woman.... The police aren't helping by their public squabbles with the coroner, she said. She dismissed the mayor's televised appearance at one death scene as "a public relations move."[66]

As law enforcement worked tirelessly behind the scenes, for the people of Columbus, fear and frustration remained the orders of the day.

Chapter 9

No End in Sight

A month passed, and then two, without further evidence of the Strangler. Perhaps it was the intensity of the police surveillance that deterred him, or perhaps the fact that many homes of the city were now newly protected by burglar bars and dead bolt locks, the residents therein armed and prepared to kill a would-be intruder. In late November, the headline "Fear of Stocking Strangler Subsiding in Area" topped an article in the *Ledger-Enquirer*.

> The fear that has gripped so many in this city so tightly has loosened a bit. Some people's minds are drifting to other things and conversation isn't always dominated by talk of the savage stranglings. Some of the older women who had left their homes to live with relatives have returned. Many of the lights which burned all night have been dimmed, police say. Behind their deadbolt locks some folks are thinking of Christmas and the holiday spirit.[67]

This emerging anticipation of a return to some sense of normalcy was not universal. Like many, Mary Kate Jenkins, a thirty-seven-year-old teacher at a local business school, feared being attacked by the Strangler. Originally living on Richard Street in the heart of Wynnton a few blocks from the site of Ms. Scheible's murder, she, her husband, and their infant child had recently moved to north Columbus, away from the killings. But even this was not far enough. Because her husband, a Georgia Power employee, was frequently out of town on business, she and her child were staying with her parents in Fort Mitchell, Alabama, about ten miles south of Columbus. It offered a refuge from the danger and a short daily commute to her job. On the foggy morning of December 15, 1977, Mary Kate was on her way to work, passing through an intersection that she had traversed a thousand or more times before. This occasion was different. A log truck emerged from the thick fog, striking her car and killing her instantly. To her family, she had become yet another victim of the Strangler.[68]

Near the end of his monthly news conference a few days before Christmas, Mayor Mickle "casually" announced his plans to "set up a task force to concentrate on solving the killings." The idea was evidently in its early stages; Mickle said he had not yet discussed it with police chief McClung. Indicating "that the police have apparently hit a wall in the investigation," Mickle said, "Maybe by putting in some new blood, new people, new talents, we will find something we've overlooked." His target date was early January, "if there is no break in the case by then."[69]

Mickle's allegations aside, the police had been tireless in their investigations and were possibly making some progress toward identifying a suspect. In their defense, or perhaps in response to Mickle's still unformed plans, on December 28th, the director of the Robbery/Homicide Squad, Ronnie Jones, prepared a summary report of their efforts to date:

> As a result of follow-up investigation by the members of the Homicide Squad of the Columbus Police Department, several hundreds of leads have been checked out. Numerous out of town trips concerning possible suspects have been made by members of the Homicide Squad. Countless overtime hours were acquired by a large portion of the entire department. Hundreds of suspects have been questioned concerning the strangulations, some suspects requiring several days by at least two men to be checked out. Sixteen telephone traps were made by the department with the cooperation of the Southern Bell Telephone Company resulting from citizens of Columbus making complaints saying the Strangler had called them saying they were the next victim. As a result of the sixteen telephone traps, two arrests were made by the Homicide Squad. Thus resulting in two individual cases of charges of terroristic threats that were not related or found to be related in anyway with the stocking strangulations. Numerous police personnel of the Columbus Police Department were placed on stakeouts in the crime scene area. They consisted of individual residents being staked out from the inside, men being located on roof tops in the area and numerous men being placed in undercover vehicles patrolling and checking the crime area over a period of several months. Close contact has also been kept with several police agencies out of state concerning homicides or strangulations involving elderly ladies. Numerous teletypes have been sent to different law enforcement agencies and numerous long-distance phone calls have been made to agencies across the country. Contact has been made to agencies as far away as

Toronto, Ontario, Canada concerning similarities in the strangulations.[70]

The report went on to say that Homicide Squad investigators had identified and were "working on two prime suspects. Both being black."

The first of the two was James Brookins, whose father had spoken
earlier to police. "A black Georgia Bureau of Investigation undercover
agent was assigned to tail James Brookins and make acquaintances with
him and see if he could find out anything of Brookins that might be pertinent to the strangulations." Shortly after the Thurmond murder, Brookins was admitted to a psychiatric hospital where he stayed for a month. He
was later arrested for impersonating a police officer. The second suspect,
an eighteen-year-old, was arrested by a patrolman after breaking into the
home of an elderly black female whom he attempted to rape. He was
"known to hang around street corners in the Wynnton area." At the time
of the report, the investigation into both suspects was ongoing.

Although unknown to the public and not mentioned in Ronnie
Jones's report, the intensive police patrols of Wynnton had been sharply
curtailed about a week before Christmas, approximately eight weeks after
the Strangler's last murder. The date of the report, Wednesday, December
28, 1977, was ironic. Undoubtedly, it would have been submitted that
morning, as the events of that afternoon would once again dramatically
change the narrative in this continuing saga.

At about 10:30 on the morning of December 28th, Tommie Stevens
arrived at the home of Ms. Kathleen Woodruff, where Ms. Stevens had
worked as a maid for some thirty-three years. Both women were seventy-
four years old and over the decades had developed a close relationship. Ms.
Woodruff was the widow of George C. Woodruff, to whom she had been
married for more than four decades prior to his death in 1968. Her late
husband, described in the press as a leading businessman and industrialist,
had been one of Columbus's most prominent citizens. In his youth, he was
a well-known football player for the University of Georgia, later serving as
team coach from 1923 to 1927. The Woodruff practice fields there were
named in his honor. Woodruff Hall was the home of the university's bas-
ketball team for many years. Prior to marrying her husband, Ms. Woodruff
had attended Sophie Newcomb College in New Orleans, later studying in
Paris, France, and Florence, Italy. Since her husband's death she had led a
quiet life in her home at 1811 Buena Vista Road. The preceding afternoon,

Ms. Stevens left work a little after five. At the time, Ms. Woodruff was sitting in the living room reading a book.

On arriving at work the next morning and not seeing her employer, Ms. Stevens later said, "I went on in down to her bedroom and looked in and the light was on and it looked like [Ms. Woodruff] was under the cover. She was covered up except for her chest and she had on the same dress she had on yesterday evening when I left.... I thought she had been reading and had dozed off." This would not have been unusual; Ms. Woodruff would often stay up late at night to read or watch television. About half an hour later, Ms. Stevens became concerned, thinking "Mrs. Woodruff does not normally sleep this late. I went through the hallway and looked into her bedroom and called for her several times and she did not answer. I went on into the bedroom and looked at her, waved my hands over her eyes to see if she would bat her eyes and she did not. I then saw a little streak of blood coming down the right side of her mouth and her face seemed like it had little bruises on it." Panicking, she called Ms. Woodruff's son, George, to tell him that his mother was dead.[71] The son arrived shortly and called the police.

Chapter 10

A Tragedy of Errors

The death of Kathleen Woodruff thrust murders attributed to the Columbus Strangler into the national spotlight, and not in a way that reflected at all well on the city. Variations on the story from United Press International (UPI) and Associated Press (AP) newswires appeared in dozens of daily papers across the country. Some, like the *Mobile Register*, implied Ms. Woodruff's murder might not have occurred if the "special police patrols which had cruised by Kathleen K. Woodruff's home every night since October 29th [had not been] called off just before Christmas because 'the Stocking Strangler' hadn't killed since October."[72] With the death of such a prominent citizen, other papers simply brought attention to what had been an otherwise regional news item. One particularly vitriolic article titled "A Tragedy of Errors in Columbus, Ga." was published in the *Washington Post* on December 30th, submitted by none other than Carl Cannon, the *Ledger* reporter who had written extensively about the case.

Noting that after Chamber of Commerce efforts to have "the rest of America hear the name of Columbus," the dream of promoting " a lovely, small, quaint Southern city was swept away by a reality of random violence.... If the rest of America was to hear of Columbus's tale of the New South, it was to hear of it because one of the most savage series of crime in the history of the South happened here—the rape-strangling of five elderly Columbus women in their homes." Cannon was especially hard on local law enforcement: "The police have shown a genius for making the wrong moves. The mayor has been single-mindedly stubborn in his refusal to call on the Georgia Bureau of Investigation for help." The "dimwitted" Jerome Livas was no longer considered a suspect by police only after a third murder occurred while he was incarcerated, and the extraction of a jailhouse confession in which he also admitted to killing presidents Kennedy and McKinley.[73]

In what had become his style of issuing his opinions directly to the press, Coroner Don Kilgore opined that he did not believe Woodruff's killer was the same person who had committed the other four strangulation murders. "In my opinion this is not the same thing. She was not brutally beaten and there was no real apparent evidence of rape," he said. The crime scene analysis and the autopsy would prove otherwise. Ms. Woodruff's lower body, like that of the other victims, had been covered up with a sheet when she was found, but was naked from the waist down. Police discovered a pillowcase, a pair of women's panties, and a garter belt with attached stockings that someone—presumably the killer—had attempted to conceal under the foundation of a small outbuilding behind the house. The medical examiner's autopsy report indicated that she died sometime between midnight and 4:00 A.M. on the 28th. Bruises on her left jaw suggested that she had been struck in the face. A scarf—ironically patterned with red, white, and black University of Georgia logos—was wrapped tightly around her neck, and her hyoid bone was fractured, both evidence of death by strangulation. Examination of vaginal fluid revealed abundant spermatozoa.

The killer had apparently gained entry to Ms. Woodruff's house through a rear window that he pried open. Though her locks had been recently changed, there were no burglar bars on the windows. Her maid, Tommie Stevens, told a reporter, "Her son and me always warned her about staying alone by herself in the big house. But she wouldn't listen. She just wanted to be by herself. She just felt nobody would bother her. I used to tell her occasionally that she must have someone to stay with her at night. But no, she didn't want that."[74] She was aware of the risk and chose to stay alone. It appeared that Ms. Woodruff may have been sitting at a desk in her living room writing a check when the intruder surprised her. Her glasses and checkbook were found on the floor. Samples of what was initially thought to be soil collected from the living room carpet and floor in the hall and bedroom turned out to be a mixture of spices, described by the state crime lab as "salt crystals and some vegetable material, probably a cooking seasoning mixture of some type." Further analysis later identified the substance as "celery salt." It had apparently been put there by the killer to conceal his scent if tracking dogs were brought in by the police. Hair samples found on the victim's bedding were described as "Negroid hair." Crime scene techs also collected several fingerprints and shoeprints.

In a funeral attended by "almost 300 of the town's most prestigious citizens," Ms. Woodruff was buried in a short graveside service, the ceremony lasting less than ten minutes. The minister read the 23rd Psalm and a brief poem by Ralph Waldo Emerson. "Little was said of the woman who was a member of one of Columbus's most influential families."[75]

The day of the funeral, Columbus's two daily papers ran editorials demanding that the mayor, police chief, and public safety director do more. "Let's Solve the Killings," the *Ledger* said, calling for "mobilizing every possible resource, including manpower, technical assistance and all the outside help...to find the person responsible. The citizenry expects no less." Noting that the "results [of the investigations] have been, from what has been made public, just about an absolute zero," the *Enquirer* demanded "outside help." "The best criminologists available from other police agencies should be asked for assistance—hired if necessary. It will be no reflection on our police force to call on the top homicide investigators in the country to bring a fresh approach and the best thinking available."[76,77]

At a special news conference the same day, police chief Curtis McClung, accompanied by Mayor Mickle, announced the creation of a "special investigative task force" to be made up of investigators from the Columbus Police Department and the Muscogee County Sheriff's Department as well as agents from the Georgia Bureau of Investigation. The director of the Robbery/Homicide division, Ronnie Jones, would act as task force leader. Despite calls for more transparency in their inquiry, McClung "repeated earlier statements that he would not disclose details of the investigative procedures used in the cases, nor any details of the crimes or crime scenes." Blaming criticism on "rumors in the community," he said, "I will not allow these critics (of the police investigation) to pressure us into revealing how we are utilizing this outside help in such a manner as to jeopardize the success of our investigation."[78] Besides police efforts, the reward for the capture and conviction of the Strangler had also been increased. With recent additions from local citizens and the Columbus newspapers, plus an increase in the amount offered by the state, the reward now approached $20,000.

As noted earlier, the intense police presence in the Wynnton district had the positive effect of reducing, but not eliminating, burglaries. Amidst the distractions of the holiday season, and even with the death of Kathleen Woodruff, some still occurred. As later events would reveal, two residential break-ins, one occurring about a week before the Woodruff murder and the other a few days afterwards, would be of importance in piecing together the puzzle then known only as the Columbus Strangler. On the night of December 20th, Mr. and Mrs. William Swift returned to their home at 1710 Buena Vista Road at about 10:30 P.M. after attending a Christmas party. The Swift home was a large two-story, six-columned Greek revival mansion, separated from the street by a large expanse of manicured lawn, and located only a short distance down and across the street from the home of Kathleen Woodruff. Ms. Swift, age fifty-eight, went on to bed, while her sixty-nine-year-old husband stayed up a while to watch television. At about 1:00 A.M., he climbed the stairs to join his wife, discovering in the process that their home had been burglarized while they were away for the evening. Jewelry and some cash were missing. The police were called and the burglary reported. A police survey of the premises at the time did not reveal how the burglar gained entry into the Swift house.

Like many homeowners in the neighborhood, the Swifts had taken precautions to protect themselves from would-be intruders, including the installation of burglar bars on their windows. About a week later, Mr. Swift noted that the bars on a downstairs kitchen window had been removed by the burglar, and then carefully put back in place so as not to be noticed. The police had missed this in searching for clues on the night of the theft. Not thinking his discovery of any importance in solving the crime, Mr. Swift did not inform the police, mentioning his discovery only to his wife.

The second burglary occurred on the night of December 31st–January 1st at the home of Mr. and Mrs. Abraham Illges at 2021 Brookside Drive. The Illges home was a large, rambling, three-storied, stone- and brick-clad structure with a slate roof, built in a style that one might find in the English countryside. Located on a heavily wooded, two-acre lot in the finest part of Wynnton, its owners were clearly persons of substance and style. The Illgeses were an older couple, Ms. Illges being seventy-five and her husband, who was in poor health, age eighty-three. Sometime during the night, an intruder gained entry through a ground floor window, ascended a short flight of steps to the main level, then a longer second flight of steps to the upper level, where the Illgeses were asleep in separate bedrooms at opposite ends of the house. They awoke the following morning to discover that during the night someone had entered both bedrooms, stealing $600 in cash and a set of car keys to their new 1978 Cadillac, which had been parked in the driveway. The missing car was discovered by police about 2:00 A.M. the following morning on Victory Drive in south Columbus in the parking lot of a Motel 6 and near a Sambo's restaurant.

As those who attended New Year's Eve parties the night of the Illges burglary must have discussed, in the four months just ended, five women had been brutally murdered, all within a relatively small area of the city. The police—so far as anyone seemed to know—appeared unable to stop the slaughter. Perhaps things would change with the New Year and the nascent task force.

Chapter 11

The Task Force

The beginning of a new year, coupled with the announcement of the formation of a task force to apprehend the Strangler, created a sense of hope that a resolution might be near. The combined holiday editions of the *Ledger-Enquirer* polled the public, asking readers for their opinion as to the top story of 1977, the year just passed. There were many options: the inauguration of Jimmy Carter as America's thirty-ninth president; the deaths of Bing Crosby and Elvis Presley; the Canary Island aircraft disaster that took the lives of 583 passengers when two Boeing 747s collided on the runway of the Tenerife Airport; and the capture of David Berkowitz, New York's elusive "Son of Sam" serial killer, to name a few.[*] In Columbus, the five strangling murders topped the list of local events.[79]

Stung by criticism from the press, on December 30th, Mayor Mickle and Chief McClung met privately with three prominent business executives and the editor of the *Ledger-Enquirer* to review the exact measures that were being taken in the search. "The four were briefed on the investigation because of a widespread feeling that Columbus police were not doing enough to solve the stranglings, especially in the area of seeking outside assistance." The men were said to emerge from the meeting reassured.[80]

Meanwhile, the new task force had set up a command post in the Civil Defense Headquarters in the basement of the government center. The mood was one of quiet optimism. "We feel strongly that we will get the person that's done this," Ronnie Jones, the task force chief, said. "Every member of this police force—every member of this squad—wants to catch the killer just as much as any person out on the street—probably more." To better track the killer, the city had been divided into 210 squares, with each square subdivided into 25 smaller squares, creating a grid coordinate system.[81] A December 31st memo from Jones and Jimmy Davis, his counterpart from the Georgia Bureau of Investigation, outlined a new investigative protocol. "In the event of another stocking strangulation in the city,"

---

[*] Berkowitz was responsible for six murders in New York City between July 1976 and July 1977. NBC news had earlier referred to the Columbus Strangler as "the Southern Son of Sam."

eighteen officers were to be assigned to each crime scene: four officers would search the scene, two officers would gather evidence, an "I.D. Tech" would be in charge of photographs, latent fingerprint collection, etc., while eleven officers would canvass the neighborhood. The diversion of resources to the Strangler investigation had the potential to leave other areas of law enforcement relatively unattended. In response, the Georgia State Patrol announced that sixteen troopers were being dispatched to Columbus to help enforce traffic laws.[82]

Over the following weeks, task force members pursued dozens and dozens of leads, none of which yielded useful information. In one interview, a possible suspect told investigators that he heard a female friend state "the male suspect we're looking for in these homicides was a white male who was planting black pubic hairs as evidence that a black male was the perpetrator of these crimes." Commonalities between the victims were analyzed looking for a unifying thread. Did they worship at the same church, seek medical care from the same physician, or perhaps share a handyman or yard worker? Schools were asked to provide lists of problematic students who might be considered as suspects. As before, hundreds called in information and tips to the hotlines. Investigators acquired a computer to cross-reference the massive amount of information that continued to pour in.† Jane Hudson, a well-known "psychic" on Atlanta's WRNG radio, predicted "the crime would be solved by the end of January," explaining that the revelation "just came through my mind" while talking to a person who called in to her radio show. Going into more detail, she explained, "The killer is a light-skinned person—if he's black, he's very light-skinned. He's young, no more than thirty. He's a psychopath. The police already have this person under surveillance and are merely waiting." Right or wrong, as events would unfold over the following weeks, her next prediction would prove to be at least partially accurate. "There will be a sixth attempt," she said. "It won't be successful, however, and it will help the police to close in on the killer."[83]

In keeping with his previous statements, Coroner Donald Kilgore acted as a bit of a rogue, issuing his own often-contrarian opinions to news media. On January 5th, he insisted the investigation into Kathleen Woodruff's murder had been "mishandled" because investigators had linked it to

---

† It should be recalled that in 1978, computer technology was still in its infancy. The first Apple computer was introduced in April 1976, and the first IBM desktop computer in August 1981.

the other four stranglings. "Nobody knows how many killers we are looking for," Kilgore said. He wanted it made clear that she had not been beaten, so "she isn't tagged as number five."[84]

With the new and expanded team in place and police patrols resumed, surveillance of the Wynnton area continued with ever greater intensity. When interviewed decades later, residents of the area at the time spoke of the nighttime patrols, officers hidden from view watching with night-vision goggles, the spotlights from police cruisers probing their lawns and casting shadows on their bedroom ceilings, the roar of helicopters hovering in the darkness overhead, and the fear that lurking somewhere in the night the Strangler waited, or worse, had managed to elude the watchers and claim yet another victim.[85]

While weeks passed without another killing, burglaries continued. Most were petty crime. Others, like the break-in at the home of Mr. and Mrs. Jack M. Passailaigue, were different. The Passailaigues lived at 1608 Wildwood Avenue, one block away from the Illges home, where a burglar had struck the night of New Year's Eve. Like many in the neighborhood, they were an older couple; Mr. Passailaigue was seventy-one and his wife sixty-nine. Set far back from the street, the Passailaigue home was large and impressive, a potential treasure trove for an aspiring burglar. With the Strangler still at large, they had taken precautions to protect their home by installing a proprietary burglar alarm system, with wireless FM transmitters attached to sensors on each potential point of entry. The transmitters could be individually disarmed via a local switch. On Friday night, January 6th, at about 11:00 P.M., Mr. Passailaigue was asleep and his wife reading when the alarm sounded. Ms. Passailaigue cut off the system, checked the house thoroughly, but did not find anything amiss. Police cars in the area were using FM radios and their interference had erroneously set off an alarm several times before. After reactivating the alarm system, she went to bed.

At about 7:00 A.M. the following morning, Mr. Passailaigue awoke and went downstairs to the kitchen. He found a bottle of orange juice sitting on the counter and, thinking that his wife had left it out the night before, returned it to the refrigerator. Walking into the den, he found a sliding glass door leading to the outside standing open. The door's alarm switch had been turned off. Curious, and in consideration of the open door and the alarm that had gone off the night before, the couple looked about and discovered that an intruder had been in their house overnight. A valuable gold-and-gemstone ring was missing, as were a small Persian rug, a small television, a .38 caliber Colt revolver, and about $162 in cash taken from the a wallet and pocketbook. A missing keyring led to the discovery that their 1972 Ford LTD station wagon had been stolen as well.

Police and crime scene investigators responding to the couple's call discovered that the burglar had initially tried to enter through French doors leading to the dining room. After cutting a screen and unsuccessfully trying to remove a windowpane, the intruder had pried open the sliding glass door to the den. They assumed that as the initial alarm the night before went off, he entered the house and concealed himself while Ms. Passailaigue checked the downstairs area and reset the alarm before going to bed for the night. After the couple were asleep, he explored the house, using a flashlight he had found in the den near his point of entry. To make his exit, the burglar simply turned off the alarm sensor on the sliding glass door, stole the Passailaigue's station wagon, and disappeared into the night. The car was discovered the same morning parked less than two miles away at the southern edge of the Wynnton district.

The crime scene was processed, yielding some latent but unidentified fingerprints. A single set of shoe tracks was discovered in the carport area and photographed for reference. On further questioning, detectives learned that on New Year's Day, the morning after the Illges burglary, the Passailaigue's son had come to visit and attempted to let himself in via the same sliding glass door through which the burglar would gain entry six days later. Unable to open the door, he discovered that someone had tried to force the lock. Mr. Passailaigue called a locksmith and had the locking mechanism replaced. Assuming that both incidents were the work of the same person, it appeared that he had been successful on his second attempt. The police report commented that the intruder must have had some knowledge of the alarm system and was not frightened away when it went off on his second attempt. The proximity and similarity of the Illges and Passailaigue burglaries was evident, "about the same thing," according to police detective Billie Jeter. The task force was investigating both.[86] The culprit, whomever he might be, appeared to be intelligent and perhaps foolheartedly bold in his criminal enterprise.

Chapter 12

The Night of Terrors (Part I)

The task force continued to probe every possible connection between the victims as well as possible motivations that would attract a killer to that particular person. A list of 111 "Questions Regarding the Victim's Background" was distributed to investigators. In addition to the usual demographics and descriptions, officers delved into such areas as the victims' past employment, education, personal habits, finances, clothing choices, legal history, etc., etc. Lists of meter readers were obtained from Georgia Power, Columbus Gas & Light, and Columbus Water Works. Physicians, pharmacists, manicurists, and hair stylists were interviewed. A federally funded "Community Awareness" program utilizing door-to-door canvassing of neighborhoods to make lower-income residents aware of government services for which they might be eligible was cancelled in Wynnton. All of the program's employees were black. "A lot of the white residents were afraid, particularly when the black men in the program would come up," Iris Buckner, the director of the program, explained. "It's understandable because everyone has the understanding that the Strangler is black." Police were quick to say that officially, they didn't know the race of the Strangler and were investigating all leads.[87]

The lack of a good visual image or description of the Strangler hindered the investigation. As a result, in mid-January investigators met once again with Gertrude Miller, the only victim to survive the Strangler's attack. Her assault had taken place more than four months earlier, and while the purpose of the interview was an "attempt to obtain an accurate composite drawing of the subject," Ms. Miller was able to relate additional information about her ordeal. In slight variance from her earlier description, she described her attacker as "a black male in his early twenties, approximately 5'8" to 5'10", medium complexion, very slender, no facial hair, wearing a black shirt with a flowered design on the front." After working with Miller for more than two hours, the agents were unable to develop an image that was "satisfactory to the victim." Regrouping, they found "a black artist," Calvin Earl, employed by local television channel 38. Earl agreed to meet with Miller and after about three hours had drawn a sketch that she rated as "very accurate" and "very similar to the perpetrator."[88] The sketch was distributed to field agents for future interviews.

Two days later, Special Agents C. S. Stone and J. C. Freeman met with Charles E. Blews and three other men—apparently his employees—in the board room of the Trust Company of Georgia. Blews was described as "a local adult book store owner and adult movie theater operator who is reported to be head of, or one of, the largest pornography dealers in the Columbus area." Agent Stone requested the meeting in "reference to any subjects who appeared to have a deep perverted interest in sado-masochistic movies and or books." They were shown the recently drawn sketch but were unable to identify any individuals who might appear similar. All agreed to cooperate with police in the investigation.[89]

Investigators "had not ruled out the possibility of a traveling killer." Task force members were in touch with numerous police agencies around the nation, including Los Angeles, where the so-called "Hillside Strangler" raped and killed nine women and girls between October and December 1977.[90]* Closer to home, on the same day that agents were meeting with Gertrude Miller, the task force received a call from Special Agent Steve Williams of the Florida Department of Law Enforcement in Tallahassee to report a crime that had taken place two days earlier at Florida State University. An unknown intruder had broken into the Chi Omega sorority house, attacking four coeds, two of whom were killed. Of the students, twenty-one-year-old Margaret Bowman had been severely beaten about the head and strangled with a nylon stocking. The similarity between her death and the five victims of the Strangler in Columbus led Williams to make the call. The suspect, who had escaped, was described as a white male, possibly in his twenties. On January 24th, two detectives from Columbus went to Tallahassee to explore any possible connections. They concluded that while the crimes might have superficial similarities, they were unrelated to those in Columbus. Several years later, just prior to his execution, serial killer Ted Bundy admitted to murdering Bowman.

At 1:46 A.M. on the morning of February 5th, a burglar alarm went off at the home of Ms. Ethyl Illges Woodruff at 1941 Stark Avenue. Ms. Woodruff, age ninety-one, shared the house with her sixty-four-year-old daughter, Emily. She was the sister-in-law of Kathleen Woodruff, the

---

* The killings were later found to be the work of not one, but two men, Kenneth Bianchi and his cousin, Angelo Buono Jr. The two were arrested in 1979 and sentenced to life in prison for their crimes.

Strangler's most recent victim, and the sister of Abraham Illges, whose home a few blocks away had been burglarized on New Year's Eve. Like most who lived in that part of Wynnton, the Woodruffs were wealthy. Emily was not formally employed, but served as a trustee of the Springer Opera House, the Springer Guild, the Springer Theater Company, and the Historic Columbus Foundation, and was a member of other charitable boards.[†]

The burglar had tried to gain entrance to the house by removing a glass pane from a carport door and reaching inside to unlock it. When the door was opened, it set off an audible alarm that frightened him away and automatically contacted the police. In addition to latent fingerprints on the door, crime scene investigators found shoeprints on a brick walkway near the house that appeared to match those of the burglar found at the Passailaigue home on January 6th. A yellow-and-black Bright Star flashlight found in the Woodruff's yard was thought to have been dropped by the burglar. Extensive efforts to track down and interview buyers of this particular model led to Ms. Ruth Schwob, who lived only one block away at 1800 Carter Avenue. Some cash had been stolen from her pocketbook a few days earlier. After being contacted, she discovered that her flashlight appeared to be missing as well, although there was no clear evidence of a break-in at her home. She tentatively identified the flashlight found at the Woodruff residence as being the same or similar to hers.

With the number of burglaries in the neighborhood, Ms. Schwob, a seventy-four-year-old who lived alone, was concerned that the Strangler might target her as his next victim. The widow of Simon Schwob, she was described in the press as "a wealthy civic leader" and "one of Columbus's most prominent and most honored citizens," recognized for her contributions to local charitable organizations. She had succeeded her husband as president of the Schwob Manufacturing Company after his death in 1954, and headed the firm for more than twenty years until its sale in 1976. In thinking of a way to be certain that help arrived quickly in the case of a break-in, Ms. Schwob convinced her next-door neighbor, Dr. Fred Burdette, that they should both have an alarm button installed at their bedsides. If either one should face an emergency, they would press the bell,

---

[†] Emily Woodruff, whose occupation is listed in an online biography as "philanthropist," was married for a brief time in the mid-1930s to actor Hume Cronyn, who in later years married actress Jessica Tandy. When asked by police, Ms. Woodruff refused to reveal the name of her former husband.

which would set off a loud alarm in the other's house that could be heard in the neighborhood. If the alarm were triggered, the police were to be called immediately. As Dr. Burdette related later, not long after the system was installed, Ms. Schwob accidently pressed her alarm button, leading to his calling the police for what turned out to be a false alarm. The next time that happened, he resolved, he would first call Ms. Schwob to be sure that it was a true emergency. Perhaps in response to the Passailaigue burglary, she had the exterior locks at her house changed on Friday, February 10th.

At around 5:00 A.M. on the morning of Saturday, February 11th, the same burglar who had broken into the 2021 Brookside Drive home of Mr. and Mrs. Abraham Illges on New Year's Eve night returned for a second break-in. Once again entering the same ground floor window he had used before, he climbed the short flight of steps to the main level of the house, but this time found the door locked. Retracing his path out of the window, he went to the house next door and obtained a tall ladder, which he propped against the back of the Illges house, enabling him to reach a higher window that opened into the breakfast room on the main level. Crawling through that window, he made his way to the foyer and approached the stairway leading to the bedrooms on the third level. This time was different, however. After the first break-in, the Illgeses had installed a concealed pressure switch under the carpet at the foot of the stairs. When the intruder stepped on the carpet, the alarm went off. The time was 5:15 A.M. The police were automatically called and arrived within minutes, but once again, the burglar was gone.

While investigators were at the Illges house, they received a call to check the Schwob residence, two blocks away. The bedside alarm of Dr. Burdette, Ms. Schwob's neighbor, rang at 5:44 A.M. Not wanting to call in another false alarm, he first called Ms. Schwob, but on receiving no answer, called the police, who met him at her house at 5:50 A.M. After surveying the exterior of the house, an officer found an unlocked kitchen window and crawled in while Dr. Burdette and another officer waited and watched outside. Exploring the darkened house by using his flashlight, he found Ms. Schwob sitting on the side of her bed, a stocking wrapped around her neck. A screwdriver lay on the floor. Ms. Schwob warned the officer that "someone was still in the house." A thorough search of the premises failed to find the intruder. Apparently the phone call had frightened him, allowing time for an escape before the police arrived. On investigation, it was clear that the burglar gained entry to the house by stepping on top of an air conditioning unit and then using the screwdriver to pry open the kitchen window. Shoeprints were found on the ground by the driveway and on several surfaces at the site of entry.

Police and investigators flooded the scene. According to the police report of the incident, a total of thirty-five people were there in an official capacity by 7:00 A.M., including Chief Curtis McClung, Muscogee County deputy sheriff Don Miller, task force head Ronnie Jones, two representatives from the state crime laboratory, the GBI agent-in-charge, and Ms. Schwob's personal physician. An intensive search of the area both on foot and with helicopters and tracking dogs failed to find the intruder.

To everyone's relief—and surprise—Ms. Schwob was relatively unharmed. After a brief trip to the emergency room, she returned home and was eager to tell her story of survival. She said she had been awoken from a sound sleep by a man straddling her. "He was on the bed and had his hand on my throat and then he wrapped pantyhose all around. He pulled the thing tight around my neck." The pantyhose were hers, she said, apparently picked up from where she had left them in the bedroom.

"I fought like a tiger," she said, but he "choked me so bad I passed out." She had no recollection of either pressing the alarm button or of Dr. Burdette's phone call. Saying that she was a bit sore but not badly hurt, Ms. Schwob said she had "a hard time" removing the pantyhose from her neck.[91] She told police that she was unable to identify the intruder. Her bedroom was dark, and he appeared to have a full facial mask of some sort. She could not tell for certain if he was black or white but indicated that it might have been a local "hippie," a white boy. Investigation of this insinuation led nowhere. Task force director Ronnie Jones spoke to the press later in the day, stating that the investigation "is proceeding on the assumption that the assailant was the same person who since September has strangled five elderly women who lived in the Wynnton Road area of Columbus. Jones's comments marked the first time during the grueling investigation that police have stated publicly that they believe all the killings were by the same man."[92] Unspoken was the obvious: the psychic's prediction had been partially fulfilled, but once again the Strangler had escaped capture.

Chapter 13

The Night of Terrors (Part II)

After an overnight low of thirty degrees, the weather in Columbus on the Sunday morning of February 12, 1978, was crisp but pleasant, with the temperature rising steadily to a high of nearly seventy degrees by midafternoon. In the words of one news reporter, it turned out to be a beautiful springlike day. For the nation at large, it was the birthday of Abraham Lincoln and Charles Darwin. Just the day before, the People's Republic of China had lifted a ban on works by Aristotle, Shakespeare, and Dickens. In Columbus, however, the mood was somber. Newspapers and television commentators reported the second break-in at the Illges home the night before and the aborted attack on Ruth Schwob. Church congregations prayed for divine guidance while on a more practical basis, homeowners checked and rechecked their dead bolts, alarm systems, and firearms.

At 11:46 A.M. that morning, police received a call from Ms. Judy Borom, the daughter-in-law of Ms. Mildred Borom. The elder Ms. Borom lived at 1612 Forest Avenue, just down and diagonally across the street from the Abraham Illges residence. Her daughter-in-law and three grandchildren had dropped by after church to pay her a visit. Ms. Borom was a seventy-eight-year-old widow whose lifestyle this late in life "was that of a loner," according to a later police interview with her family. She was said to have "no close personal friends except for family members and seldom left the house." Her son, Perry Borom, was the vice president of the Woodruff/Brown Company, whose president was George Woodruff Jr., the son of Strangler victim Kathleen Woodruff. Family members had last seen and talked with Ms. Borom two days earlier at about 3:30 P.M. on Friday afternoon. Judy Borom called police when Ms. Borom failed to answer either her doorbell or the phone. Her grandson discovered that a screen had been removed from one of the windows on the side of the house and a glass pane broken in what appeared to be an attempt to gain entry.

Two detectives arrived promptly and began to check the house. A series of tennis shoeprints which appeared to match those seen at the Schwob home the day before were found under a front window and on a walkway. Within minutes, task force director Ronnie Jones, accompanied by a GBI special agent, arrived to assist in the search for an entry point.

All the exterior doors were locked, and none of the windows could be opened; it was discovered later that Ms. Borom's son had all of them screwed shut to thwart a possible intruder. With a strong suggestion of foul play, Director Jones ordered one of the detectives "to kick the back door open." In a short hallway leading to a bedroom, detectives found Ms. Borom's body lying on its back, a blue dress pulled from a nearby closet covering her face and breasts, but her nightgown pulled up to expose her pubic area. Ms. Borom had apparently struggled with her killer. An unnamed police source described the scene in the adjacent bedroom as looking like "a battlefield." A bedside table was turned over. Pieces of a broken lamp and bedsheets were strewn on the floor.[93] Two jewelry boxes on a dresser had been opened and their contents partially removed. The contents of a blue ladies' handbag had been dumped on a small rug next to the bed. A small television continued to play, tuned to WRBL, Columbus Channel 3. For the second time in two days, ground-based investigators, search dogs, and helicopters above were brought in to scour the immediate neighborhood, but nothing was found.

Like the other victims, Ms. Borom had been strangled, however this time with a "curtain draw cord" cut from the drapes of a bedroom window. It had been tightly wrapped twice around her neck, then fixed with a single knot. An autopsy done later in the day found "multiple abrasions and excoriations" of her cheeks and face, with cuts on her lip and chin. The hyoid bone was fractured at multiple sites. Vaginal fluid contained spermatozoa, consistent with "recent sexual intercourse." It was clear that Ms. Borom had been dead for some time when her body was found. Her death was estimated to have occurred as much as thirty hours prior, which would potentially place it as early as 6:00 A.M. on Saturday morning, the 11th.

Perhaps overcome by yet another murder, task force director Ronnie Jones was reported to have "collapsed at the scene," complaining of chest pains. He was hospitalized for observation but was back at work two days later. Police chief McClung commented, "Seems to be exhaustion. He's been working real hard and long hours since September."[94] If anyone could have been singled out as the man in charge, it would have been Jones. The Borom murder was the sixth in five months, yet investigators were no closer to finding the perpetrator than they had been at the outset.[95]

Based on the evidence, investigators developed a disturbing scenario as to what might have happened: Mildred Borom appeared to have been strangled in her home while police were investigating the Schwob strangling attempt a few hundred yards away. Based on the estimated time of death, it was theorized that the Strangler first entered the Illges home but was frightened off after tripping the burglar alarm when he stepped on the pressure switch under the hall carpet at 5:15 A.M. Fleeing the police, he then went to Ms. Schwob's home, a place he had possibly burglarized before. In the midst of strangling her with a stocking, he was again frightened by the alarm in the house next door and the persistent ringing of the telephone at Ms. Schwob's bedside. The time then was 5:44 A.M. Realizing police were on the way, he fled back in the direction of the Illges home, perhaps hiding in Wildwood Park, a several-acre neighborhood green space only about two hundred feet from the rear of Ms. Borom's house. Coroner Kilgore commented, "If he'd been to the Borom house first, it wouldn't have made sense for him to go to the Schwob house." Detective Commander Herman Boone agreed, saying "he had no way of knowing for sure whether the attempt on Ms. Schwob or the strangling of Ms. Borom came first, but didn't argue with the scenario that the killer, frustrated in his attempt to strangle Ms. Schwob, picked another target."[96] With the windows and doors all locked at the Borom house, there was no obvious evidence of how the Strangler gained entry. Ms. Borom was known to be an early riser, and the television was on when police entered her home. Police theorized that he may have simply rang the doorbell. Ms. Borom "may have opened the door without knowing it was her killer who was to enter."[97]

The relative assurance offered by the creation of the task force had been shattered. After a hiatus of more than a month, the Strangler had struck again, this time not once, but possibly three times in a period of less than twenty-four hours. It had been "The Night of Terrors," in the words of District Attorney William J. ("Bill") Smith. Smith had been an assistant district attorney for several years, moving up to the head position in early January 1978 when the former DA, Mullins Whisnant, was chosen for a newly created Superior Court judgeship.* Commenting on the Strangler's new crimes, Chief McClung said, "It's obvious he's playing with us. He's become somewhat reckless."[98]

Journalists and news editorials over the following days expressed frustration with the police and political establishment while demanding more transparency in regard to the progress of the investigation. Bev Greer, a columnist for the *Ledger*, opined that the "unwanted secrecy...has served no purpose other than to cause panic, confusion, rampant rumor, and

---

* Smith would later play a major role in the Strangler case.

finally, distrust of the police department and a lack of confidence in their abilities." Dissing Mayor Mickle, she said, "We know that at each scene of the slayings, except that of Mrs. Borom, the mayor had been on the scene along with [Safety Director] Darrah, waving to friends, strolling in and out of houses where possible evidence was being examined by investigators, ambling around yards and conferring with police officials."[99] The day after the discovery of Ms. Borom's body, the *Enquirer* called for greater protection "for our elderly women," going so far as to suggest calling in the National Guard.[100] A later editorial demanded "a more open, responsive policy by police," averring that Columbus citizens "deserve to know what's going on."[101]

For whatever good it might do, the death of a sixth victim allowed Gov. George Busbee to add an additional $1,000 to the reward for the capture and conviction of the Strangler. The total now stood at $21,000.

Chapter 14

The Ku Klux Klan Steps Up

In the wake of a sixth death, the calls for increased transparency in the murder investigations grew ever more strident. "Columbus police officials are not serving the public well by their reluctance to reveal essential facts about the strangulation-slayings of six elderly women," the *Enquirer* declared.[102] By the day after the discovery of Ms. Borom's body, rumors began to spread that a local man had been arrested in the case, an event the police were quick to deny. "In a way, the spread of rumor is understandable," the *Ledger's* editorialist explained. "People are frightened. They want to believe that the Strangler has been caught, and are eager to spread the word that he has been.... It's unwise to keep the community so much in the dark that rumors mushroom. Openness is the best weapon against fear and panic. Let's have some openness."[103] Caving to public pressure, a few days later police chief McClung took responsibility and agreed to daily briefings on the investigation.

Word had leaked that shoeprints found at the scene of Ms. Borom's murder appeared similar to those found under the kitchen window at Ms. Schwob's, suggesting that one person might be responsible for both break-ins. Detective Commander Herman Boone told reporters that the crime lab was working on this, but otherwise could not comment further. "Boone said the only other information the police know about the killer is speculative, based on a psychological profile pieced together by experts from throughout the nation."[104] While rumors had circulated for months about the race of the Strangler, Boone officially confirmed for the first time in a later interview that the killer was believed to be black "because black hairs were found on or around at least three of the six strangling victims."[105] After two criminologists from the state crime labs in Atlanta and Columbus, contacted by reporters, dampened Boone's assessment by saying the suspect might, for example, be of mixed race, the commander equivocated on his earlier statement, explaining the police felt they were "just not in a position to know one way or the other. If we were sure he was black or white, I'd tell you," Boone said. "We'd want to know because then we wouldn't have to look at both black and white suspects. It would cut down the work for the task force." Coroner Kilgore, outspoken as usual, called on the police to clarify their position. "If he's black, then the police should say it so the community knows more about who to look for."[106]

For whatever they might have contributed toward educating the public, Kilgore's comments served mainly to open old wounds of racial animus. Several days later, the Rev. Johnny Flakes, a local NAACP official, called a press conference to condemn Kilgore for "casting a cloud of suspicion over every black in this community without substantially aiding the search for the killer." Hoping to stem a growing controversy, Mayor Jack Mickle hastily arranged a meeting between Kilgore and Flakes, plus another NAACP officer, the Rev. Charles Blake. Mickle, who with mayor pro tem A. J. McClung, attended the meeting in the role of mediator, stated afterward that the hour-long discussion "cleared the matter up." In sharp contrast, Rev. Blake commented, "I don't think [the coroner] really sees how much damage his remark has done to race relations. He felt we were blowing it out of proportion."[107] Matters became worse two days later when Mark Stuart, a member of the local branch of the Knights of the Ku Klux Klan, announced that Klan members were planning to start "automobile patrols through the Wynnton Road area to help Columbus police" catch the Strangler. Permission for the patrols had been obtained from David Duke, the Klan's Grand Wizard in Louisiana. A news article announcing the Klan's plan pointedly noted, "The announcement by the Klan comes on the heels of speculation that the killer is black."[108]

The city of Columbus had a long and sad association with the various incarnations of the Ku Klux Klan. During the Reconstruction Era of the late 1860s and early 1870s, local regulatory and vigilante groups, loosely referred to as "klans," operated in the Columbus area before fading away in the latter part of the century. In 1915, a failed Methodist minister named William Joseph Simmons, inspired by the movie *The Birth of a Nation*, organized a beneficial fraternal order which he named the Knights of the Ku Klux Klan. As a state-chartered, tax-exempt entity, this new Klan was founded primarily as a money-making scheme for Simmons and his associates. For the first few years of its existence, the Klan's membership was primarily limited to Georgia and Alabama. Klansmen were active in Columbus during the World War I era, supporting the war effort and troops from Camp Benning. Both local papers of the day, the *Ledger* and the *Enquirer-Sun*, expressed their approval. Starting in 1920, the Klan spread rapidly throughout the nation, and by mid-decade boasted an estimated five million members in all forty-eight states. Attracted by its mantra of "One Hundred Percent Americanism," prominent men from many walks of life joined, including politicians and members of law enforcement. In Columbus in the early 1920s, the Klan held meetings in the armory above police headquarters and was endorsed by both Columbus's mayor and chief of police (who were themselves presumably members).

Hidden behind its public persona, the Klan of the 1920s was a thoroughly corrupt organization, manipulated by its leaders to extract political power and personal wealth. One of the few public figures who acknowledged this was Julian Harris, editor and later owner of the *Enquirer-Sun*.[*] Despite threats to his life and economic harm to his paper, Harris took a firm stand against the fraudulence of the Klan. In part for this, the paper was awarded a Pulitzer Prize for "the most disinterested and meritorious public service rendered by any American newspaper in 1925." By the late 1920s, Americans had begun to understand the Klan's iniquity, and membership in the order plummeted. The Knights of the Ku Klux Klan officially dissolved under pressure from the IRS in 1944. The raison d'être of the post-World War II Klans was anti-black racism inspired by the civil rights movement. Perhaps needless to say, the prospect of Klansmen independently patrolling the neighborhoods of Wynnton in search of the Strangler produced cries of alarm.[†]

The announcement that the Klan was planning patrols brought an immediate reaction from Rev. Charles Blake. "We don't want any Ku Klux Klan.... It's going to put every black man in Columbus on the spot.... A black man can walk down the street that night and get shot. We don't need that sort of thing." In reference to Coroner Kilgore, with whom he had met two days earlier, Blake said, "We tried to tell him this thing was far-reaching. He didn't think that way. Somebody's going to get killed...about a man making a statement that should not have been made." In response, the coroner said the blacks were "overreacting." "I will not retract anything I've said. I gave my personal opinion." "The pubic hairs found were 'black, Negroid pubic hairs—and that's a fact,' Kilgore said." Declaring the lab tests as "ninety-five to ninety-nine percent accurate," he

---

[*] Julian Harris was the son of famed journalist and writer Joel Chandler Harris, best remembered for his collection of Uncle Remus folktales.

[†] The history of the Ku Klux Klan of the 1920s is both a disturbing and fascinating episode in America's past, when, for a few years, a group that could be accurately compared to contemporary fascist movements in Europe seemed destined to have a voice in the nation's future. The Klan of this era and Julian Harris's experiences with the Klan in Columbus are discussed in detail in *The Second Coming of the Invisible Empire* (Mercer University Press, 2016).

continued, "Facts are facts and you have to face facts." In response to the statements of Blake and Kilgore, Klansman Mark Stuart said "the patrols are not based on the reported race of the suspect. 'There is no racial bias involved.'" Few seemed to believe him.[109]

Not unexpectedly, the police were upset. Police chief McClung threatened to arrest any Klan members who hindered law enforcement's work. Ms. Carolyn Ferguson, a thirty-five-year-old guidance counselor and mother of two, presented Mayor Mickle with a petition reading, "We do not want the Klan or any unauthorized private vigilante group patrolling our neighborhood." It had been signed by 484 Wynnton residents. Stuart was nonchalant: "I don't believe there's anything legally that they can do," he said. "As law-abiding citizens they can't stop us from driving the public roads. It was done in New York with the Son of Sam, and they're doing it now in Los Angeles with the Hillside Strangler. It's been tested plenty of times." Klan patrols began February 27th.[110,111]

One of the biggest blows to the credibility of the Columbus police, and by extension the Strangler investigation, came the preceding week when an article focusing on an interview with Muscogee County Superior Court judge John H. Land appeared in the *Washington Post*. "I don't have too much confidence in the investigative ability of the Columbus Police Department," Land was reported to have said. "If you had a department in which you had confidence, it would be a tough case. But the real emphasis [in Columbus] is on traffic enforcement. I heard one of [the police officials] say the other day that they'll get the Strangler the first time he runs a traffic light." Referring to the Livas case, Land said, "It concerned me when they tried to lay the first stranglings on him (Livas). I appointed a public defender to keep the police department from framing him." The article also "quoted local mortician and political leader George Ford, Jr. as saying Kilgore's statements have made 'young blacks as mad as hell.'" Both the mayor and the police chief refused to comment on Land's statements.[112,113,‡]

An opinion piece in the *Ledger* described the feeling that seemed to have taken over the community: "We're like a non-swimmer in water over his head. The instinct is to fight back. To kick and grab and scream. We've reached the point of near panic in our frustration over the elusive terrorist.

---

‡ To be fair, Judge Land's disdain for the Columbus Police Department may have had its origin in politics, as he had earlier supported an alternative candidate for the police chief position then held by Curtis McClung.

So we lash out at each other. Why can't the police do something? Why hasn't the task force arrested someone? The questions are asked all over Columbus."[114]

Chapter 15

The Forces of Evil

As if the Klan's unwanted entry into the search for the Strangler and the resulting outcry from the black community and residents of Wynnton were not enough, there was more to come. On March 3rd, police chief McClung received a letter that read as follows:

> March 1, 1978
> To Chief of Police:
> Dear Sir:
> We are an organization composed of seven members. I'm writing this letter to inform you that we have one of your Columbus women captive, her name is Gail Jackson. Since that coroner said the Strangler is black, we decided to come here and try to catch him or put more pressure on you. I see now more pressure is needed. At this point Gail Jackson is still living. If that Strangler is not caught by 1 June 1978, you will find Gail Jackson's body on Wynnton Road.
> If he's still not caught by 1 September 1978, the victims will double. This is the break we have been looking for. Tell that coroner thanks a lot. From now on black women in Columbus, Georgia will be disappearing until the Strangler is caught. Don't forget that date, Gail Jackson's life depends on it. From now to 1 June Gail Jackson is with us. You better answer us somehow, TV or radio. If we don't hear some type of reply in two days we will take it as though you don't care. If we take it that way, Gail Jackson will be executed. You have until Sunday for a reply. Don't think we are bluffing. Better yet, I'll give you until midnight Monday....
> P.S. We are called The Forces of Evil, we are an organization within an organization. By the way, anyone can get ahold of military writing equipment.[115]

The letter was written on military stationery. It would be the first of six letters from the Forces of Evil received over the next month.

Despite the ominous tone of the letter, the initial reaction held that it was a hoax of some sort. Chief McClung turned it over to the identification section of the police department. The name "Gail Jackson" was not found in a search of missing persons reports.

On March 13th, Chief McClung received a second, longer, and more rambling letter from "the Chairman of All the Forces." Once again, he said their hostage would be executed unless the Strangler were caught but gave another option: "Get ten thousand dollars to us by 1 June 1978." The letter ended with a threat:

> Don't think we are bluffing. We are an organization within an organization. We are an organization that makes our own laws and rules and punishments. Please help Gail Jackson live, she's only twenty-one years old and will be twenty-two in September. I'm the one that's keeping her alive, but the rest of the forces want her executed. Please let us hear from you no later than 11:00 P.M. Friday night. We will not write to you anymore, Chief. This is no prank or joke, so don't take it that way please. Can't you see I, the chairman, want Gail to live? We will continue on getting black women here in Columbus until the Stocking Strangler is caught.

This was followed by a signature of sorts and a postscript:

> The Forces of Evil. We are here in Columbus, Georgia. We came from Chicago, Illinois. We are here to make justice.
>   P.S. Thank that coroner for saying the Strangler is black. We are patrolling, also, but you just don't know us. We better hear something from you no later than 11:00 P.M. Friday night or we won't wait until June 1, 1978. I hope you will make the right decision. Good luck.

In response to the second letter, Chief McClung gave an interview to a local newspaper reporter "asking the Chairman of the F.O.E. 'to contact me in any way he sees fit. We'll be glad to talk with him about any matters he wants to discuss, including ransom demands,' the chief said at the time."[116]

On March 27th, McClung received two more letters from the "Chairman," both postmarked two days earlier. In response to McClung's interview, the writer said,

This is in reference to that column that you wrote about us in the newspaper. So you think that this is a hoax; believe me, this is no hoax. To prove it to you we have captured another of your Columbus, Georgia, black women. Her name is Irene. We don't know her last name, she refused to tell us. Now we have Gail Jackson and Irene. Since you people think this is a hoax, Gail Jackson will be executed in fourteen days. We will keep Irene alive until 1 June 1978. We captured Irene 16 March 1978 walking towards her home, but she never did reach home. I apologize for taking such actions on their lives, but Gail Jackson could have been spared if you didn't think that this was a hoax.

The letter continued, taunting McClung, threatening to "capture" more black women, and declaring—as if there were any doubt—that "we are an all-white organization."

The fourth letter, received on the same day, advised McClung that "the US Army Military Police Desk Sergeant" would receive a call on April 1st informing them of where Gail Jackson's body could be found. The writer said her body would be "in bad shape." "One of her arms will be broken, and the style of execution will be a sharp blow to her head to cause instant death." In response, Chief McClung ran an advertisement in the local newspaper asking "the Chairman" to contact him.

A fifth letter to the *Columbus Ledger* was postmarked March 25th and apparently mailed at the same time as the two others sent to McClung. Again "the Chairman" announced that Gail Jackson would be killed on April 1st because the police chief had called his letters "a hoax" and "in a roundabout way ma[d]e fun of one of my member's handwriting." Referring to the other captive, "Irene," the letter continued,

You people in Columbus, Georgia better wake up. The Chief of Police is playing with your lives. If he should call this a hoax like the first one with Gail Jackson, then Irene will die, and we will just get another black woman. It's up to the black citizens of Columbus, Georgia to wake the police department up and meet our demands. The black women in Columbus, Georgia lives depend on it. Good luck, you people need it. It's the Chief's fault that Gail Jackson has to die.

On March 30th at 12:53 P.M., Sergeant George Thompson, a military policeman working the police desk at Fort Benning, received a brief phone call from an unknown party telling him "where to find the body." He was instructed to look in an area in the woods off Cusseta Road just past the Sand Hill Bar and Grill. Cusseta Road was one of the major routes leading south into the Fort Benning reservation. Approximately a minute later, Sergeant James Harris, a military policeman working in Fort Benning's provost marshall's office, received a similar phone call. He was told to "bring a shovel." At 4:18 P.M. that afternoon, Laverne McNeal, the "complaint clerk" at the Columbus Police Department, answered a third call giving the same instructions. The caller this time said he was "the F.O.E., Forces of Evil." In later testimony all three unequivocally identified the caller as "a black male."

The first two calls resulted in officers being dispatched to the area described by the caller. At approximately 1:45 P.M. William Wanninger, an Army Criminal Investigative Division agent, discovered the partially nude body of a black female in a shallow grave "partially covered with twigs, pine needles and leaves." It was evident that the person had been dead for some time. Crime scene investigation and later autopsy revealed that she had suffered "violent blows to each side of the head" with a metal object—later found to be a tire tool—so severely that her entire facial structure was destroyed and missing, with pieces of jaw, teeth, and facial bones found at a distance from the body. Fingerprints obtained from the corpse matched those of Brenda Gail Faison, a twenty-one-year-old who had moved to Columbus from Miami, Florida. Faison was working as a prostitute, using the aliases of Gail Jackson and Gail Bogen. She was last seen on the evening of February 27th by her boyfriend.

At about 1:15 P.M. on April 3rd, Sergeant William Smith, who was manning the police desk at Fort Benning, received a call from "a black male" telling him that the body of "Irene" could be found at the Maertens Range (a military firing range) on the Fort. The caller, who identified himself by saying "I am a member of the Forces of Evil," was familiar with Fort Benning and gave specific directions as to how to get to the site. Approximately two hours later, searchers found the nude body of a black female hidden behind a stack of logs at the site described by the caller. As later described by William Wanninger, the officer who was also present at the discovery of Gail Faison's body, "the head was missing. There was an enormous amount of maggots, decomposition was obvious, gaping holes in the chest, as though the body had been there for a couple of weeks." Examination of the body at autopsy was consistent with the head having been destroyed by "massive blunt force trauma" in addition to multiple rib fractures. The body was eventually identified as that of Irene Thirkield, a known prostitute who had last been seen at Vice Mitchell's Teen Tavern on Cusseta Road on the evening of March 15th.

A sixth letter from the Forces of Evil, postmarked April 4th, was received by Chief McClung the following day. It said that a third "black woman" had been kidnapped the night before. Once again, the writer demanded that the Strangler be caught, but this time added that once in custody he be turned over to the Forces of Evil. In addition, he wanted a personal apology from McClung "for calling us a hoax and talking about our handwriting." As events unfolded, however, by the time McClung received the letter, "the Chairman" was already in police custody.

On April 4th, the day after the discovery of Irene Thirkield's body, a military officer reviewing the recordings of the phone calls giving the location of the bodies recognized the voice as that of Pvt. William Henry Hance, a twenty-six-year-old black male ammunition handler for the 10th Artillery. He was arrested that same day and confessed to both crimes, giving details of the murders and the weapons used. The evidence against him was overwhelming. In addition to his detailed confession, which he later recanted while proclaiming his innocence, his fingerprints were identified on one of the letters from the F.O.E., and handwriting experts were able to say with assurance that Hance wrote the letters himself. Witnesses identified him as being with Irene Thirkield on the night she disappeared. In addition to the murders of Faison and Thirkield, Hance admitted to the unsolved September 1977 murder of Pvt. Karen Hickman, a twenty-four-year-old Fort Benning soldier whose battered body was found on the base.

In the end, the Forces of Evil did not exist. Hance, a serial killer himself, was using the presence of another serial killer in Columbus in an attempt to divert attention and cover up his own crimes.[*]

---

[*] Since the body of Gail Faison was found on civilian property and the bodies of Thirkield and Hickman were found on the military reservation, Hance was tried in both court systems. Military courts-martial convicted him of the Thirkield and Hickman murders, sentencing him to life in prison at hard labor. A December 1978 trial in Muscogee County Superior Court convicted him of the murder of Gail Faison, for which he was sentenced to death. After a series of appeals, one of which led to a retrial of the sentencing phase of his case and a reaffirmation of his punishment, Hance was executed by the state of Georgia in March 1994. Although the case was never brought to trial, Hance was later identified as the murderer of another young black woman at Fort Benjamin Harrison, in Indiana, where he had been stationed earlier. (R. K. Ressler and T. Shachtman, *Whoever Fights Monsters* [New York: St. Martin's Press, 1992], 183.)

Chapter 16

Another Murder

In a perverse way, the fact that the Forces of Evil murders were not connected to the Strangler seemed to provide some sense of relief for the residents of Wynnton. The Strangler's last known victim, Mildred Borom, was killed on February 11th. More than two months had passed without an incident, empiric evidence that the intensive patrols of the area appeared to have deterred further attacks. Near the end of March, several detectives assigned to the task force were transferred to other duties "because there were so few fresh leads coming in that there was little for them to do."[117] All was soon to change.

On Thursday, April 20th, Janet T. Cofer, a normally punctual sixty-one-year-old widowed kindergarten and first-grade teacher at Dimon Elementary, was not in her classroom at the start of the school day. Though she lived alone and fit the profile of the Strangler's victims, her modest one-story brick ranch home located at 3783 Steam Mill Road was more than two miles from the heart of Wynnton in what was described as "an integrated neighborhood." Her adult son, Mike, who worked in a hardware store in nearby Manchester, Georgia, spent most weeknights at her house, returning home on weekends to be with his family in Dallas, northwest of Atlanta. Ms. Cofer had a dog named Buffy, a small dachshund that slept under her bed. A buzzer system to alert a next-door neighbor had been hooked up in her kitchen. "I think they were going to run it into the bedroom, but they never got around to it," a friend said. "She had Mike and her dog. She felt safe."[118, 119]

Mike spent Tuesday night, the 18th, at his mother's house, but breaking his routine, returned to Dallas the following night to be with his family. Her dog, Buffy, had been run over by a car a couple of weeks earlier. On Wednesday evening, the 19th, Ms. Cofer attended choir practice at the Wynnton United Methodist Church, where she was an active member. Among the last to see her was her friend and fellow choir member Vivian Tyler, who said Ms. Cofer remarked that she needed to go home and look over some tests she had given her students earlier in the day. They left the church in separate vehicles about 9:15 P.M. When Ms. Cofer failed to report for work the following morning, her principal, Jack Hendrix, called her house but received no answer. Concerned, Hendrix and a female school police officer drove to her house to check on her. Shortly after arriving, they noticed that the screen on a front living room window had been cut and rolled up, and the window itself was slightly raised. They immediately called the Columbus police.

Columbus police detective Sally Mitchell entered the house via the open front window. Inside, in the bedroom, she found the body of Janet Cofer laying face up on her bed, naked except for a purple top that had been pushed up over her breasts. A nylon stocking was wrapped tightly twice around her neck. Her face was covered with a pillow. Blood was found on the bedsheet, and there was bruising around the face and legs, indicating that she had been beaten. An autopsy revealed evidence of rape. The estimated time of death was between 4:00 and 5:00 A.M. on the morning of April 20th. At the crime scene, investigators found the window had been pried open with a screwdriver. A trail of coffee grains discovered leading from the house to the shrubbery outside was intended to deter tracking by bloodhounds, and were apparently dumped out of a coffee can taken from the house. According to police sources, shoeprints similar to those recovered from the yard of Mildred Borom were found at the Cofer crime scene as well.

Reactions to Ms. Cofer's murder ranged from sorrow to anger to frustration. Praised by her friends, neighbors, and coworkers alike, she was described as a fine Christian woman who, widowed at an early age, had put her life on hold to work and send her two sons to college. She was said to be an enthusiastic and dedicated teacher who cared deeply for her students. One neighbor, both frightened and angry, said, "I'm just going to have to sell my house. With Janet gone in this terrible way I can't stay here any longer." Another said, referring to the Strangler, "I don't understand why they haven't found him. I think it is the government dragging their feet."[120] The Rev. William B. Howell, a black activist and local president of Jesse Jackson's Operation Push, suggesting that law enforcement personnel might somehow be involved, called on Mayor Jack Mickle, Safety Director Gordon Darrah, and Muscogee County sheriff Jack Rutledge to administer lie detector tests to all "law enforcement officials." "We have the utmost respect for our law enforcement agencies without questioning their honesty and credibility. However, in order to clear the air of erroneous misconception of the integrity of our body of law enforcement...we feel this is necessary." Police chief McClung refused to comment on Howell's statement.[121]

Members of the police and task force expressed both frustration and an ongoing commitment to apprehending the killer. McClung immediately announced that the task force patrols were being expanded beyond their previous coverage area, despite a manpower shortage. Work shifts were extended from eight to twelve hours, with additional state troopers sent in to assist. Investigators searched for two unknown men reported to have been seen in the neighborhood on the night of Ms. Cofer's murder. Both were identified and interviewed in a matter of days, but were determined not to be suspects. By executive order, Gov. George Busbee boosted the state's contribution to the reward fund to $70,000—$10,000 for each murder victim—making the total more than $85,000. The increase was made possible by a bill proposed in response to the Strangler murders and passed by the current legislative session.

It had been sixty-seven days since the Strangler's last murder. The small amount of calm the interval had brought was now shattered. A widowed friend of Ms. Cofer told a reporter, "I look out the window, see somebody walking by and wonder if that's him, if that could be the Strangler. All of a sudden, everybody looks suspicious."[122]

Chapter 17

A Cold Case

Beyond the reality of the Strangler's seventh victim, a shadow world of fear, rumor, and suspicion swirled throughout the community. In late May 1978, a "rumor control center" opened in Columbus, launched by local businessmen with the stated purpose of "head[ing] off any rumors which may lead to racial polarization or hurt the investigation in the Stocking Strangler case." The fallout from Coroner Don Kilgore's comments regarding the race of the Strangler were cited as one specific reason that led to the center's creation. Open from noon to 8:00 P.M. five days a week, fifteen to thirty callers a day posed such questions as "Is my neighbor a suspect?" or "Do you have any fingerprints?" Initially staffed by community-relations specialists from the Columbus Police Department and Georgia State Patrol, it was hoped that these personnel could be replaced by volunteers at some point.[123] Beneficial or not, the mood of the public appeared to slowly improve. In the latter part of June, police spokesman David Hopkins commented that "the people of Columbus seem to be trying to put the senseless killings in the back of their minds. It's not the topic of conversation it used to be around here. People don't think about it like they used to." Hopkins expressed his concern that elderly women in Columbus might be developing "a false sense of security."[124]

At his regular news conference on July 20th, three months after the Cofer murder, Chief McClung warned citizens "not to relax because of the long hiatus," while expressing "a personal feeling of frustration" about the search. The mood of the investigators was "one of alertness," he said.[125] In a change in tactics apparently precipitated by the stalled investigation, police requested the public's help by releasing information that had previously been held confidential. Under the *Ledger*'s headline "Police Seek Gun Stolen in Wynnton," the task force solicited information on the .22 caliber blue-steel Ruger automatic pistol that had been stolen from the Sanderson and East residence in early October 1977. Accompanied by a photo of a similar pistol and the serial number of the stolen weapon, McClung was quoted as saying, "There is absolutely no evidence that the Strangler committed this particular burglary, but there is no evidence that he did not....We are going over all the events in the area because something may be of importance."[126] Requests for information and photos of the pistol were also shown on local television channels. These appeals, like others, bore no fruit.

Three days later, police released the sketch of Gertrude Miller's attacker, which had been obtained six months earlier and previously shown only to law enforcement personnel. Saying vaguely that it resembled a man seen in the Wynnton area between September and December 1977, McClung justified the delay in releasing the drawing with the thin excuse that police were "waiting until enough witnesses described the man's appearance." At the same time, a more detailed description was provided of the individual, in which he was described as "a black or dark complected white, up to 6'2", of slender build, weighing 140 to 170 pounds," with "dark hair and a light to medium brown or reddish-brown complexion." Seeking to avoid the obvious racial implications of the sketch and description, McClung said the police simply wanted to talk with the man. "I want to emphasize that at this point the individual we are seeking is a witness and there is nothing, absolutely nothing, to tie him to any of these crimes."[127] With the sketch and the description, McClung was basically confirming that the Strangler was thought to be black, the same assertion from Don Kilgore that had earlier spawned racial discord. His equivocation and convoluted explanation appeared to be an attempt to avoid offending the black community. By the following day, task force director Ronnie Jones said his "investigators had received dozens of telephone calls" concerning the sketch, leading to interviews with several individuals. "This is not a breakthrough," Chief McClung warned. "It is an investigative procedure we want to follow. Most of the logical leads have expired and we are going back."[128]

Up until this point in the investigation, there had been no substantive mention of its cost. Now, nearly ten and a half months since the death of Ferne Jackson, the Strangler's first murder victim, and more than three months since that of Janet Cofer, his last, the open-ended nature of the search, its lack of success, and its cost was attracting attention. In loosely veiled words criticizing the task force's failure to apprehend the Strangler, a *Ledger* journalist noted, "The human price of his continued freedom has been the lives of seven elderly women. In money, the cost to the city, state and federal taxpayer has been $1,062,448."* Since the formation of the task

---

* Adjusting for inflation, based on the US Bureau of Labor Statistics Consumer Price Index, this figure would roughly be equal to $4.2 million in 2020. It

force in late December 1977, more than fifty investigators had logged in excess of 100,000 man-hours. Since Ferne Jackson's murder, the investigation had cost the combined governments of Columbus and Muscogee County $443,857, the Georgia Bureau of Investigation $156,794, and the Georgia State Patrol $213,000. Local, state, and federal grants, much of which had not yet been spent, totaled $213,797. Law enforcement personnel uniformly agreed the cost had been worthwhile, despite the lack of meaningful results. When asked "How much more will it cost to catch the Strangler?" Columbus police commander Herman Boone replied,

> I don't think I can answer that. Every time a lead comes in, we hope that this will be the one. We believe—no, I'm sure—that eventually we will catch the Strangler. We are here to catch the man, to do the investigation. It could come to the point where there's no more money to run the investigation at this level. Then we'll do it with what we've got. I'm sure the day will come when we have to pull some of those men. But as long as he's (the Strangler) still out there, these cases will never be closed and we'll always be pursuing them."[129]

The following months passed without significant progress. Occasionally there were leads that held promise, but uniformly they came to naught. In the Democratic primary in early August, former state senator Harry Jackson defeated incumbent Jack Mickle in the race for Columbus mayor. Jackson was the brother-in-law of Ferne Jackson, the Strangler's first murder victim. His appeals to voters emphasized the lack of progress in the Strangler case under the Mickle administration. Jackson would defeat his Republican challenger in the November election and serve as Columbus's mayor until 1982. A summary of the past year's events on the one-year anniversary of the Strangler's first murder noted "rewards for information leading to the arrest of the Strangler are now approximately $100,000, but leads are dwindling even as investigators check out the most improbable clues." Task force investigators were said to be "working on other murders as well." There was speculation as to why the murders had stopped. Ever confident, Ronnie Jones "said that if he ever begins to think the task force will not capture the Strangler, he will resign as commander of the force."[130]

---

should be noted that broad assertions regarding the time-value of any currency are speculative at best.

Jones would step down by the end of the year to accept a position investigating credit card fraud for Columbus Bank and Trust Company.

While there were no murders, there was at least one suspicious attack on an elderly white female that followed the pattern of the Strangler.[131] At approximately 1:00 P.M. on the afternoon of Thursday, February 15, 1979, police were called to the St. Francis Hospital Emergency Room for a possible assault on eighty-three-year-old Essie Jones. Ms. Jones lived alone in room 308 on the third floor of the Ralston Towers, a former hotel in downtown Columbus that had been converted into an apartment building for senior citizens. Ms. Jones had been taken to the ER on the supposition that she had suffered severe injuries from falling in her room, but examination soon proved otherwise, leading to the police being summoned. Ms. Jones was scheduled to see her doctor that day and was to be picked up by a friend at about 11:30 A.M. She had her hair done earlier that morning, and around 10:30 A.M. spoke with her next-door neighbor, Bobbie Windham, in the hallway. As they were talking, an unfamiliar young black man walked down the hall, pausing long enough "to look in Mrs. Jones's room real good" before continuing on his way. Ms. Windham described him as being "between twenty and thirty years old." A few minutes later, as she left to go shopping, Ms. Windham incidentally noted that Ms. Jones's door was closed. At around the same time, two residents on the floor above observed a neatly dressed "handsome" young black man in their hallway. They thought his presence was unusual as "he didn't live there" and "was trying to hide his face from us," they later told police. Around 11:00 A.M., a friend came to visit Ms. Jones, discovering this time her door was ajar and a "groaning noise" could be heard coming from her room. Stepping inside, she found Ms. Jones on the floor, with "blood all over her" and her face so bruised and swollen that she was not recognizable. A building manger was called and went to room 308 to offer assistance. Ms. Jones was unable to communicate clearly due to her injuries, but kept repeating "choke, choke." It was assumed that Ms. Jones had fallen and injured herself.

Though severely injured, at the hospital Ms. Jones was able to tell doctors that she had been attacked by a "black man," the same one who passed her and Ms. Windham in the hall. Returning a few minutes later, he barged into her room and began beating her for no apparent reason. Examination revealed that she had suffered fractures of the facial bones, a broken jaw, and the dislodging of several teeth. Her undergarments had been torn off, and emergency room personal saw blood between her legs.

Examination by a gynecologist showed bruising around the vaginal introitus, presumptive evidence of rape or attempted rape. Vaginal washings did not contain spermatozoa. Ms. Jones later said she passed out during the ordeal and was unable to give detectives more information. The friend who was to pick up Ms. Jones and take her to the doctor had called by telephone during the time that the attack was presumed to be taking place. Like the phone call that disrupted the Strangler's assault on Ms. Ruth Schwob almost exactly a year earlier, it is possible that this phone call interrupted the attack on Ms. Jones, in the process saving her life. An intensive investigation of the crime scene and the surrounding neighborhood produced no actionable clues or definite suspects.

With a victim and a style of assault similar to that of the elusive Strangler, police were nonetheless reluctant to definitively say that this crime was his work. Descriptions of a possible assailant collected from several residents of the building were variable and inconsistent. There was little or no physical evidence otherwise found. In response to questions from the press, police spokesman David Hopkins said, "No description of the assailant [is] available," adding, "There is no evidence to indicate that this may be the work of the so-called Stocking Strangler." Within days, the event had faded from the news.[132]

By April 1979, the first anniversary of the Strangler's most recent murder, attention had, for the most part, turned elsewhere. Richard Gilbert, writing for the *Enquirer*, reported, "There is no suspect. There are no urgent clues. Strangling tips trickle in at the rate of two or three a week. And investigators have had to make some changes." Nighttime patrols of the Wynnton area had been reduced by fifty to sixty percent. The Strangler Task Force, now on its third director, had been drastically reduced in size, its members reassigned to other duties.[133] The odd tips and offers of assistance still arrived: A twenty-two-year-old convicted murderer serving a life sentence in Oregon offered to help. A writer from Macon, noting that psychics had offered advice on capturing the Strangler, advised, "Don't say you've tried everything until you've tried Jesus." A psychologist from Charleston, South Carolina, wrote to say that he had developed a list of traits that could identify the Strangler. Suggesting a proposed advertisement with the headline, "Do You Know the Strangler?" readers could check off characteristics that fit the pattern of the killer such as "He takes frequent walks or drives and angrily resents being asked where he is going. On rare occasions he exhibits severe outbursts of temper, then retreats into silence. He is not currently an active member of any clubs, civic organizations, or activity groups. He is single, separated, divorced, widowed or unhappily married. He may profess to be religious, but no longer attends church." Police decided against printing the advertisement as the traits fit thousands of Columbus citizens.[134]

In what may have been one of the sadder changes to mark the one-year anniversary of the Strangler's last murder, the homes of all seven victims had been sold to new owners, or, in the case of Ms. Scheible's apartment, rented to another tenant. The new owners were, as a rule, younger and often first-time home buyers. Having been murder scenes, the sale prices of the houses had plummeted significantly below market value—as much as forty percent in at least one case. When interviewed by a reporter for the *Enquirer*, the new owners showed little concern for the history attached to their homes.[135]

Asked for his perspective, Chief McClung replied,

> This has been one of the biggest career disappointments to me, our inability to clear these cases on a timely basis. I am confident they will be cleared. It will remain our number one priority.... Based on the best information we can get from experts in sex crimes and behavioral experts, offenders of this type usually continue until stopped by incarceration or other reasons. Looking at that, I am at a complete loss to explain the stop. However, we have given such extensive coverage, we may have prevented further stranglings. He could be incarcerated or dead. Just that he has stopped is the second best thing we could have. The first is to have him arrested and charged."[136]

Months passed without any progress. Periodic reports of a new suspect would be followed days later by the announcement that the person identified could not have committed the murders. When interviewed again in April 1980, near the second anniversary of the Strangler's last murder, Chief McClung painted a dim picture of the investigation. Police had "exhausted all logical leads," and while investigators had evidence collected from the crime scenes, they were no closer to solving the case than they had been two years earlier. McClung retired the following month, only to be replaced by a political rival from within the police department, O. P. Carlile, who had been appointed by the city's new mayor. At the same time, police announced the formation of a new "Stocking Strangler search unit" to replace the "abandoned" Strangler Task Force. The new unit was formed to provide a "fresh look and new ideas" in the search for the killer.[137]

Although the occasional rumor of a new clue or suspect was still mentioned, no progress was made toward the identity or capture of the Strangler. As the details of the crimes faded from the public's collective memory, attention turned to other, more immediate issues. While not completely forgotten, for practical purposes, the active search for the Strangler had ceased. The case had grown cold.

Part II

The Suspect

Chapter 18

Serial No. 13-70073

Shortly before 4:00 A.M. on Sunday morning, March 12, 1984, the manager and two employees of the Bombay Bicycle Club, a restaurant located at 3201 Macon Road in east Columbus, finished up their duties for the evening and headed home. As they left via the rear door of the restaurant, a figure dressed in a black ski mask emerged from the darkness, jamming a pistol into the manager's side and ordering that they all go back inside the building. Once inside, he demanded that the manager give him the key to the liquor closet, a large storeroom for alcoholic beverages. He locked the three inside. Fearing for their lives, they barricaded the door with cases of beer and liquor, hoping to keep the robber out should he return. Within minutes, he was back at the door, after apparently not finding what he was looking for. He ordered his hostages to open up, then tried to force his way in. Unsuccessful, he gave up and left, not realizing that when he had first ordered the door to the liquor closet open, it had set off a silent alarm.[138]

Meanwhile, the alarm company had notified Columbus police that they had received a burglar alarm from the restaurant. A call went out to police on duty and was answered by Thomas Michael Bowen, nicknamed "Spanky" by his colleagues, who was patrolling alone nearby. As Bowen, twenty-six-years-old and a seven-year veteran of the force, was pulling into the restaurant, he observed a 1977 blue Pontiac Grand Prix "tearing across the parking lot with no lights on." He flipped on his blue lights and radioed the dispatcher that he was giving chase. The fleeing car headed north on Auburn Avenue at a high rate of speed. After about two-thirds of a mile, the street dead-ended into Edgewood Road, a quiet residential neighborhood of single-family homes. Attempting to make a sharp left turn, the driver of the Grand Prix lost control, careening through several front yards before hitting a parked car and coming to an abrupt halt. No one emerged from the wreck. Bowen parked his patrol vehicle and approached the Grand Prix from the driver's side, a flashlight in one hand and his radio in the other. As he peered into the car's window, he was shot twice in rapid succession, both bullets striking him in the forehead. He fell backwards to the ground, his weapon still clipped in its holster. Within minutes, a second patrol car arrived. A call for assistance went out immediately, but the driver of the wrecked car had disappeared. A neighbor later told police that she had heard the wreck and the gunshots and shortly thereafter had seen a white male fleeing the scene. Spanky Bowen died soon after arriving at the emergency room. He was engaged to be married and had been recently accepted for a position with the Georgia State Patrol.

Det. Sgt. Mike Sellers and his partner, Det. Lem Miller, were called to investigate the shooting. The wrecked vehicle was rapidly identified as being registered to the girlfriend of Lonnie Gene Botts, who she said was driving her car that night. A machinist who two years earlier had worked in the same restaurant building, Botts was familiar with the lockable liquor closet and knew to ask for the key. No gun was recovered from the Grand Prix, but police found two spent .22 caliber shell casings, suggesting that the murder weapon was a semiautomatic pistol. Botts apparently escaped the area on foot by following the course of a nearby small waterway, Lindsey Creek, some two to two and a half miles to his mother's house. There, several hours later, Detective Sergeant Sellers found muddy wet clothes in a laundry hamper and an empty gun case for a Ruger pistol. In the gun case were several .22 caliber cartridges that were of the same type as the shell casings found in the Grand Prix. Botts's mother was told her son appeared to be in serious trouble.

Later, around midafternoon the same day, Botts, accompanied by his mother, showed up at Columbus police headquarters to turn himself in. Having been advised by an attorney not to say anything, he initially refused to give a statement to police. The next day, however, Botts admitted to a jailer that he regretted shooting Patrolman Bowen but asserted that he was acting in self-defense. As recovery of the murder weapon would be important to the prosecution of Botts's case, detectives began an intensive search for the missing gun, scouring the banks of Lindsey Creek, interviewing neighbors, and poring over pawnshop records.[*]

In an apparently unrelated event, on April 9th, Henry Sanderson called the Columbus Police Department to inquire about his stolen .22 caliber Ruger semiautomatic pistol. It had been taken in a residential

---

[*] Botts was indicted for murder and other crimes. The prosecutor, Bill Smith, indicated that the state would seek the death penalty. In November 1984, Botts accepted a plea bargain carrying a life sentence with possibility of parole, plus twenty years. As of early 2021 he remained incarcerated in the Georgia prison system.

burglary in October 1977, some six and a half years earlier. Although no direct connection existed between Sanderson's pistol and the stranglings of 1977 and 1978, the events had occurred during the same time frame. Investigators hoped that finding the missing gun might provide a clue to the killings, as the burglary took place in Wynnton a few houses away from the site of the Scheible murder and within several blocks of the sites of the attacks on Jackson, Borom, and Schwob, as well as the burglaries of the Illges home. Newspaper articles and television coverage during the summer of 1978 asking for assistance in locating the missing gun had produced no leads. Like the Strangler case, the search for this weapon had gone cold as the years passed.

Henry Sanderson insisted that he had received a call from someone telling him that his gun had been recovered. He wanted to let the police know that he had moved and, of course, wanted to retrieve his missing property, if possible. Investigators were puzzled; Sanderson's gun had not been recovered, and so far as could be determined, no one had called him. Sanderson's family said that he was developing signs of dementia and was at times confused about present and past events. It was this call, in the midst of the search for a similar type of pistol, that raised the chance—however remote—of a missed clue and a connection between the long-ago Sanderson burglary and Patrolman Bowen's murder, and possibly the Stocking Strangler. Word of Sanderson's call was passed on to Detective Sergeant Sellers. He was familiar with the missing stolen gun, having helped search for it while working with the pawnshop detail during the search for the Strangler years earlier. On April 11th, Sellers sent out a teletype to police agencies nationwide requesting information on the Ruger pistol, serial number 13-70073.

The following day, Sellers received a response from the Michigan State Police in Lansing, the state capital, indicating that a Ruger semiautomatic pistol with the same serial number had been registered several years earlier by a black male named Aaron Sanders, a local contractor who lived in Kalamazoo.[†] The Kalamazoo Police Department was contacted,

---

[†] At the time, Michigan was one of the few states in the Union to require the registration of handguns. Of all the thousands of law enforcement agencies that received the teletype, the response from the Michigan State Police was the only one received. In this era before most records were digitally archived, clerks manually searched through more than a thousand records kept on three-by-five-inch cards before discovering information on the missing pistol.

and an officer, Tom Baarda, was dispatched to follow up on the information. Aaron Sanders still had the pistol. He stated that it had been given to him by his mother, Lucille Gary Sanders, several years earlier, and insisted on the police taking the weapon, saying he wanted nothing to do with it if it was stolen. When investigators contacted Ms. Sanders, a resident of Gary, Indiana, she said that she had been given the pistol by her brother, Jim Gary, when he had visited her around 1979 or 1980. There had been a break-in at her house, and she felt that she needed a gun to protect herself. Jim Gary was a resident of Phenix City, Alabama, just across the Chattahoochee River from Columbus. The trail now led back to the area where the gun had been stolen years earlier.

On Friday, April 16th, Detective Sergeant Sellers, accompanied by Det. Lem Miller and Capt. Tommy Boswell from the Russell County, Alabama, Sheriff's Department, paid a visit to Jim Gary. Gary was initially evasive, saying he often bought and sold guns and was not sure about the particular one police were searching for. He finally admitted that he bought a similar gun from "a dude at Little Joe's Package Store," a known hangout for petty criminals. Asked if he had obtained a bill of sale, Gary said the fellow who sold it to him—whose name he didn't know or couldn't remember—was illiterate and simply put his "X" on a piece of paper to document the transaction. Detective Sergeant Sellers advised Gary that the stolen pistol could be involved in a murder investigation and the vagueness of his memories might indicate that he was either involved or covering for someone else. Sellers said he would return the following Monday, hoping in the meantime that Gary's memory would improve.

On Monday, April 19th, the officers returned to Gary's house. This time they brought a pistol similar to the stolen one, hoping to jog his memory. Over the weekend, Gary's attitude had changed. He admitted he had purchased the gun several years earlier from his nephew, Carlton Gary, paying forty dollars for the weapon. He could not recall the exact date he bought it, but stated that Carlton came back "about a month" later telling him that he needed to get the gun back because it was "hotter than a .38." This was apparently around the time that Columbus police had put out newspaper and television requests for information on the stolen pistol. Gary said that he was suspicious of his nephew and lied to him. "You know, I paid him forty dollars for that gun," Gary explained. "I still had it, but if I gave him that gun I'd never see it or my forty dollars again. So I just told him I'd sold it." When asked about Carlton's current whereabouts, Gary said that he had been in prison "in one of them Carolinas" but apparently had been released and was staying in the Columbus area at the time. About a week earlier he had come by to see his uncle, wanting to buy another pistol. Carlton said he needed to make some money and was planning to buy drugs in Florida and bring them back to Columbus to sell. When told that the pistol had originally been sought because of its connection to the stranglings six years earlier and that his nephew might be involved, Gary replied, "Aw, he wouldn't do anything like that. He's just a petty thief."

The revelation that Carlton Gary might still be in town led to a search for where he had been in prison. His parole officer, assuming he had one, should know his location. Detective Miller set out to find him. Fortuitously, the first call he made yielded an answer. Gary had been incarcerated at the Goodman Correctional Institution in Greenville, South Carolina, where he had been a trusty.[‡] But he had not been released. He had escaped on March 15, 1984, a month earlier. Thinking that their prisoner might head home, South Carolina officials had notified Columbus police. At the time, though, there was no reason to suspect that Gary was any more than another low-risk escaped prisoner who would most likely end up back in the system once he ran afoul of the law again. Sensing that there might be a connection between Gary and the Strangler murders, Sellers requested a copy of the ex-prisoner's fingerprints.

The set of Carlton Gary's fingerprints arrived from the South Carolina prison on Monday, April 30th. Sellers and Miller took them to the I.D. Division of the Columbus Police Department, giving them to Sgt. Doug Shafer with the request to check them against the unidentified prints that had been collected at the scenes of the stranglings in 1977 and 1978.[§] The index print, one from a window screen from Ms. Kathleen Woodruff's house and almost certain to have been made by the intruder,

---

[‡] A "trusty" is a prisoner who has been given special privileges or responsibilities, generally based on good behavior. It is pronounced with an an accent on the first syllable, but often confused with "trustee," which is pronounced with an accent on the second syllable. The latter word refers to a person holding a position of trust, most commonly fiduciary.

[§] In 1984, most fingerprint identification and verification were done by the same basic methods that dated to the early twentieth century: a visual identification and classification of patterns and subsequent comparison of these data to other fingerprints when seeking a possible match. A copy of this "index print" was widely distributed to law enforcement agencies in the state and region. In the early twenty-first century, much of this process has been digitized and automated.

was the first one Shafer chose for comparison. Sellers and Miller waited outside the half door, watching Shafer as he hunched over the fingerprint cards, studying their whorls, loops, and arches through a magnifying loupe, going back and forth between the newly arrived prints from South Carolina and the print collected from the murder scene. His pace quickened. He seemed agitated. Finally, raising his head, Shafer demanded, "Damn, man! Who is this?"

"Why?" Sellers replied.

"It looks like it's going to be a match," Shafer exclaimed before resuming his intensive examination. A few minutes later he turned to the waiting detectives and declared, "By god, it's him! I didn't think I'd ever find the match. We've looked at thousands of prints..." One of Carlton Gary's fingerprints was an exact match for a latent print from the Strangler's entry point into the home of Kathleen Woodruff, the Strangler's fifth victim. Sergeant Shafer, now assisted by others from the department, immediately began the tedious process of comparing Gary's prints to others from the scenes of the Strangler's murders. Within two hours, two more matches had been identified.

Turning to Miller, Sellers said, "Now we know who the Strangler is. But he's loose. He's back in Columbus."

Chapter 19

A Motel Room in Albany

Carlton Gary was, in fact, back in the Columbus area. He had been arrested on April 18th, less than two weeks earlier, in the parking lot of Smitty's Lounge at 1417 Benning Drive in the southern part of the city. Vice Squad officers observed a man smoking marijuana in a burgundy Ford LTD in the bar's parking lot. When they tried to arrest him, he pushed them away and ran toward a nearby wooded area before being caught. Gary was charged with misdemeanor possession of marijuana and obstructing an officer. After he was booked, fingerprinted, and had his mugshot taken, he was released on a $500 cash bond paid out of the $600 he had in his possession when taken into custody. The one thing Gary did not have, however, was any form of identification. So far as police knew at the time, the man they arrested and charged that night was Michael Anthony David, the name he gave them and the name that appeared on his police record.

With the matches between Carlton Gary's fingerprints and those found at the Strangler murders, Sellers and his superior officers met with Columbus police chief Jim Wetherington to plan the next step. Lt. Charles Rowe, Det. Sgt. Mike Sellers, Det. Lem Miller, Sgt. Jim Warren, and Det. Ricky Boren were tasked with following what the chief described as "the strongest lead we've ever had." The date was April 30th. If Gary discovered police were actively searching for him, he was sure to flee, so some degree of confidentiality was necessary. With information from the South Carolina prison system now in hand and several of Gary's aliases known, Sellers immediately sent out a memo to law enforcement in the area requesting assistance in his apprehension. Gary had a long criminal record and was currently a suspect in connection with "numerous" armed robberies in Georgia, Florida, and Alabama, including an April 3rd armed robbery and rape of an employee at a Po' Folks restaurant in Phenix City.

The officers began an intense search of the Columbus and Phenix City areas, a geographically huge region with a combined population of 200,000 or more individuals.

Judge William Slaughter signed an arrest warrant the next day, charging Gary with the October 1977 burglary of Ms. Callye East's home during which the Sanderson pistol was stolen.

After confessing in late February 1979 to a string of armed robberies in Greenville and Cherokee Counties, South Carolina, Gary was given a twenty-one-year sentence, which he began serving at Kirkland Correctional Institute, a high-security prison in Columbia. While in Kirkland, he worked in the prison library and became acquainted with Capt. Earl Watson, a correctional officer who kept in touch with him during his sentence. After serving nearly five years, Gary told Watson that he had "seen the light" and was ready to "do something for his fellow man."[139] On March 1, 1984, he was transferred to Goodman Correctional Institution, a minimum-security facility in Columbia, where he was made a trusty and assigned a job as a staff barber. Two weeks later, Gary and another inmate, Paul Moore, simply walked away. Moore was captured about a month later; Gary remained at large.

Columbus and Phenix City police began an intense search for their suspect. On May 1st, police learned that one of Gary's close friends was staying at a Holiday Inn in Phenix City. At midday, two detectives went to the hotel only to learn that Gary had left the room some six hours earlier. A man and a woman were arrested there, charged with possession of marijuana and cocaine. They told police that Gary had traveled back and forth between Phenix City and Gainesville, Florida, at least seven times since he arrived in the area in March, most recently returning on April 29th. Gary was a suspect in Gainesville in the robbery of a business on April 28th.[140]

At around 2:00 A.M. the next morning, Phenix City police spotted a rented 1983 Lincoln Gary was said to be driving. It was parked outside of the Coweta Apartments where Gary was alleged to be "visiting a woman." (Gary later said that police had turned their spotlight on the building, alerting him to the fact that they were nearby and allowing him to escape.) Having barely missed him again, police tapped the woman's phone lines hoping to get additional information. Gary had been tipped that police were searching for him but didn't know for what offense he was being pursued. He "called the Coweta Apartments resident and told her a Columbus woman would pick up some cocaine from her and take it to him in Albany [Georgia] .... Albany police were notified that Gary might be in a hotel there, possibly registered under the name of a woman with whom he was traveling."[141]

At about 1:00 P.M. on May 3rd, Albany police confirmed that Gary—or someone matching his description—was staying in room 254 of the Holiday Inn there, registered under the name of twenty-four-year-old Robin Odom. Police set up surveillance on either side, in rooms 252 and 256, and observed Odom leave the room and return a couple of times. On the likelihood that Gary was armed, the local SWAT* team was on standby to make the arrest. Shortly before 4:30 P.M., Odom left the room again, but this time she was grabbed by officers and questioned out of sight of room 254. She said the man in the room was "Michael Davis"—one of Gary's known aliases—and that he was armed with a pistol. The arrangement was that he would let her back in the room only after a "special knock" to let him know that it was her and not someone else. Odom was advised that "Davis" was a wanted fugitive and agreed to cooperate in getting Gary to open the door.

As two members of the SWAT team, James Paulk and David Noel, both dressed in camouflage fatigues, waited just out of sight, Odom knocked on the door and then fled back down the hall. As Gary cracked the door, Paulk, armed with a MAC-10 .45 caliber submachine gun, and Noel, armed with a .45 caliber pistol, "hit the door at a run." A struggle ensued as Gary grabbed for Noel's pistol. After about a minute, the two men managed to force their way in. When Gary saw Paulk aim the submachine gun at him he gave up and raised his hands as other Albany police officers followed the SWAT team members into the room. Gary's weapon, a chrome-plated .38 caliber revolver with its serial number ground off, sat just out of reach on a small nightstand between the beds.

Carlton Gary and Robin Odom were arrested and taken back to the Albany Police Department, where they were photographed and finger-printed while awaiting the arrival of officers from the Columbus Police Department.

---

* Special Weapons And Tactics.

Chapter 20

A Long Night

Columbus police were notified shortly after Gary and Odom were taken into custody. At about 5:50 P.M., May 3, 1984, the five officers left for Albany in two vehicles—Boren, Rowe, and Sellers in one, with Miller and Warren in the other. It would be the first time any of them had seen this mysterious person, quite possibly the serial killer who had murdered seven elderly women and terrorized the city of Columbus years earlier. Who was he? What was he? A former member of the Strangler Task Force recalled, "We always wondered what he looked like. Did he have two arms, two legs? So many people were picturing a hunchbacked monster, but [my partner] and I thought he was a smart, clever burglar."[142] Capt. Earl Watson, the South Carolina correctional officer who knew Gary during his five years in prison there, described him as "an extremely brilliant young man. His I.Q. is genius level. He's not your average mugger-street robber type." Referring to Gary as "a well-educated person," "a con man," and "a ladies' man," Watson said "he was the type of individual who had the idea that he was smarter than the average police officer. And maybe he was."[143] After arriving in Albany about 7:15 P.M., the Columbus officers saw Gary for the first time: a tall, handsome, articulate black male, shackled hand and foot, quietly awaiting his transfer and an unknown future.[144]

After completing the requisite paperwork, the officers and their two charges left Albany about 8:00 P.M. to return to Columbus. Robin Odom rode with Miller and Warren. Boren drove the other vehicle, with Rowe in the front passenger's seat, Sellers in the left rear behind the driver, and Carlton Gary, still shackled, in the right rear. There were no plans to begin interviewing Gary before reaching Columbus, but per routine protocol, he was advised again regarding his rights as a prisoner: the right to remain silent with the knowledge that anything he said could be used against him in a court of law, the right to a lawyer, and the specific right to have a lawyer present during any questioning. Gary acknowledged the notification but was quick to reply, "The last thing I need right now is a lawyer."

After a brief period of silence, Gary asked what he was being charged with. When told it was for a 1977 burglary, he replied that he "didn't do burglaries." After a few more questions, and the explanation that the burglary took place on Eberhart Avenue in Columbus, he admitted that he had some knowledge of it. Gary said that he and a friend of his, Theopolis Joe Preston, drove over to Callye East's house in a truck. He stayed in the truck while Preston burglarized the house. To that, Detective Boren asked, "Well, how do you explain, then, that your prints were in this house if you never went in?" In truth, his prints had not been found in the house, but Gary had no way of knowing that. Boren was not being intentionally untruthful. He was aware that Gary's prints had been found at several crime scenes but did not know which ones. After a moment's reflection, Gary said, "Enough of this bullshit. I'll tell you the truth."

Over the following minutes, Gary explained in detail how he and Preston had gained entry through a kitchen window that they pried open while standing on a porch rail. He admitted taking some money and the car keys that belonged to the Toyota parked outside. The gun—the missing Ruger automatic—was stolen from the car, which they took and later abandoned on a street off Old Buena Vista Road. (Later, back at Columbus police headquarters, Gary was shown the actual gun and identified it as the one "I sold to my Uncle Jim.")

Gary was asked if he had been involved with other burglaries. He admitted that he had broken into a "castle" in the same neighborhood as the East house. He said someone else—an unnamed person—was with him, that they had stolen a Cadillac, and that they ran when an alarm went off. Lieutenant Rowe, recalling that in some ways the Illges home resembled a castle, asked Gary if he had burglarized it twice. This time he described, again in detail, how he and his unnamed accomplice had broken in the first time after prying open a basement window with a screwdriver. He spoke of exploring the darkened house and finding "an old man" and "an old woman" asleep in separate bedrooms on the upper floor. After stealing "a lot of money" and car keys from a pocketbook, they stole the Cadillac parked in the front driveway, later abandoning it near a motel and restaurant off Victory Drive in south Columbus.

The second time, the two gained entry through the same basement window, but this time found the door accessing the upper part of the house locked. They then stole a long ladder from the house next door and pried open a second-level kitchen window to get inside. As they started to climb the steps from the foyer to the next level, a hidden alarm was triggered. The two split, fleeing the house separately. Gary said he ran out the front door and down the long driveway, where he hid in some bushes across the street as the police responded to the alarm. A few minutes later,

Lieutenant Rowe asked Gary to explain how "his prints were found in one of the houses where one of the old ladies had been killed." Gary replied "that he had a small business at that time, where he would go around and do odd jobs, he would paint houses, and he would clean curtains and so forth, and his prints might have been in that house for that reason."

By this time, the two vehicles were back in Columbus, arriving at police headquarters at about 9:40 P.M. to find the street crowded with media vehicles and the hallways nearly blocked by curious cops and a gaggle of reporters and photographers eager to see and photograph the Strangler suspect. Gary, dressed in a red sweatshirt, gray sweatpants, and white socks with no shoes, was led in by officers on either side of him, his feet and ankles still shackled. He "flashed nervous grins as he took small steps up the hall," appearing to enjoy the attention.[145,146,147] He was taken to the I.D. Division, where he was photographed, fingerprinted, and samples of blood, hair, and saliva were collected.

With the booking formalities completed by about 11:30 P.M., Gary seemed eager to resume talking with the officers who had brought him back from Albany. No written record or recording had been made during the trip, so this time he was asked if the conversation could be recorded, or at least written down. Gary said he did not want that. He said he first wanted to meet with Robin Odom.* Officers allowed the two to talk for a few minutes, quietly observing. Gary kept asking her, "What should I do? What should I do?" as if he were torn between several alternatives. Odom replied that she simply did not know. By the time the conversation finished, Gary appeared to have made a decision. "Okay, I'm ready to tell you the truth," he said. "I did go into some of the houses where you have my fingerprints." The conversation resumed. "The first thing he said was that he had gone into a house on Buena Vista Road, and he believed that the lady's name was Mrs. Woodruff." This was the first time her name had been mentioned. As described later in trial testimony by Detective Sergeant Sellers:

> And then after that he said that he had also gone into a house where there was an old lady in the front yard on a walker. And we started to ask him about it and to elaborate about it and then he started to shake, and he started to rock back and forth in the chair and he said but I was not alone. And we told him, we said,

---

* Odom was soon released from police custody without being charged.

what are you talking about, what do you mean? And it took him about five minutes and he blurted out that there was somebody else with him. And we asked him who, can you tell us who, and he...just looked like it was a big labor for him to finally push this name out.... He seemed really tormented with it, rocking back and forth, of whether he should tell or not, but he finally said that a friend of mine went in, and we said what's his name and he said Malvin Alamichael Crittenden, and I was kinda stunned at the name, you know? I thought he might come up with some-body like Joe Smith or John Doe or something like that, but he came out with this guy's name.

His alleged accomplice now identified, Gary gave a meticulous account of how he and Michael, or Mike, as he referred to Crittenden, had robbed Ms. Florence Scheible days after the Callye East burglary. In this case, though, and the others to follow, he made it clear that "I did the burglaries and Michael killed the old ladies." Asked about other break-ins, he mentioned a house on Buena Vista Road and "other houses he could tell us about, but could show us better, because he couldn't tell us where they were at, but he could show us," Detective Sergeant Sellers later testi-fied. Even though by this time it was well after midnight, Gary seemed willing to talk. As long as he wanted to do so, the officers were ready to listen. As Sellers explained, "This guy was just caught up in what he was doing, he was. He was just reliving and recapping all this stuff, and he was just continually talking and talking and so, you know, he never even said anything about being tired. He never said anything about let's stop, or an-ything like that. He wanted to go. He wanted to talk. He wanted to tell it, so we let him tell it." After discussing the options, and despite the late hour, the officers agreed to take Gary up on his offer, to let him show them houses he had burglarized during the time of the killing spree attributed to the Strangler. Gary and the three officers, Rowe, Boren, and Sellers, seated in the same places as before, got back in the police car and headed toward the Wynnton district. It was about 1:30 A.M. on May 4th.

For more than an hour the officers and their prisoner cruised the quiet residential streets of Wynnton, with Gary sometimes giving directions. He pointed out the "castle," the Illges house that he had burglarized twice, and where he hid the second time after the alarm sounded. He described the details of the nearby Borom house, even though the officers were not fa-miliar with it. Ms. Borom had struggled with her attacker before she was killed, a detail confirmed by Gary's comment that "Michael told me he had trouble with the woman, he said she was big and strong but everything came out all right." He pointed out the Schwob house "where Michael almost got caught by the alarm going off." He identified the Scheible house "as where I saw the old lady in her front yard with the walker," as well as the nearby Callye East house, "where I got the gun from that I sold to Uncle Jim." At the Dimenstien house, he remarked "there's the door that [Michael] took the hinge pins off." He recognized Ms. Martha Thurmond's house, commenting that she was a schoolteacher and acknowledging her name. At the site of Ms. Woodruff's house, Gary said he and Michael had gone in through a back window, commenting that "she was sitting in a chair in the living room" when Michael attacked her, and that he recalled something about a scarf.[†] He pointed out the Swift house on Buena Vista Road, with its distinctive six columns that he and Michael allegedly burgled just before Christmas in 1977.[‡]

It was after three o'clock in the morning by the time the group arrived back at police headquarters and turned Gary over to the jailers. Mike Sellers went home, sat down at his kitchen table, and made notes of all that had taken place over the preceding hours, knowing that Gary's admissions would be vital in the prosecution of his case. Conversations with Gary would continue over the following days with other voluntary revelations about his life, his past crimes, and his relationships with women and family. The nighttime ride through the streets of Wynnton did not include a visit to the area of Ms. Janet Cofer's home, but Gary revealed details that would be important later. He said that one night he and Michael were riding about, looking for a place to rob. They chose a house on Steam Mill Road next door to another house where "an old firetruck" was parked in the carport. Gary described how they broke in by cutting the screen on a front window then prying it open with a screwdriver. He said he saw Michael assaulting the woman, but he left the house and returned to where they had parked their car.

It had been a long and strange night. Why would this man, Carlton Gary, voluntarily and with such eagerness provide information on these crimes? He was sure to be charged, even if he were not the murderer. Why would he so readily implicate his friend, Malvin Alamichael Crittenden?

[†] Ms. Woodruff was the only one of the victims strangled by a scarf.

[‡] The officers and Gary did not ride past the site of the Cofer murder, which took place on Steam Mill Road, outside of the Wynnton district.

The answer would become clearer as the investigation proceeded, but for the moment, it was another strange twist in an already bizarre and horrific tale.

Chapter 21

Who Is Carlton Gary?

With a suspect now in custody, the public and the press were eager to define him. Was he, as his uncle Jim had suggested, "just a petty thief," a hapless soul who had naively fallen in with evil companions in the form of such men as Theopolis Joe Preston and Malvin Alamichael Crittenden? His reluctant admissions to the detectives on the night of his arrest might suggest as much. Or alternatively, did the façade of a smiling young man with his neatly trimmed afro and cropped Fu Manchu moustache hide a vicious fiend capable of beating, raping, and strangling defenseless elderly women? Reporters fanned out across the area in search of answers.

Gary's mother, Carolyn Lucille Davis, a former maid, lived in south Wynnton in a modest shotgun house at 2708 Thomas Street, only blocks from Gertrude Miller's home and the locations where the stolen vehicles of Ferne Jackson and Jean Dimenstien had been found. She was adamant about her son's innocence. "I'm his mother, I know that, and I am prejudiced, but I believe he is one of the finest young men God ever put breath in," she told a reporter for the *Enquirer*. "A person can be accused of a lot of things, but that's not saying you're guilty. I just hope people realize that." Ms. Davis and Carlton's father separated before he was born. She was not sure how well he knew his father, if at all. She said she last saw her son on Valentine's Day in 1980 when she visited him in prison in South Carolina. As to his innocence, she declared, "He could not have done all those things they said he did. If he would have been here then, I would have known about it." She asserted that he was being "railroaded" because he was black and was not sure he could get a fair trial. Part of her son's problems were due to the police, she alleged. "Every time he would start something he could never complete it because [the police] were always picking him up. It all seems like a nightmare."[148,149]

While Ms. Davis's comments were no doubt given sincerely, the facts belied her opinions. Most of the front page of the May 5, 1984, combined edition of the *Enquirer* and *Ledger* was devoted to the events leading to Gary's arrest, his criminal history, and the fact that a special session of a Muscogee County Grand Jury had indicted him the preceding afternoon for the murders of Florence Scheible, Martha Thurmond, and Kathleen

Woodruff. Under the bold headline "Grand Jury Indicts Suspect in 3 'Stocking Stranglings,'" most of the paper's front page was taken up by a photo of a smiling Carlton Gary in handcuffs juxtaposed with a map of the east coast of the United States and a long list of criminal offenses in New York, South Carolina, Georgia, Florida, and Alabama that he had been charged with, confessed to, or was suspected of committing between 1967 and April 28, 1984, less than five days before his arrest in Albany.

Gary's first known arrest occurred at age seventeen when he was a student at Lincoln High School in Gainesville, Florida, where his family had moved in the 1960s. Charged at that time with breaking and entering an auto, he was arrested again in Gainesville the next year on an arson charge. In 1970 and the years that followed, he was arrested multiple times in New York state, finally escaping from Onondaga Correctional Institution in Jamesville in 1977 and returning to Georgia. The following year saw a string of armed robberies in South Carolina resulting in his imprisonment in 1979, and the escape in 1984 that led to his return to Columbus. In the month before his arrest, he was a suspect in an armed robbery and rape in Phenix City, Alabama, and an armed robbery in Gainesville.* His mother's assertions aside, the facts strongly suggested that Gary might be best described as a career criminal.

The intense interest in Gary's criminal history revealed several important facts. Among them was the recognition that he frequently used aliases, among them Michael David, Michael Davis, Carl Michaels, Carlton Michaels, Micky Davis, and Micky David.† Because of this, there were several missed opportunities that might have implicated Gary earlier as a Strangler suspect. During the months in 1977 and 1978 when the Strangler was active in Columbus, Gary was one of thousands of individuals stopped by police for routine "field interviews." For each of the six times he was questioned, he gave them a different name, a different date of birth, and a different Social Security number. Because of this, his data, when

---

* Gary's offenses and arrest records are extensive and become important in this saga as events unfold. A more complete and detailed listing can be found in the appendix of this book, but it is reasonable to speculate that the entire extent of Gary's criminal history will never be known.

† In one interview with a reporter, Gary's mother said that his given name was simply "Carlton Gary." He sometimes gave his name as "Carlton Michael Gary," but she insisted that he did not have a given middle name.

entered into the task force's computer system, did not flag him as a suspicious individual.[150]

Between mid-September and early December 1978, an unknown gunman held up five steakhouses in the Greenville, South Carolina, area, usually showing up near closing time, earning him the nickname of "the Steak House Bandit." In mid-February 1979, Gary was arrested about forty miles away in Gaffney, South Carolina, following a similar robbery of a Po' Folks Restaurant. The details of Gary's arrest are interesting. A patrolman cruising by the restaurant shortly before 10:00 P.M. noted a young waitress fleeing the building and running across a major street "without looking." Curious, he turned into the Po' Folks parking lot. Just as he did, the back door opened and a man (later identified as Gary) emerged with a C&S Bank money bag in one hand and a .357 Magnum Trooper revolver in the other. The man ran for the nearby woods. As fortune would have it, state-police tracking dogs were nearby working on another case and were able to arrive at the robbery scene within thirty to forty-five minutes. For the next three hours the dogs tracked Gary, who was finally captured about 2:00 A.M. on February 16th. When questioned by police, Gary gave his name as Michael Anthony David. He said that he and a man named Malvin Crittenden had staked out the restaurant with plans to rob it. He alleged that as police arrived, he and Crittenden took off towards the woods. When captured, Gary did not have in his possession the gun, the money, or the keys to a blue Firebird with Georgia license plates parked nearby, alleging they had been taken by Crittenden. He said it was Crittenden who robbed the restaurant while "he waited outside as the lookout." When told by investigators they did not believe his story, Gary gave his true name. Later, on the day of his arrest, Gary saw the same police officer who had confronted him the night before as he emerged from the restaurant and said to him, "I should have killed you while I had the chance."[151] Uncertain of how much evidence the police had against him, a few days later Gary confessed to the string of South Carolina robberies and was sentenced in a plea bargain to twenty-one years in prison.[‡]

[‡] Gary would escape and return to Columbus five years later. The astute reader will note that this robbery took place on the same day as the attack on Ms. Essie Jones at the Ralston Towers in Columbus, but roughly ten hours later. During the investigation of Gary's criminal history after his 1984 arrest in Albany, a pattern emerged in which he would commit a crime and immediately leave town, presumably to avoid apprehension. In 1979, the drive from Columbus to Gaffney could

Because he was from Columbus, where a string of similar robberies had occurred earlier in 1978, South Carolina authorities contacted the Columbus police when he was apprehended in 1979. On March 10th, Dets. Richard Smith and Bruce Berreth were dispatched to Greenville to interrogate him. After a deal was made with Gary's court-appointed attorney "that he would only talk about...five specific robberies and that he would not be prosecuted for them," the officers interviewed him for a total of six hours. In a three-page written confession, Gary admitted to robbing the five restaurants in Columbus between April and October 1978. The cases were then "exceptionally cleared," a term meaning they were solved without an arrest being made. Because Gary was facing a sentence of more than two decades in South Carolina for his robberies there, it was felt that any attempt to prosecute him in Columbus would be superfluous. Detective Smith's written March 28, 1979, report includes a notation that "a copy of Carlton Gary's fingerprint card" was returned to the Columbus Police Department. For whatever reason, these fingerprints were evidently not compared to those of the suspected Strangler on file there. When asked about this more than five years later, after Gary's arrest, a police source "said that no questions were posed concerning the stranglings, that no physical evidence was obtained, and that fingerprints were not requested."[152,153] This statement appears to be in error.

Some expressed surprise that Gary was indicted so rapidly, less than twenty-four hours after his capture. Muscogee district attorney Bill Smith said, "We felt it was appropriate under the facts and circumstances of this case. It is unusual, but it's certainly not unprecedented. We've done it on a number of occasions in the past." Smith said he could not discuss the evidence presented to the grand jury, nor the evidence planned for use at a trial. He refused to say why Gary, under both his given name and several of his aliases, was indicted on only three of the seven slayings, but would not rule out the possibility that one or more of the other four cases attributed to the Strangler would be brought before the grand jury at a later date.§ Smith was unequivocal in stating that he would be seeking the death penalty once the case came to trial.

---

easily be accomplished in far less than ten hours. While Gary was never formally accused of the attack on Ms. Jones, and the issue not raised at trial, authorities feel that he was most likely the perpetrator.

§ Later, Smith said his decision to indict Gary on the three cases was based on the fact that at the time, they were the prosecution's strongest in terms of evidence.

Now in custody, Gary was being held in the Muscogee County Jail, but not as part of the general jail population, according to Sheriff Gene Hodge. "We have incarcerated him by himself," the sheriff explained. "When we have a prisoner that is charged with a serious offense, we put them by themselves so we can monitor them, especially in the beginning." Hodge also noted that Gary had a history of escape and that protection from other prisoners was a consideration. "We are aware there are feelings about him that would not be true of every prisoner, but we think our jail is secure."[154]

Shortly after his indictment, Gary's mother asked local African American attorney John Allen to represent him. Allen first met with Gary on Saturday, May 5th, the day after his indictment. After an initial interview, he called Chief Superior Court judge John Land to inform him that he was now acting as Gary's attorney and to instruct the police that there were to be no further interviews with his client. Early the following week, however, Allen requested the court to appoint another lawyer for Gary's defense, stating that his caseload would not permit him to undertake what was obviously a complex death penalty case.** On May 9th, Judge Land asked William L. Kirby II to take the case on a public defender basis. Kirby, a thirty-six-year-old attorney who had been practicing in Columbus for ten years and had been involved in three other death penalty cases, met with Gary early the next morning. In an interview afterwards with a reporter for the *Enquirer*, Kirby attacked the state's case. While admitting that he had not discussed any details with his client, he implied that Gary's rapid indictment might be an effort on the part of the prosecution to hide evidence or prevent him from examining witnesses. He suggested that he might seek a change of venue. The following day, Judge Land appointed twenty-eight-year-old Columbus attorney Stephen Hyles as a second member of the defense team. Gary's first appearance in court was scheduled for May 15th, "little more than a formality," or "the kickoff in a football game," as Kirby described it.[155]

The hearing was brief and uneventful, one of a series prior to Gary's formal arraignment, at which time he would hear the charges against him

---

Gary had admitted to police officers that he was present at the times of the break-ins at the homes of Scheible, Thurman, and Woodruff, and his fingerprints were found at each crime scene.

** Allen would later become a superior court judge in the Chattahoochee Judicial Circuit.

and be asked to enter a plea of guilty or not guilty. Judge Land set the arraignment date for July 17th, more than two months hence. In the interim, both the prosecution and defense would have the opportunity to file motions relating to the case. Gary was escorted into the courtroom "surrounded by sheriff's deputies," a white Bible tucked under his right arm. Shackled and dressed in the same red sweatshirt and gray sweatpants he was wearing when arrested, he spoke only once "in a clear voice," answering affirmatively when asked by Land if he was satisfied with his defense. His mother and sister, each clutching Bibles, sat on the front row. Gary "puckered his lips and blew a kiss" toward them as his mother said out loud, "We love you."[156]

Two days later, the Rev. Dr. D. A. DuBois, calling himself Carlton Gary's spiritual advisor, delivered to reporters a one-page statement written by Gary. DuBois, who identified himself as the chief prophet at the El Shaddai Miracle Temple, where Gary's mother was a member, had met with Carlton at the jail the day before. He wanted to make it clear that "the man accused in the strangling of three Columbus widows is an ordained minister, a black belt in karate and is not a murderer." "Mr. Gary feels the media has misrepresented him and drawn a bad appearance of him," DuBois said. "The first question I asked him was if he was guilty. I told him not to lie to me and God. He said he didn't do it and he was confident that he'd be found not guilty." Among other assertions, Gary's statement alleged that he had simply found the Ruger pistol that he sold to his uncle, and that while "he had committed many other crimes including robberies and other burglaries with women alone in their houses," he had never hurt anyone. In an oblique reference to the fact that all of the Strangler's victims were white, Gary said the "many ladies that I have do not believe in interracial relationships." DuBois alleged that Gary's knowledge of the details of some of the stranglings came from what he read in the newspapers. "Gary thinks police believe him to be an uneducated black man, DuBois said. He said Gary attended Atlantic Union College in South Lancaster, Mass., Chipola Junior College, Marianna, Fla., and Oakwood Seminary in Huntsville, Ala., and is an ordained minister." Contacted by a reporter, "registrars at the three colleges said...they have no record of a Carlton Gary ever being enrolled." In summary, DuBois acknowledged that Gary "'is a criminal—just not a murderer.' He depicted him as a 'modern-day Robin Hood' because 'he robbed from the rich' and would 'share with his lady friends who might be on welfare.'" When contacted, Gary's attorneys refused comment on his statement.[157]

In a brief news item published elsewhere the same day, Gary was said to have "apparently attempted suicide" on May 10th and had "been skipping some meals." In explaining the former episode, Sheriff Hodge said, "He tore up his sheet and stuck it through the sprinkler head on the ceiling and tied it off. It was an apparent suicide attempt, but we don't know his intentions." As to the latter, Hodge said "he has refused some meals, but he has bought lots of things from our concession stand." The Rev. Dr. DuBois said, "He is afraid of being poisoned."[158] Though the torn sheet was hung from the ceiling, Gary did not put it around his neck or attempt to hang himself. The consensus among the police was that it was an attempt to force a transfer to a mental institution, or a similar facility offering greater opportunities for escape.

Chapter 22

The Dance Begins

Gary's arrest, his indictment by a grand jury for capital crimes,* and the provision of court-appointed attorneys marked the beginning of a legal saga that would last for nearly three and a half decades. A bedrock principle of American jurisprudence is the concept of a defendant's innocence unless or until adjudged otherwise by a jury of his peers. To reach such a verdict, the state, represented by the prosecutor, must affirmatively prove the accused's guilt beyond a reasonable doubt. The defendant, represented by his attorneys, has no obligation other than having to stand trial on the issues for which he has been indicted. He cannot be forced to testify, nor to answer in any way the accusations against him. If a jury finds the state's case insufficient proof of guilt, then they may render a verdict of "not guilty." This does not mean that the defendant is innocent but rather that, in the opinion of the jurors, the whole of the evidence presented was insufficient to render a guilty verdict. The prosecutor is limited to presenting facts in the form of evidence and testimony. The response of the defendant's attorneys is often one of attacking the system and the process that led to their client's arrest and indictment. In the absence of exculpatory evidence in favor of their client, tactics of delay, obfuscation, and accusations of prosecutorial and systemic bias are common.

Over the following weeks, Kirby and Hyles filed a number of motions on behalf of their client. These included a request for a change of venue, alleging that the sensational press coverage of Gary's arrest made it impossible for him to receive a fair trial in Columbus. They requested a separate trial for each of the seven felonies for which he had been indicted—three of murder and four of burglary. They demanded "an independent scientific examination of all physical evidence in the possession of the state which is capable of scientific comparison." Citing the fact that Gary had been indicted without a preliminary hearing in Recorder's Court, at which time evidence against him would have been presented, the attorneys demanded immediate full disclosure of all evidence held by the state, alleging (with some degree of hyperbole) "approximately 20,000 persons were

---

* A "capital crime" is an offense for which the death penalty is a legally permissible punishment.

interviewed, approximately 2,000 suspects were uncovered and several millions of dollars were expended." In asking that Gary be "given a full and complete psychiatric and psychological examination," the attorneys noted "such evaluations are necessary to ensure the defendant is capable of understanding and comprehending the nature and extent of the charges against him." They objected to the state's intention to seek the death penalty for Gary should he be convicted, alleging that such a punishment discriminated against blacks accused of killing whites, and against defendants who were poor and male.[159,160,161] In an issue that would become important later in the case, Kirby and Hyles requested funds to hire an investigator to assist them in Gary's defense. Judge Land did not rule immediately on most of the defense's motions, deferring them instead for later consideration. He did, however, agree with the need for an investigator working on behalf of the defense, and approved the hiring of former sheriff's deputy and experienced legal investigator Don Snow in that position. Land rejected the demand for immediate full disclosure of all evidence, terming it overly broad.

On July 17th, 1984, the day scheduled for his arraignment, Gary appeared in court neatly dressed in a light-colored double-breasted coat offset with a slim dark tie of contrasting hue. Except for "one flurry of emotion" in response to the judge's ruling on a defense request, he sat passively throughout the proceedings. The majority of the day was devoted to additional motions before Judge Land, "with the lawyers jockeying for legal positions," in the words of one journalist.[162] Land ruled in favor of the defense that the statute of limitations had expired for the four burglary indictments, effectively dismissing those charges. He agreed with the defense's request by ordering that Gary undergo physical, psychological, and psychiatric testing, but rejected the motion that bypassing a preliminary hearing prior to his indictment had violated his rights. The issue of a change of venue was deferred to the time of jury selection. Near the end of the day, Gary, through his attorney, pled "not guilty" to each of the three murder charges. Judge Land tentatively set a trial date for early December.

While Gary's attorneys were formulating their strategy for the defense of their client, the prosecution was diligently working to assemble a case that would convince a jury of his guilt. Within days of Gary's arrest, prosecutor Bill Smith requested that the detectives who assisted in his apprehension and were familiar with the case be temporarily assigned as investigators for the prosecutor's office. It was assumed that this would be for a few months only. Officers Sellers, Rowe, Boren, Miller, and Warren thus became part of the prosecution team, not realizing that it would be more than two years before Gary's case would finally come to trial.[†] Though Gary had been indicted on only three of the seven slayings thought to be committed by the Strangler, all of the crimes shared many common elements: the stocking strangulation of an elderly white female who lived alone, forced entry into the victim's home, a crime committed at night, the location in or near the Wynnton area, the covering of the murder victim, etc. Furthermore, while driving through Wynnton with the detectives on the night of his arrest, Gary had shown familiarity with several of the sites of the murders. Gary's rap sheet, which both investigators and the press had obtained shortly after his arrest in May, listed other offenses committed while he was living in cities in New York and Connecticut prior to 1977. Investigators theorized that if there were commonalities, they might be reflected in Gary's previous crimes. Richard Hyatt, reporting for the *Ledger*, commented, "Although no one here will talk about why these cities are related to the three local cases, sources believe the prosecution is attempting to show a pattern of violence in the subject's past."[163] One possible example was the 1970 case of Nellie Farmer in Albany, New York.

In 1970, Gary was implicated in the rape and murder of Nellie Farmer, an eighty-three-year-old retired welfare caseworker. On April 14th of that year, Albany police were called to room 604 of the Wellington Hotel, then used as a residence for senior citizens. Ms. Farmer's body lay face down on the floor, partially covered with articles of clothing. Further examination revealed blood and feces on her lower body and legs; an autopsy confirmed that she had been raped and sodomized. The cause of death was given as strangulation as evidenced by a fracture of the hyoid bone. Her room had been ransacked, including a large steamer trunk that held a latent fingerprint clearly identified as that of Carl Michaels, the alias that Carlton Gary was using at the time. Gary (as Michaels) was indicted for Ms. Farmer's rape and murder. As with the deaths attributed to the Strangler and the attempt to name another suspect when he was captured after robbing the Po' Folks restaurant in Gaffney, South Carolina, Gary tried to shift blame to someone else by turning state's evidence against an

---

[†] Sellers, Rowe, and Boren would continue to work with the prosecutor's office through Gary's trial. Shortly after completion of the initial investigation, Miller and Warren resumed their previous duties with the Columbus Police Department.

alleged accomplice, in this case John Lee Mitchell. Interviewed for the *Ledger* by Hyatt, Albany County assistant district attorney Daniel Dwyer said that "he (Gary) planned the robbery but testified he was not involved in the murder. The woman was killed with a stocking or an article of clothing." Mitchell was subsequently brought to trial for Ms. Farmer's murder, with Gary as the star witness against him.

> Gary said he had entered the room to rob her and that she was dead when he came in. Gary said he had been a lookout while Mitchell had gone inside Miss Farmer's room.... The state's case [against Mitchell] was damaged when a handwriting expert testified that Gary was the real author of a statement supposedly written by another jail inmate. The statement claimed Mitchell had confessed to being Miss Farmer's murderer in conversations with the inmate.

Mitchell was acquitted.[164] After a plea bargain for his role in the robbery alone, Gary was sentenced to ten years in prison, but was released on parole in March 1975 after serving less than five.

Dwyer also mentioned another murder case, that of Marion Brewer, a sixty-two-year-old social worker who lived alone in a nearby retirement hotel and was found strangled "with an article of clothing" on February 12, 1970. "We never could connect the cases even though the *modus operandi* was very similar," Dwyer said. The case remained unsolved nearly a decade and a half later.[165,‡]

On August 2nd, a Muscogee County grand jury reindicted Gary on the four counts of burglary that Judge Land had dismissed two weeks earlier. District Attorney Smith noted that there were exceptions to the statute of limitation laws, and they were applicable to this case, specifically

---

‡ At the time, Gary was living in Albany, New York, with Sheila Dean, who was interviewed after Gary's arrest in 1984. Notes made by investigators after his arrest include the following statement: "Marion Brewer, WF, lived at Room #404, Hampton Hotel, Albany, New York. She was strangled in her room. The Hampton Hotel is near the Wellington Hotel. Carlton lived very close to both hotels at this time. Also, about this time Sheila Dean recalls Carlton came home and told her she should be careful because he had 'just killed someone.'"

because Gary was not a resident of Georgia and his identity was unknown. Defense attorney Kirby refused to comment on this reversal.§

In a surprising change, in a handwritten note filed on August 28th, Gary requested that Atlanta attorney August F. ("Bud") Siemon be allowed to head his defense team and "to select any other member of the bar as co-counsel, as he deems necessary." Siemon, age thirty-six, had been a member of the bar for eight years, and had previously served as a public defender in Douglas, Georgia, and Waycross, Georgia. Contacted by a reporter, Siemon said, "He wanted me to represent him and I agreed to do it." Meanwhile, William Kirby, who had been serving as court-appointed lead counsel, seemed to be taken by surprise. He "wouldn't comment on Gary's action, but said he hopes to learn in the next days his status in the case. 'It's a little up in the air at this point,' he said." In a motion that accompanied Gary's note, "Siemon asked for a temporary delay in the case and a postponement of any consideration of any motions until he has 'an opportunity to make a professional assessment' of the case."[166]

Within weeks, Siemon filed a motion requesting that Gary be allowed a second state-paid attorney and an investigator to assist with his defense, specifically citing Kirby and Snow to fill these positions. At a September 25th hearing, Judge Land denied his request, "ruling that Gary opted for his own attorney instead of Kirby. 'Mr. Gary has exercised the alternative and...does now have the counsel of his choice,' Land said."[167]

Throughout the fall months, the two sides continued to build their cases. The trial date, originally scheduled for December, had fallen by the wayside with no definite time yet chosen. During a lengthy hearing held before Judge Land on December 14th, Siemon once again requested state funding for a co-counsel, this time local lawyer Gary Parker, saying that "failure of the court to appoint and pay Parker would result in a denial of Gary's rights" to due process and equal protection under the law.** Once again, Judge Land refused, commenting, "Mr. Gary, of his own choosing, selected another counsel." Parker indicated that he was willing to volunteer some services and would continue to do so. Siemon also expressed concern about his client's health, saying Gary "has lost a lot of weight since he's

---

§ The legal term is that the law had "tolled," meaning in this case the time limits did not apply. In a brief October 11th hearing, Gary would plead not guilty to these charges.

** This was the same Gary Parker who years earlier seemed to justify crimes by blacks against whites by terming them "the have-nots after the haves."

been in custody and has suffered from food poisoning." Sheriff Hodge, consulted later about this allegation, "said he knew of no health problems except for a stomach virus that affected some inmates," commenting that Gary had access to medical treatment if needed.[168]

By the end of the month of December 1984, Carlton Gary had been in police custody for nearly eight months. With a trial date still uncertain, to an outsider, the legal process might have appeared to have ground to a halt. Behind the scenes, however, the struggle continued.

Chapter 23

A Year of Rotating Judges, Claims of Abuse, and an Escape Attempt

Reflected in the "speedy trial" clause of the Sixth Amendment of the United States Constitution, the legal maxim "Justice delayed is justice denied" is one of the fundamental operating principles of the American judicial system. Except, of course, when the perceived judicial outcome is potentially negative for one party or another to the case at hand. In those situations, delay and postponement of a trial via legal challenges become the order of the day.

On February 8th, 1985, Bud Siemon, now joined in Gary's defense by Atlanta attorney Bruce Harvey, filed another flurry of motions on behalf of their client. They requested funds to conduct a "community prejudice survey," alleging that "due to the massive volume and prejudicial nature of the media coverage in this case there is a dangerous possibility that actual prejudice may involve the jury box." They asked that any statements made by Gary after his May 3, 1984, arrest not be allowed into evidence at trial. The motion contended that Gary, "while not confessing to murder, made statements admitting to alleged criminal activities." These statements were "contradictory," indicating that their client had been confused by a police "strategy of coercion and inquisition." Another motion requested that defense attorneys be given office space in Columbus's Government Center, to include "a telephone, word processor, typewriter, and a receptionist during the pre-trial hearings and the trial."[169]

Perhaps the most significant motion called for Judge Land to recuse himself from the case. The day after Gary's indictment, his mother had requested representation from local attorney John Allen. After Allen interviewed his new client and advised him to remain silent, he discovered that Gary was still talking with police investigators, apparently of his own volition. Concerned that Gary would make statements that could be used against him, Allen contacted Judge Land to express his concern. As the issue of the admissibility of Gary's statements to police might come up later at trial, Land could be called as a witness for the defense, thus disqualifying him to serve as an impartial judge in the case. This motion was addressed in a March 14th hearing before Houston Judicial Circuit judge

Willis B. Hunt Jr., chosen to preside as the issue questioned Judge Land's objectivity.

The hearing, with Gary present, began with disruption. Manacled when led into the courtroom, Gary accused a deputy of "manhandling" him, shouting, "I'm going to get you. You can count on that." Pointing his finger at one of the deputies, Gary threatened, "I'm going to kill him." The prisoner had to be quieted before the hearing could start. Gary's attorneys requested that Land be removed from the case. Gary's former attorney, John Allen, testified that in the May 1984 phone call to the judge, Land said "your boy [referring to Gary] might not be telling you the truth." Land denied saying this and stated that he had not formed an opinion as to Gary's guilt or innocence. Siemon alleged that Land "had an active role in obtaining statements" and had already shown "a degree of bias" in the case. Hunt did not rule on the merits of the arguments, instead taking the matter under advisement.[170]

In a May 3rd order, Hunt said that Land should recuse himself from the case in order to remove any doubt as to his objectivity if he continued to serve as trial judge and thereafter the case was reviewed on an appeals court level. Land agreed, stating, "I think I should get out of the case altogether."[171] A few days later, Hal Bell, administrative judge for the Third Judicial Administrative District, appointed Superior Court judge E. Mullins Whisnant to take Land's place. This appointment cleared the way for pretrial motions to be heard and the subsequent beginning of Gary's trial.

Within days, Gary's attorneys publicly objected to Whisnant's appointment, citing the fact that he had been the Chattahoochee Circuit district attorney during the Strangler's first several murders in 1977, alleging this role might impair his ability to hear evidence objectively. Even though nearly six and a half years had elapsed between Whisnant's transition to the judgeship and Gary's arrest, Bud Siemon said, "You can't be the prosecutor on a case and then turn around and be the trial judge on the same case. It obviously disqualifies him." He said he would file a motion to have Whisnant removed if he refused to recuse himself.[172] Facing opposition, a week later Whisnant sent a letter to Judge Bell asking to be removed from the Gary case. The same day, Bell announced that Chattahoochee District Superior Court judge Kenneth Followill had been appointed to take Whisnant's place.

With an acceptable presiding judge now in place, Siemon and Harvey filed a habeas corpus petition on June 12th alleging that Gary had lost some forty-five pounds since his arrest due to "inadequate dietary provisions and psychological stresses" related to solitary confinement and "harassment" by jailers.* Jailers were allowing "unauthorized persons" into Gary's area "for the purpose of exhibiting Mr. Gary...as one would exhibit an animal in a zoo." In addition, the petition said Gary was not being given opportunity for "exercise, recreation and personal hygiene." This supposed mistreatment was damaging his ability to participate in his own defense. Asked for a response, Sheriff Hodge said Gary "definitely has not been mistreated," but refused to comment further. Judge Followill scheduled a hearing for July 2nd to hear this and multiple other pretrial motions.[173,174]

In a hearing that lasted over two days Gary, dressed in a "stylish gray suit," served as the prime witness to his own alleged mistreatment at the hands of his jailers. Correctional personnel had brought curious visitors and family members by to gawk at him in his cell, he said. His religious views, at first Muslim and later Seventh Day Adventist, forbade him from eating pork, yet it was often served to him at the jail. Other witnesses testified that Gary had lost between twenty and fifty pounds since his incarceration, but no documentation was offered to support these estimates. In rebuttal, prosecutors assured the court that if anything, Gary had been given special treatment. Detained in a private seventy-square-foot cell equipped with television and radio, he was afforded "extended time for visitors in a special area and allowed to hang his drawings and family photos on the wall." District Attorney Smith characterized the complaints of abuse as "naked allegation without an iota of proof." Jailers testified that Gary often did not eat his three daily meals, "instead buy[ing] as much as nine dollars' worth of candies, cakes and other sweets from the jail's store." As to the pork issue, "jailers said pork dishes like streak-o'-lean and sausage [were] gone from his plate when they retrieve[d] the dishes from his cell." Again, defense attorneys renewed their call for funding to hire experts and investigators to support their case, the cost of which could exceed $100,000 by one estimate. Deferring a ruling on most of the issues presented, Judge Followill strongly criticized defense attorneys for having interviewed only ten to fifteen of the prosecution's estimated 350 to 400 potential witnesses. "That takes me aback," Followill said. "Evidence that you

---

* A writ of habeas corpus is an order requiring that a prisoner be brought before a court (or other legal authority) to determine if he/she is being legally detained. The name and concept have their origins in Medieval English common law. In this case the defense attorneys were alleging that the condition under which Gary was detained were in violation of his constitutional rights.

have interviewed ten witnesses in the last ten and a half months doesn't go a long way toward impressing me on how you use your time."[175,176]

Weeks passed. In late August, Followill told a reporter that he expected Gary's trial to begin toward the end of fall, only a few months away. In anticipation, he had turned his judicial duties over to other judges in order to prepare. Responding, Gary attorney Bruce Harvey said mounting a proper defense would not be possible without "financial help." At a five-hour hearing on October 7th, Siemon and Harvey again alleged prosecutorial misconduct in the failure to timely turn over evidence and case-related documents, complained about their client's treatment in jail, and continued their demands for funding. As with Judges Land and Whisnant, they accused Judge Followill of "bias" based on the statements he made about a potential trial date before the end of the year, alleging he knew that the defense could not be ready for a trial by that time. Without filing a formal motion, Siemon suggested that Followill recuse himself and call for an outside judge to conduct a hearing on the issue. Responding strongly to the defense's demands, Followill denied motions to dismiss Gary's indictments or provide funding for defense investigators or experts. If they genuinely wanted him removed from the case, he said, they could file the proper motions and proceed accordingly.[177]

Monday, December 16, 1985, marked the last full week before the beginning of the Christmas holidays. Judge Followill had scheduled a pre-trial hearing for that day on the major issue of the admissibility in court of statements made by Gary to police shortly after his arrest in May 1984.[†] More than nineteen months had elapsed with a trial date yet to be determined. Gary's statements to police in the hours following his arrest were critical to the state's case. At the start of the hearing, Bud Siemon delivered a long oral plea to the judge, hoping to have the hearing deferred until such time as other issues he deemed important to the defense could be decided. Bringing up again the issues of alleged "judicial bias," inadequate notice of the hearing, lack of funding for defense experts and witnesses, and others unrelated to the potential introduction of Gary's post-arrest

---

[†] Such a proceeding is known as a Jackson-Denno hearing based on the 1964 US Supreme Court case of *Jackson v. Denno*, 378 US 368. The purpose of the hearing is to determine whether a defendant's statement(s) was (were) voluntarily given to an officer and whether the defendant was advised of his or her rights. Such a hearing is held outside the presence of a jury, with the judge subsequently making a determination on whether the statements will be admissible as evidence.

statements at trial, his aim appeared to be yet another attempt to delay his client's day in court. Asked for a response to Siemon's statements, prosecutor Smith replied, "Well, Your Honor, we are here on the order of the Court to have a Jackson-Denno hearing. We are prepared to go forward. Counsel (referring to Siemon) seems to go back and argues at some length the issues that have been decided by the court, that have been ruled on by the court." The hearing, addressing the issues of Gary's testimony as planned, resumed shortly.

For the remainder of the day and continuing through Wednesday, the 18th, the court heard witnesses from both the Columbus and Albany Police Departments testify in detail about the circumstances of Gary's arrest and his questioning in the hours and days that followed. Officers Rowe, Sellers, and Boren all stated that Gary had been advised of his rights and acknowledged them. Two documents signed by Gary confirming this were introduced into evidence. All three officers agreed that Gary had spoken freely and eagerly. The following morning, Gary, who was present during the hearing, told the court he wanted to take a lie detector (polygraph) test because "the public is being deprived of the truth." Alleging "these police are not beyond lying, and in a case like this, are bound to lie," he requested that they be made to take a polygraph test as well. He accused Judge Followill of bias, blaming the judge's failure to grant several defense motions on "skin color." "There is no kind of value placed upon a black person's life." The hearing ended Wednesday morning with Followill stating that he would make a final ruling on the admissibility of Gary's statements after he reviewed the evidence presented during the hearing. In reference to polygraph testing, he said that the attorneys for the state and defendant could discuss a possible agreement to allow such. He granted Gary Parker's request to withdraw as one of Carlton Gary's attorneys, both for economic reasons and the fact that Carlton Gary had requested that he be dismissed from his case.[178,179] Despite aggressive efforts by defense counsel to postpone and delay, completion of the hearing meant that the case was moving ever closer to trial, now predicted to begin in February 1986.

At approximately 4:00 P.M. on the afternoon of Sunday, December 29th, jailers discovered that Gary had tried to escape. They had grown suspicious because their prisoner had "been unusually quiet during the past two weeks and played his television set louder than normal." Having manipulated the light to darken his cell so jailers could not see inside, Gary had managed to cut a hole measuring roughly eight by eight inches in the concrete blocks above his lavatory. This was accomplished by using a twelve-inch steel leg that he had removed from his bed. The hole was in a wall where he had pasted some of his drawings. He had concealed it with a piece of cardboard on which he had placed four or five photos. Gary was moved to another cell. Sheriff Gene Hodge commented that already tight security would be "snugger" from then on.[180]

Chapter 24

Delays

Under a February 2, 1986, headline of "Defense Attorney Calls Upcoming Gary Trial 'A Farce,'" *Ledger-Enquirer* staff reporter Ken Elkins wrote,

A poster on the office wall of one of Carlton Gary's Atlanta attorneys shows an electric chair with the inscription, "Cruel and Unusual." The poster tells much about August "Bud" Siemon and Bruce Harvey's defense of the accused Columbus Strangler. The defense will be a fight against the death penalty by attorneys who specialize in such cases. Privately, the two have told local attorneys that they will fight the death penalty through appeals instead of before a jury.... A date for Gary's trial, which Siemon estimated would take two to four months, hasn't been set, although both the defense and the prosecution believe the trial is imminent.

The defense method apparently chosen by the attorneys seems to presume that Gary will be found guilty and sentenced to death, said one local attorney who has discussed the case with one of Gary's attorneys. Siemon and Harvey will focus on the appeal of the conviction, seeking to overturn a conviction on one or more technicalities or legal grounds, said the attorney, who asked to remain anonymous.

Complaining chiefly about the failure of the Columbus judges' refusal to pay most of the expenses requested by the defense, Siemon referred to the upcoming trial as a "farce."[181] By the end of the week, Judge Followill had set the trial date for March 10th, just over a month away. Evidently not pleased with Siemon's comments to the press, on the same day, Followill issued a separate gag order barring court officials, including attorneys, from giving their "opinion as to the fairness of the proceeding." Specifically, the order prohibited comments on

Gary's criminal record; the existence or content of any confession or Gary's refusal to make a statement; tests performed or Gary's refusal to take any test; the identity, testimony or credibility of prospective witnesses; an opinion about Gary's guilt; an opinion on the fairness of the trial, appropriateness of the date of the trial, its length or the amount of resources expended in preparation for the trial; or any personal remarks concerning counsel, the trial judge, the accused or the officers of the court.[182]

The press, normally opposed to such orders, editorially endorsed the decision. Referring to Siemon's comment on the scheduled trial being a "farce," the *Ledger* opined that "Followill is going the extra mile to see that the attorney's comment does not become a self-fulfilling prophesy."[183] The *Enquirer* referred to the ban as "a reasonable balancing of the public's right to know and the accused's right to a fair trial."[184] Noting that cameras and members of the media would be allowed in the courtroom, both papers assured their readers that the trial would have full coverage.

In the days that followed, Siemon and Harvey once again sought to delay Gary's trial "in order to show a need for court-ordered funds to interview hundreds of potential witnesses in thirteen states." Based on their alleged previous statements regarding fighting their client's case on the appellate level, as well as the fact that such a request had been denied before, it appeared that they were building a case on which to challenge an adverse outcome in the trial, now scheduled to begin in less than two weeks. The issue was addressed in a hearing on February 26th. Gary appeared briefly at the start of the proceeding, answering Followill's question about whether he thought he was receiving an adequate defense. Referring to and echoing his attorneys, Gary said, "I feel they're doing an excellent job, but it doesn't seem to matter.... I already know the outcome of every motion. It's just racism and politics...all these hearings are just a farce." He complained of his eyes and said he had been unable to maintain "basic personal hygiene." Speaking for the prosecution, Bill Smith referred to the defense's demand for funds as a request for "a blank check." Judge Followill rejected the motion. Without the requested funding from the court, Siemon commented that "we're going to be unable to defend this man in what is probably one of the most important criminal cases in the history of this state."[185]

On Sunday, March 9, 1986, the *Atlanta Journal-Constitution*'s front-page story featured the upcoming trial of Carlton Gary, scheduled to start the next day in Columbus. By this time, the "Stocking Strangler" case had become national news, on a par with New York's Son of Sam and Los

Angeles's Hillside Stranglers. Under the headline "'Strangler' Defendant Gary, Man of Contradictions, Going on Trial," a detailed account variously described him as a "sensitive artist," a "careful bandit," a "ladies' man," and "a personable, highly intelligent...chronic talker." The article briefly described Gary's life and past criminal history as well as the crimes with which he was currently charged. With the enthusiasm of a sports reporter covering opposing teams on the eve of the big game, the paper's reporter featured bios of prosecutor Bill Smith and defense attorney Bud Siemon. A quote from one of Gary's many former girlfriends seemed to sum up the thrust of the article. Commenting that the charges against him were "alien to everything I know about him," she also said, "I expected him to be cleared before now, and the longer it goes on, the more doubt I have."

Brimming with anticipation, the headline on Columbus's morning paper the next day announced in bold font "Trial of Accused 'Stocking Strangler' Opens." "Preliminaries to Columbus's most important trial of the decade began today," the article read, going on to briefly refer to Gary's alleged offenses, the judge, the attorneys for both sides, and the courtroom preparation. Coverage "by regional and national news organizations" was expected.[186] Some hours later on the same day, an even bolder headline on the city's evening paper declared, "Strangling Trial Delayed for Tests."[187] The date would be pushed back once again, this time to allow for evaluation of Gary's competency to stand trial.

The abortive trial had begun routinely enough that morning with the first matter being the choosing of a jury. Some ninety-four prospective jurors were waiting to be interviewed with an additional 150 summoned to appear later in the week. Gary, however, initially refused to get dressed to come to court. Shortly after 11:00 A.M., he was brought into the courtroom dressed in a white prison uniform. In sharp contrast to his appearance at a hearing less than two weeks earlier, Gary's "hair was matted and he walked unsteadily." When court convened shortly thereafter, Siemon and Harvey presented Judge Followill an unusual handwritten motion stating that they intended to raise the issue "mental incompetence." If there was any question of Gary's ability to understand the charges against him and to assist in his own defense, an adverse verdict in a subsequent trial could be overturned on an appellate court level. This maneuver forced Judge Followill to abandon the idea of beginning a trial and instead hold an impromptu hearing on the defense's motion.[188]

In the thirty-minute hearing that followed, the only witness Bud Siemon called to testify was Bruce Harvey, Gary's other defense attorney.

Referring to their client, Harvey said, "He rambles; he's not very fixed in reality," noting that he had seen a deterioration in Gary's physical and mental condition over the past four to five months. "I don't think [Gary] understands what I recommend and can follow legal advice reasonably." In response to a question from prosecutor Smith, Harvey said, "I can ask him about Bill Smith and he will answer about a purple cow." Obviously displeased with the direction events were taking, Smith asked, "They've represented him for two years. We've had six to eight hearings. We set the trial date two months ago. Why raise this issue today?" Siemon replied, "We came to court today to strike a jury. We raised the issue because Carlton Gary refused to come to court this morning." Faced with no other options, Judge Followill postponed the start of Gary's trial indefinitely, instead ordering that he first undergo psychological and psychiatric evaluation. Asked for a response to the morning's turn of events, both sides refused comment based on the earlier gag order. Siemon simply stated, "Our motions speak for themselves." Bill Smith said, "I can't talk about what happened, but you can see from my face how I feel."[189,190]

The determination of Gary's competence injected not only a delay in the date of any potential trial for the crimes for which he was charged, but also added another layer of complexity. He would require a formal assessment of his cognitive and psychological status, after which a separate *civil* jury trial would need to be held to decide formally whether his *criminal* trial could proceed.* On March 24th, Gary was transferred to Central State Hospital in Milledgeville, Georgia, to undergo testing. Various estimates held this could take as long as forty-five days. As if this evaluation would not be enough, Gary's attorneys said that they would "also like an independent evaluation—one conducted by a qualified 'expert' not associated with any state agency."[191] Noting that Siemon had said Gary had shown signs of poor mental health for many months, an editorial writer for the Ledger asked,

> So why does the question of Gary's competence to stand trial not arise until the day the proceedings are scheduled to begin? We're

---

* *Criminal trials* are held for offenses that violate a law and are generally prosecuted by a governmental entity, such as the state. *Civil trials*, on the other hand, involve disputes between persons or entities (e.g., corporations) and are held to settle issues involving, in this case, the legal and/or constitutional rights and/or obligations of a person or entity.

not told. A gag order on officers of the court and principals in the case prevails. This delay could push the beginning of Gary's trial until May, or even later. No one—not the defense, not the prosecution, not the families of the murder victims, and not the public—stands to gain by what appears at first blush to be an unnecessary stall, a delayed delay, so to speak.

If Carlton Gary is eventually found not guilty, this belated concern for his mental competence will only have prolonged the agony of an innocent man. If he is convicted, then we all will have been put through an apparently ill-timed delay in order to determine something that could and should have been determined during the past year. In either case, justice is the loser.[192]

Chapter 25

A Puzzling Life

Gary's stay at Central State Hospital was brief—surprisingly so. By 7:00 P.M. on Friday, March 28th, 1986, he was back in his jail cell in Columbus. Sheriff Gene Hodge, who was responsible for taking him and picking him up, expressed ignorance of what, if anything, happened in Milledgeville. "They call—we haul," he said simply. If anyone knew why the testing, originally anticipated to take many weeks, was over in less than five days, they were not speaking. Judge Followill's gag order remained in place. It took the better part of two weeks for the answer to leak out: Gary had failed to take the court-ordered tests to determine his sanity. Unnamed officials reported that he had either refused or was unable to cooperate with the testing. His lawyers could not be reached for comment. In the meanwhile, Followill scheduled the competency trial for April 21st.

Before and during the news vacuum created by the gag order, *Ledger-Enquirer* reporter Richard Hyatt had been digging deeply into Carlton Gary's life and background. For many, Gary remained a mystery: the suspect in the Stocking Strangler cases; the man who robbed restaurants in Columbus, Phenix City, and South Carolina; the man who had spent much of his adult life either behind bars, on parole, or as an escapee on the run from the law. For three months Hyatt explored Gary's past, traveling more than 2,500 miles and interviewing more than forty people in six states, including "lawyers and police, wary criminals and quiet people who live unspectacular lives." From these interviews, as well as police, court, and prison records, he was able to construct the first detailed look at the man whom he described as "an elusive, enigmatic figure," "a puzzle whose pieces don't fit." This became the feature story on the front page of the April 13th, 1986, edition of the *Ledger-Enquirer*. For the first time, readers learned the details of Gary's early life, his abandonment by his mother, and a childhood spent bouncing from the home of one relative to that of another in Georgia, Florida, and North Carolina. There were details of his "life of crime" ranging from his first arrests in Gainesville, Florida, shortly after his seventeenth birthday, to drug dealing and armed robberies in New York, Georgia, Florida, and South Carolina that became the main means of sustaining his lifestyle. There were multiple prison escapes, including the one from Onondaga County Correctional Institute in Janesville, New York, on August 22, 1977, that led to his return to Columbus just before the Strangler's killings began. A retired city cop who knew Gary as a teenager in Florida said, "It seemed that everything that happened, his name came up. Robbery, assault, even murder. Carlton Gary was involved. He's always been a crook." While imprisoned in Dannemora, New York, Gary claimed to have college degrees in theology and physical education. On testing there, his IQ was determined to be 114, well above average. "Psychological tests found him 'self-righteous and self-assertive.' No indication of a mental disorder was found but he was said to exhibit 'a severe antisocial personality.'"[193]

Perhaps the most revealing section of Hyatt's article was his assessment of Gary's relationship with women, one he described as "often a mixture of love and hate." "The common thread to the tapestry of Carlton Gary is women," Hyatt wrote.

> He is a latter-day Svengali, controlling and manipulating women through charm, flattery, kind words—and brutal force....He loves women, leaves them and often they wait for him to do it again....Lovely women clustered around him, drawn by his looks, his eyes and his endless rap. Mesmerized ladies were soon renting motel rooms and luxurious cars for him and acting as twenty-four-hour couriers of messages and drugs....Sources say that in Connecticut and New York, [Gary] was a working pimp with a stable of prostitutes. At times he was sadistic, whipping them like field hands.[194]

Among and between relationships and dalliances, Gary once estimated that by the time of his arrest in 1984 he had fathered fourteen children.[195]

On Monday, April 21st, jury selection began for the civil trial on Gary's competence. The first matter was the selection of twelve jurors and two alternates to be chosen from a pool of thirty-six. After questioning by attorneys over that day and the next, all were rejected, most because they admitted they had discussed the case or read newspaper articles about it. Siemon speculated that the prospective jurors may have read Hyatt's article on Gary's criminal record and already formed an opinion. On Wednesday, a fresh panel of fifty-one more prospective jurors was brought in, but this time "kept from other jurors and monitored by bailiffs and deputies to ensure they didn't discuss the case or read or listen to news reports" on the upcoming trial. It was Thursday morning before the twelve-juror panel was formed, nine whites and three blacks who were to decide on Gary's mental fitness for trial. Immediately after the jury was chosen, Siemon called for a mistrial, alleging that prosecutor Smith and assistant prosecutor Doug Pullen had "systematically excluded blacks" during the selection process, an accusation that the prosecution team denied. The makeup of the jury pool did not exactly reflect the racial makeup of Columbus, whose population was thirty-three percent black. Judge Followill rejected the motion, clearing the way for testimony to start on Friday morning.[196,197]

After opening arguments in which Bill Smith described Gary's refusal to cooperate with psychological testing as "'a sham or a show' as part of a decision 'to avoid a criminal' trial," expert witnesses from Central State Hospital confirmed they found no reason to believe that Gary was either mentally ill or incompetent. "Central State psychologist Jerold S. Lower said Gary played volleyball and talked with low-level workers during his five days in Milledgeville but refused to talk to psychologists." While playing "very skillfully" and interacting with other players, he "failed on four occasions to respond to efforts to test him, blocking psychologists' efforts to determine if he's mentally able to stand trial." Gary Parker, Carlton Gary's former defense attorney and now a witness in his case, described him as being "withdrawn" and "very paranoid," a process that had begun a year or more earlier. The probative value of Parker's testimony was lessened on cross-examination when Bill Smith read him excerpts from a hearing only slightly more than four months earlier when Parker said Gary was competent to understand the details of his case and make decisions in assistance of his defense. Bud Siemon referred to Gary as "irrational and paranoid" and suffering from memory loss, much of which he blamed on the conditions of his client's incarceration. In testimony that continued through Saturday and Monday, the jury heard from Sheriff Gene Hodge, who testified that Gary had burned his city-supplied television set about three weeks earlier, placing it on top of a pile of newspapers and magazines which he set on fire in a corner of his cell. Gary, dressed in prison garb, sat at the defense table during the testimony. Most of the time he kept his head in his hands or on the table, occasionally making groaning or snoring noises.[198]

In his closing argument, Smith said Gary began faking when "he began to perceive the nature and strength of the state's case." Siemon said, however, "You can't put someone in a box for two years and expect them...to keep wanting to go on." Gary had become unable to assist in his defense in any meaningful way, he said. For a fourth time during the trial,

Siemon called on Judge Followill to declare a mistrial, and for the fourth time Followill refused. After four days of jury selection and three days of testimony, on Monday, April 28th, it took the jury approximately eighty minutes to declare Gary competent to stand trial.[199,200,201]

Two days later, the US Supreme Court issued a ruling in the landmark case of *Batson v. Kentucky*, declaring that the Equal Protection Clause of the Fourteenth Amendment of the Constitution forbids a prosecutor from excluding prospective jurors solely on the basis of race. Referring to the decision, Siemon and Harvey alleged that "District Attorney William J. Smith and First Assistant Douglas Pullen systematically excluded blacks from Gary's seven-day competency trial." Smith was quick to deny the charge, noting that Judge Followill's gag order prevented him from saying more.[202,*]

In his column in the *Enquirer* following the close of Gary's competency trial, Richard Hyatt wrote,

> Monday's decision and even the upcoming murder trial are no more than dress rehearsals for the main event. Carlton Gary's fate won't be decided here. It will be decided elsewhere. Another jury. Another day. And the prospect of future appeals can't be ignored.
>
> Every word that is spoken goes into the transcript which will become the script for those appeals. Every word is weighed. Every decision is measured. It is a game of words on a judicial playground. The definition of a word is not as important as the color of the word. But the game goes beyond semantics. Similar games are played with issues....
>
> Now the case is back to where it was four months ago. Followill will set a trial date, probably in June. But what legal rabbits Siemon will pull out of his hat, no one knows. A change of venue motion remains an option, and Gary can always fire his lawyers.
>
> In his closing statement, [prosecutor] Smith suggested the jury ask itself these questions: "Who's in charge here? Are we going to let Carlton Gary control this case? Who's in charge? Who's going to be in charge from here on?" Valid question. But when you wade through the courtroom mumbo-jumbo,

---

* Since the original ruling, the precedent set by the case of *Batson v. Kentucky* 476 US 79 (1986) has been broadened to other related situations.

Followill's not in charge, Siemon's not in charge, Smith's not in charge, and Gary's not in charge. The people in charge wear black robes and work in a marble building in Washington. And it will be those eight men and one woman who may someday make the final decision.[†]

His words would prove prescient.

[†] In case Hyatt's reference is not clear to the reader, he is referring to the US Supreme Court, which at the time was composed of eight men and one woman.

Chapter 26

Two Steps Forward and One Step Back

May 3rd and 4th, 1986, marked, respectively, the two-year anniversary of Carlton Gary's arrest and indictment. Despite his incarceration and the passage of time, he was scarcely closer to coming to trial for his alleged offenses than he had been when first taken into custody. The delay had multiple causes, not the least of which was the sheer complexity of the case. A major reason, however, was a seemingly deliberate attempt on the part of Gary's defense attorneys to postpone his trial for as long as possible. The results of these delays were, paradoxically, said to be the causes of further necessary delays. The need for a competency trial, for example, was alleged to result in part from the amount of time Gary had spent in jail. There were other matters as well, real, perceived, or alleged. These included the nebulous issues of juror bias, and race, and whether a "fair trial" could be had in Muscogee County. Should Gary be convicted, a single error heard on appeal could lead to an order for a new trial, thus starting the entire process all over again.

After considering the issue for a bit more than a week, Judge Kenneth Followill set Monday, June 9th, as the day to begin the second attempt to try Gary for murder. The first ended when it became necessary to conduct a separate civil trial on the defendant's competency. Like that proceeding, this new criminal trial would start with the tedious task of choosing jurors. One hundred and one potential jurors were sworn initially, first to be qualified as eligible, then to be placed in a group from which twelve trial jurors and four alternates would be chosen. Once again, Gary was present as juror selection got underway, neatly dressed in a peach-colored, long-sleeved T-shirt and white prison slacks. In sharp contrast to the competency hearing, however, he seemed to pay attention to the proceedings. The change was not to last.

Around 11:30 A.M., about an hour after the start of jury selection, Gary said he did not feel well and asked to leave the courtroom. A doctor was summoned and examined him in his jail cell because he refused to go to the examination room in the jail complex. He found Gary lying on the floor of his cell, his head and shoulders beneath his bunk and his body covered with a blanket. He was uncooperative for an exam. Siemon demanded an exam by an "independent doctor," instead of Gary being evaluated by a city-paid physician. Arrangement was made for him to be seen in the hospital emergency room, but he refused to leave his cell.

Matters proceeded slowly. Most of the first day was taken up by Gary's alleged illness and various motions from the defense. When both sides were asked by Judge Followill if they were ready for trial, Siemon replied that he was not, again citing lack of financial and material support by the court. Despite the jury finding that Gary was competent to stand trial, Siemon predicted, "You're going to see outbursts from Carlton Gary during this trial, judge. I can guarantee it. He's not the same stable person I met two years ago."[203]

On the second day, Siemon again asked Judge Followill to recuse himself, alleging that he had violated his own gag order by speaking to a reporter on a point of law. Followill refused and denied the motion. Gary again repeatedly interrupted proceedings, complaining of back pain and other medical issues. This time he agreed to go to the emergency room but once there refused to cooperate with an examination. Bruce Harvey requested that the trial be recessed until the defense could find a "medical expert" for their client. The motion was denied. Gary was excused from the trial for the remainder of the week. As before, jury selection proceeded slowly as most of the day was taken up by defense motions. By Wednesday, June 11th, the third day of the trial, only eight of the 101 people in the jury pool had been interviewed.

On the fourth day, Siemon renewed his efforts to remove Judge Followill, this time referring to an article in the *Atlanta Constitution* that mentioned the comments that had resulted in the recusal request two days earlier. Again, the issues of funding and the possible need for a change of venue were discussed. Siemon and Harvey expressed fear that if the trial location were moved, it could be to a place with an "all-white jury." Evidently ignoring the implicit issue of juror bias in his own statement, Siemon said, "We've got to see to it that Carlton Gary gets some people on the jury that at least can understand him and the life he has had." Prosecutor Smith "vehemently denied Siemon's complaints that the prosecution [was] aiming for a white jury."[204] The same themes and distractions marked the Friday and Saturday sessions of court. By the end of the week less than a third of the original jury pool had been questioned and qualified.

When jury selection resumed on Monday, June 16th, once again Siemon called for Judge Followill to step down, this time accusing him of describing the requirements of jury duty differently to two prospective jurors, one black and one white. Referring to prosecutor Smith, he said, "I'm shocked and surprised that in 1986 a district attorney could be as big a racist as he is." Judge Followill reprimanded him for the comment. With continued efforts at jury selection, and continued complaints from defense attorneys of "racism" in the process, shortly after noon on Tuesday, Siemon filed a motion for a change of venue of the trial. This brought the jury selection process—which had already consumed seven days—to a halt and would, of necessity, involve one or more unrelated hearings on the motion. Siemon requested that the hearing start the following week. Judge Followill refused, stating, "I'm not going to delay the trial any longer." In preparation for the hearing, Siemon and Harvey issued subpoenas to three local newspapers, three local television stations, and at least five radio stations demanding production of all news items related to the "Stocking Strangler" crimes that had been published, broadcast, or recorded since 1977.[205]

On Wednesday, June 18th, Judge Followill granted the defense motion for a change in venue, citing Richard Hyatt's April 13th article on Carlton Gary in the *Ledger-Enquirer* as well as extensive pretrial publicity of the case. For the first time in a week, Gary was back in court to hear the decision, this time well-groomed and dressed in a black jacket, white shirt, tan pants, and matching suede boots. Instead of moving the trial to another location, however, the jurors would be chosen elsewhere and brought to Columbus, an arrangement allowed under the then-recent Uniform Rules pertaining to Georgia Superior Courts. Prosecutor Smith did not oppose the motion, though he regretted the time wasted and costs involved in eight days of attempted jury selection, accusing the defense of having "toyed with the court." The location where a new jury would be chosen was to be decided by the judge. Smith requested a quick decision, noting, "I've had three witnesses die of natural causes since the arrest of this man."[206,207]

After two weeks of consideration and research, on July 2nd, Judge Followill announced that the third attempt at Carlton Gary's murder trial would begin on July 28th with jury selection to take place in Griffin, Georgia. Once a jury was selected, the trial (and jurors) would return to Columbus. The county seat of Spalding County, Griffin was seventy-eight miles northeast of Columbus and forty miles south of Atlanta. According to the 1980 census, Spalding County's black population made up about twenty-seven percent of its residents, as compared to Muscogee County's thirty-four percent. Bruce Harvey immediately reacted to the decision, saying, "On the face of it, the demographics would appear to be a problem." Within days, Siemon and Harvey filed three motions. Pleading personal financial distress, Harvey requested that Followill either formally appoint him to represent Gary—which would include his being paid by the county—or allow him to withdraw from the case. One of Siemon's motions protested the choice of Griffin as the site where trial jurors would be chosen. The motion charged that Followill picked the site "with the express intention of minimalizing black participation" in Gary's trial, as well as attempting to "maximize the potential for prejudicial impact of pretrial publicity." Another motion asked that Followill be removed from the case based on his acting "in a racially discriminatory manner." Both motions asked for a hearing before another judge.[208,209] It was scheduled for July 21st in Columbus, a week before the scheduled opening of Gary's murder trial.

With Chief Judge C. Cloud Morgan from the Macon Judicial Circuit presiding and Judge Followill now sitting under judgment in his own courtroom, Siemon argued that the racial disparity between Spalding and Muscogee Counties would deny Gary his right to adequate black representation on a jury. The decision to choose Spalding County was grounds for Followill's dismissal. "We submit to you that we've got not the appearance of impropriety, but the stench of impropriety," Siemon alleged. Gary was present in the courtroom as well, this time dressed in an ivory-colored suit jacket, gray slacks, and dress shoes. After three hours of presentation including rebuttal from prosecutors, Morgan said he would rule in a few days.[210]

In a terse, four-paragraph ruling issued on July 24th, Morgan denied the motion to remove Judge Followill, stating that he found the defense arguments "unpersuasive." He did not rule on the motion challenging juror selection in Spalding County, or Harvey's request to be excused as Gary's attorney, leaving these up to Judge Followill. As it was Followill who chose the location of jury selection, Morgan's decision effectively affirmed the change as appropriate. It would be up to Followill to decide on Harvey's request. Most importantly, however, Morgan's ruling cleared the way for Gary's trial to begin on the scheduled date of July 28th.[211]

Chapter 27

The Trial—Part I: Preliminaries

The third attempt at Carlton Gary's murder trial began at 10:00 A.M. on Monday morning, July 28th, 1986, in Griffin, Georgia, the site of jury selection.* Once a panel had been chosen, the court—including the jurors—would move back to Columbus for the rest of the proceeding. A total of 225 potential jurors had been summoned by the court. From this group, fifty-eight would need to be qualified to serve, from which the final group of twelve, plus four alternates, would be picked.† Perhaps not unexpectedly, the day opened with motions from Bud Siemon challenging both the site of jury selection and the racial makeup of Spalding County's pool of jurors. Both were dismissed by Judge Followill, who did grant Bruce Harvey's earlier motion to withdraw as Carlton Gary's attorney. Gary, who was present for the first day of jury selection, approved of the change but compared the judge and prosecutors to Ku Klux Klan members holding a lynching. "Most of you, you just wear the suits now. You don't have the hoods.... You're just trying to send someone down the road, the only thing missing is some hoods and a tree," Gary said bitterly.[212]

Jury selection proceeded slowly with the judge and both prosecution and defense attorneys interviewing prospective candidates in order to rule out real or potential bias, or preconceived notions of Gary's guilt or innocence. As this was a case in which the state was seeking the death penalty, candidates who stated they could not support this option in case Gary was convicted were excluded. Seven of the necessary fifty-eight were "qualified" on Monday, with an additional ten the next day. On Tuesday, Gary again lashed out at the court, complaining of harassment in the Spalding County jail, alleging that he had not eaten in thirty-three days, and that

---

* Unless otherwise referenced, in this and the chapters that follow on the trial of *State v. Gary*, quotes and observations are drawn from the written trial transcript and/or video records of the trial.

† To explain the number of fifty-eight, the defense had twenty peremptory strikes, and the prosecution half that number, or ten. So, if both sides used all their strikes, a pool of forty-two candidates would be needed to choose twelve jurors. For the remaining sixteen potential alternate jurors, the defense had eight strikes and the prosecution four, leaving four qualified alternates.

he suffered from back pain. There was no point in his being present, he said. "You got the money. You got the lawyers. You got the press. I ain't got nothing. If we had some money this whole thing would have been over a long time ago. This (trial) ain't nothing. This is a big joke." With that, Judge Followill honored his request and sent him back to the jail "until further notice."[213] By Thursday afternoon, July 31st, thirty-two jurors had been qualified, of which only five were black. Siemon argued frequently that the process was biased, that the racial makeup of Spalding County was significantly different from that of Muscogee County, accusing the court of qualifying "death-prone" jurors "while excusing those opposed to the death penalty."[214] Five more jurors were qualified on Friday before court adjourned for the weekend.

When court resumed on Monday, Gary was back in the courtroom, this time barefooted and wearing a jail uniform. Jury selection continued, with Siemon complaining that the juror list did not appear to be randomly selected as required by law. Citing as evidence that the list included a woman named Willis, two people named Williams, and three more by the name of Jones, he asked for funds to hire "an independent expert to analyze the jury list." Followill denied his request.[215] By Wednesday afternoon, the group of fifty-eight had been chosen. The final group of twelve jurors and four alternates were selected the following day. The twelve, nine men and three white women, whose ages ranged from twenty-three to sixty-eight, were drawn from a diverse group of occupations including mill worker, airline mechanic, registered nurse, and Baptist minister. Three of the jurors and two of the alternates were black. They were immediately transported by Muscogee County sheriff's deputies to Columbus, checking into the Columbus Hilton later that afternoon, where they were to be sequestered for the remainder of the trial, cut off from outside news of the case. Predictions held that the trial could last for three months.

With the jury chosen and shielded from events taking place in the courtroom, Judge Followill could hear motions and testimony in reference to the state's case against Gary, in the process making critical decisions that would have a profound influence on the outcome of the case and the jury's verdict. While more technical in a legal sense, the consequences of these deliberations and the judge's rulings on the admissibility of certain facts and evidence would shape the course of the rest of the trial. Also, for the first time, the defense—and the public, via news reports—would learn how the prosecution had chosen to present its side of the case. Two major points would be at issue this day and the next: the admissibility of fingerprints, blood, hair, and saliva samples taken after Gary's arrest and the prosecution's efforts to show that the crimes with which he was charged were similar to, and followed a pattern of, other crimes that he was known or believed to have committed, but for which he was not being prosecuted at this trial.‡ The legal strategy for presenting the latter point raised an often-asked question: if, in fact, Gary was thought to have committed all of the seven horrific rapes and murders attributed to the Strangler, why was he only charged with three of them? The answer, as given by prosecutor Bill Smith, was simple:

> We felt that these were our strongest cases. In the indicted crimes, Gary had admitted to being present and participating in each of the crimes, and his fingerprint was found at each of the crime scenes. In the four others, only one of these elements was present. In Ferne Jackson's murder, his print was found, but he made no admission. In the murders of Dimenstien, Borom, and Cofer, he admitted to being present but no fingerprint was found.

The hearings began on Friday morning, August 8th, and continued through the following day. The issue of admissibility of fingerprint, blood,

---

‡ This is an important legal point. Among the previous cases Smith quoted in support of introducing evidence of other crimes was a 1983 Georgia Supreme Court decision (*Williams v. State* 312 S.E.2d 40) regarding the case of another serial killer, Wayne Williams, implicated in more than two dozen child murders in Atlanta in 1979–81. The justices wrote, "We have held that evidence of other criminal acts of the defendant may be admitted if it 'is substantially relevant for some purpose other than to show a probability that (the defendant) committed the crime on trial because he is a man of criminal character....' The purposes for which evidence of extrinsic offenses may be offered include motive; intent; absence of mistake or accident (each is aspect of intent), plan or scheme (of which the crime on trial is a part); and identity. To render evidence of extrinsic offenses admissible for any of these purposes, the state must show that the defendant was the perpetrator of the extrinsic offenses, and that there is a sufficient similarity or connection between the extrinsic offense and the offense charged, such that proof of the former tends to prove the latter." In his arguments before Judge Followill, Prosecutor Smith specifically noted that there were twenty-five armed robberies that were committed by Gary with the same modus operandi. But, he emphasized that these were not being introduced into the case as they had no direct relationship to the three cases for which Gary was being tried, and should they be admitted, they would only show that he committed these crimes "because he is a man of criminal character, and no more."

and pubic hair samples collected at the time of Gary's arrest was rapidly settled when Judge Followill denied the defense's motions to exclude this evidence. The remainder of the day was devoted to the presentation of the state's request to enter into evidence the details of some fourteen similar crimes which Carlton Gary was known or suspected to have committed. The relationship of these other cases to the murders and rapes of Florence Scheible, Martha Thurmond, and Kathleen Woodruff were drawn through similarities in location; time frame; the victims' ages, race, and sex; the details of the individual crimes themselves; and, most importantly, a strong connection with the defendant. In addition to the four other Columbus murders attributed to the Strangler, there were the attacks on Gertrude Miller and Ruth Schwob, both of whom survived. There were the burglaries at the homes of Callye East, the Swifts, and the Illgeses. From New York, the rape and murder of Nellie Farmer, and the assault, rape, and robbery of Jean Frost displayed the same pattern. When in custody and confronted with evidence against him, Gary had regularly attempted to shift the blame to a co-conspirator, naming at various times Malvin Alamichael Crittenden, John Lee Mitchell, Theopolis Joe Preston, or Dudley Harris. Taken together, the consistency of the modus operandi in each of these cases and their association with Gary represented one of the prosecution's most powerful arguments in favor of his guilt.

During a four-hour presentation illustrated by a large chart displaying the commonalities among the crimes attributed to Gary, prosecutor Smith outlined the state's case. As reported by the *Ledger-Enquirer*,

> Smith's charts connected the Wynnton murders by neighborhood, mode of entry into the homes, and mode of attack— rape and strangulation using a woman's stocking, scarf or other cord, with the bodies left covered, usually in the bedroom. The Wynnton burglaries were part of a pattern because each occurred just a few houses away from a strangling victim's home and during the same time period as the stranglings, Smith said. Also, a gun stolen from a car at one of the burglaries later was linked to Gary.[216,217]

With Smith's presentation completed, Bud Siemon began his argument against the inclusion of other crimes, claiming initially that the court's refusal to grant funds to the defense had hampered his ability to conduct his own independent investigation. Apparently aware that the state had strong legal precedent for its plans, Siemon offered not to oppose the admission of other crimes if the court would "grant us the funds to do the same type of investigation that Mr. Smith and his legions of investigators have been able to do." Judge Followill denied his motion. In a brief rebuttal thereafter, Siemon attempted to point out the dissimilarities between the other crimes while downplaying the factors they had in common and ignoring their relationship to his client. It had been a long day and was now past 6:00 P.M. Followill adjourned court until the following morning, saying he would review the facts and rule on the issues thereafter.

In contrast to the previous day's hearing, the proceedings on Saturday morning were brief, lasting just over two and a half hours. At issue was the admissibility of statements made to police by Carlton Gary when he was initially charged with the murder of Nellie Farmer in Albany, New York, in 1970, and after he was captured in February 1979 following the Po' Folks robbery in Gaffney, South Carolina.[§] Both times he tried to shift the blame for the crimes to someone else, John Lee Mitchell in New York and Malvin Alamichael Crittenden in South Carolina. Retired Albany Police detective Anthony Sidoti and South Carolina detectives Jack Blanton and Glenn M. Purvines testified about Gary's questioning following his arrests in the two states. The prosecution was seeking to assure the court that in both instances, Gary had been informed of his Miranda rights and that his statements had been given freely and voluntarily.

Gary, who had been absent for the preceding day's hearing, was in court this time, having been brought there at the prosecution's request. Sidoti was able to identify him as the person he knew in New York as Carl Michaels, the alias Gary was using at the time. Blanton identified Gary as the man known as Michael David, another of Gary's aliases. (Based on his fingerprints, South Carolina authorities were later able to identify "Michael David" as Carlton Gary.) Questioning of the witnesses was occasionally punctuated by short outbursts from the defendant: "Damn," "Oh, boy," "Unbelievable," "Jesus, it's unreal, I'm telling you," "Lying, that's what the motherfucker done," etc.

Despite objections from Bud Siemon, Followill found "from a preponderance of the evidence, the defendant was advised of each of his Miranda rights, that he understood them, that he voluntarily waived them, that he thereafter gave the statement[s] freely and voluntarily, without any

---

[§] In legal parlance, this was a Jackson-Denno hearing. See footnote in chapter 23.

hope of benefit or fear of injury." The judge also approved the introduction into evidence the extrinsic crimes presented by the prosecution the day before. These rulings cleared the way for the formal portion of the trial to begin on Monday, August 11th, more than two years and three months since Gary's arrest, and nearly nine years since the rape and strangulation deaths of Florence Scheible, Martha Thurmond, and Kathleen Woodruff.

Chapter 28

The Trial—Part II
Opening Statements

The formal trial began shortly after 9:00 A.M. on Monday, August 11th. The day began with Bud Siemon objecting to Carlton Gary's presence in the courtroom while dressed in "jail clothes." Commenting on his client's weight loss, Siemon said, "He's got a due process right to be tried and to look like something besides a jailbird sitting here at the defense table." Judge Followill suggested that Gary change to civilian clothes, but he did not want to do that. Allowed to speak to the court, Gary complained that he had not eaten in "forty days," that he had been abused by his jailers, that he had been refused medical care, and that he did not "care about this circus you got going on up here." He requested to be allowed to return to his cell. Followill refused.

The trial was to begin with opening statements from each side. As the prosecution's case was complex, Bill Smith advised the court that his opening statement would be lengthy. With a hint of sarcasm, Siemon suggested that since the defense had not been given funds by the court to do their *own* investigation, then perhaps time allotted for the prosecution's statement should be limited to "about twenty-five minutes," the amount of time he expected his opening statement would last. Again, Followill denied his request, granting Smith unlimited time. His presentation would consume the remainder of the day.

With the jury now in the courtroom and duly sworn, Followill explained that opening statements were designed to give the jurors an overview of each side's case and were not to be considered as evidence. He reminded the jury that when considering their verdict in a criminal case, the state had the burden of proof. Smith began his presentation by explaining that Carlton Gary was charged with three counts of rape, three counts of murder, and three counts of burglary* from the attacks on Florence Scheible, Martha Thurmond, and Kathleen Woodruff. These three

---

* The term "burglary," as used in this sense, means "entering or remaining in the dwelling house or place of business of another without permission or consent, with intent to commit another felony," in this case, murder.

crimes were part of seven nearly identical crimes committed between September 1977 and April 1978. The evidence to be presented would show that the crimes had a number of common characteristics: The victims were all elderly white females who lived alone and whose ages ranged from fifty-nine to eighty-nine. With one exception, the crimes occurred at night. In each case there was evidence of actual or attempted forced entry. The victims were raped and murdered. The cause of death was "ligature strangulation": in five of the seven cases by the use of a female stocking, in one by a scarf, and in another by a curtain cord. All the victims were physically abused by being beaten before their deaths. All the victim's bodies were covered afterwards. Six of the seven crimes occurred in the Wynnton area. Finally, evidence pointed to the fact that Gary was the perpetrator in all seven crimes. Gary's fingerprints were found in each of the three cases with which he was charged, and in the home of Ferne Jackson, one of the uncharged murder cases.

Smith's presentation was accompanied and illustrated by a map displaying the physical locations of the murders attributed to the Strangler as well as the places that Gary was living during the eight months in which the murders took place, and a timeline correlating the series of events. In addition to these crimes, the map displayed the burglaries at the residences of Callye East, the Swifts, and the Illgeses. There were the two instances of victims who survived the Strangler's attack: Gertrude Miller, who was scheduled to testify later in the trial, and Ruth Schwob, who had died in the eight and a half years since her ordeal. From New York, there were the cases of Nellie Farmer and Jean Frost. Farmer was raped and murdered by strangulation in April 1970. Gary's fingerprints were found in her room, but he convinced police officers that he simply committed the robbery and blamed the rape and murder on John Lee Mitchell. In an attack that was nearly "identical" to the rape and attempted murder of Gertrude Miller in Columbus, Jean Frost was attacked in her Syracuse, New York, apartment, raped, strangled with a scarf, and left for dead in January 1977. Gary was arrested the next day and found to have in his possession a watch stolen from Ms. Farmer's dresser. When confronted by the police, he pled guilty to the lesser charge of possessing stolen property, while blaming the attack on another friend, Dudley Harris.

After being brought back to Columbus following his arrest in Albany, Georgia, on May 3, 1984, Gary pointed out to police officers the homes of five of the Strangler's seven victims, denying that he was the perpetrator but relating details of the crimes and their locations that would only be known to someone who was there. Again, while admitting to breaking and entering the homes, he blamed the rapes and murders on Malvin Alamichael Crittenden.

Other than his fingerprints, the physical evidence connecting Gary to the Strangler's seven murders was limited. At the time of the trial, prior to the technology that led to DNA analysis useful for forensic purposes, investigators often relied on other types of physical evidence. Smith presented two: hair analysis and blood-group identification based on bodily fluid secretion. Experts agreed that the foreign pubic hairs found on and around the bodies of the rape victims were of "Negroid" origin; beyond that, they could not match samples obtained from Gary with those found at the crime scenes. Three experts described the findings as "inconclusive," that is, neither implicating nor exonerating the defendant.

Evidence of the blood type of a suspect can sometimes be obtained from analysis of bodily fluids, specifically saliva or tears, and semen in males or vaginal secretions in females. Approximately eighty percent of humans secrete markers that can be used to identify blood type, while the other twenty percent do not. Based on analysis of the vaginal fluid of the rape victims as well as determination of their blood type, crime laboratory investigators were able to determine that the rapist had type O blood.[†] This is the most common blood type, found in about forty-five percent of the American population. Carlton Gary was found to have type O blood and was one of the eighty percent of people who are secretors. While this evidence did not directly implicate Gary, neither did it exonerate him. Instead, it confirmed that he *could have* committed the rapes attributed to the Strangler.

In summary, Smith told the jury, "Based on this evidence which I have outlined to you, obviously in great detail, and which we expect to be presented from the witness stand during the course of this trial, the state intends to ask you at the conclusion of the trial to return a verdict of guilty on all counts." It was nearly 5:00 P.M. by the time Smith finished the state's opening statement. Allowing for brief recesses and two hours taken for lunch, the presentation had lasted nearly five hours. Bud Siemon opted to give his opening statement the following morning.

In sharp contrast to Bill Smith's careful detailing of the facts the state intended to prove, Siemon's presentation was brief—lasting only about forty minutes—and based on generalities and attempts to cast doubt and

---

[†] There are four blood types: O, A, B, and AB.

aspersion on the state's case. He asked the jury to recall "everything that Mr. Smith told you yesterday was not evidence. It was just [what] *he* expects the evidence to prove. What I am telling you today, this morning, is not evidence, it's just what *I* expect the evidence to prove."[‡]

Siemon began by attacking conclusions based on hair analysis. After arresting his client, and after indicting him in less than twenty-four hours, the fact that the pubic hair analysis was not a definite match posed a "problem with their case." Stating unequivocally that Gary had been "excluded by hair evidence," Siemon accused the state of attempting to find a well-paid "expert" who would make excuses for the failure to establish a definitive connection between the hair evidence and the defendant. Dismissing the prosecution's arguments, he referred to the hair analysis as "opinion evidence. Anybody can look at two hairs and give an opinion on whether or not they match." He dismissed the importance of Gary's fingerprints found at the crime scenes with "you don't know when fingerprints were left" and "they don't prove that he's the murderer."

Siemon questioned why the interviews with Gary on the ride back from Albany and his later tour of the Wynnton area with the detectives were not recorded, stating, "They didn't want to make a recording of what he said," implying that the police reports of those events were fabricated. Since Gary had not lived in Columbus for more than a decade prior to returning in 1977, he could not have known the streets of Wynnton as detailed in police reports. "There are facts contained in those statements that the police wrote down that are just not true." And furthermore, how could he have chosen the victims of the crimes, or committed them with the intense law enforcement presence in the area at the time?

Describing his client as "a career criminal," Siemon said, "One thing about Carlton Gary, one thing we know about him, is that when Carlton Gary commits a crime he gets caught.... The one thing about his crimes, though, the ones that they have caught him on, the ones that they've convicted him of, is that nobody's ever been hurt." As an example, he pointed out that when Gary was confronted by a policeman after the armed robbery of the Po' Folks restaurant in Gaffney, South Carolina, he did not shoot the officer. "Carlton didn't shoot because he doesn't. His crimes, people don't get hurt."

The evidence and testimony against Gary were "manufactured, in large part, by the police officers who were ordered to fill in the blanks in

---

[‡] Emphasis added.

their case." Although some things in the reports "have the ring of truth," he said, Siemon portrayed his client as a victim of police corruption:

> The evidence is going to show, ladies and gentlemen, that the police in this case decided Carlton Gary was guilty as soon as they arrested him. That they ignored evidence.... We're going to prove at least that he wasn't the murderer, and that he wasn't the person that actually committed the crimes, and that since they've been trying to, and instead of going out and getting the evidence, and then deciding on a suspect..., they did it the reverse way, they got a suspect and then went out and tried to mold the evidence to adhere to what their case was.

In closing, Siemon called on the jury to "give us a fair trial," well aware that his client's future and possibly his life would depend on the outcome of the events of the days that would immediately follow.

Chapter 29

The Trial—Part III
Witness Identifications

Bud Siemon's brief opening statement left the remainder of the day free for the start of witness testimony. Having the burden of proof, the state was required to present its case first, followed by the defense. The state's first witness was Gail Newman, who was delivering telephone books door-to-door on October 21, 1977, the day of Ms. Florence Scheible's murder. At about 10:30 A.M., she saw an elderly lady with a walker, presumably Ms. Scheible, in the front yard of 1941 Dimon Street. The lady, apparently having some visual impairment, at first did not see Ms. Newman as she placed the book in a chair on the front porch. When Ms. Scheible did see her, she appeared concerned and asked what she was doing. Ms. Newman explained that she was delivering phone books. Ms. Scheible "seemed real relieved" and said, "Well, that's all right, you know, just can't be too careful these days." These were Ms. Scheible's last known words. A second witness, Dorothy Harcourt, who lived directly across the street from Ms. Scheible, testified that she, too, had seen her with her walker in her yard about 11:00 A.M. She observed Ms. Scheible go back inside her apartment around 11:30 or shortly before. Other than her murderer, Ms. Harcourt was apparently the last person to see Ms. Scheible alive.

Ed Gibson, a patrolman with the Columbus Police Department, responded to a call to the Scheible residence shortly before 3:00 P.M. that afternoon. He was met there by Col. Paul Scheible, Ms. Scheible's son, who informed him that his mother was inside and he thought that she was dead. Col. Scheible and his wife waited outside while Gibson went in the apartment. In the bedroom he observed "a person lying on the bed, and the person was covered up with the bed covers and so forth, and there was a pillow laying over the head of the body." Lifting the pillow, it was obvious that she was deceased. He called for backup.

Next, C. Frank Simons testified. At the time, he was a detective with the Columbus Police Department Robbery and Homicide Squad. After an I.D. technician photographed the scene, Simons removed the covering. Underneath, he observed the body "of an elderly white female laying on her back. She was wearing glasses, her dress was pushed up above her waist, and one stocking was on, her face was bloody. There was a stocking wrapped around her neck. Her pubic area was bloody."

Dr. Joe Webber, the Muscogee County medical examiner, described the findings from Ms. Scheible's autopsy done later that afternoon. Before her death, she had been severely beaten, with "massive hemorrhage" between the scalp and skull. After the stocking was removed, her neck revealed "a deep groove" due to the ligature, and "the classic findings of strangulation," including the fracture of her hyoid bone. The upper two cervical vertebrae were broken as well, "probably due to [the] blow to the head." The vaginal area showed "a massive laceration" and spermatozoa in the vaginal secretions, indicating "strong evidence of rape." As photographs documenting Dr. Webber's testimony were introduced into evidence, Siemon objected, describing them as "gruesome photographs that prove nothing." He was willing to stipulate that the victim had been strangled and raped, so "their evidentiary value is zero." Smith responded that the photos were evidence in support of the exact crimes with which Gary was charged and were not introduced for sensational purposes. The objection was overruled.

The next witness, a state crime laboratory technician, testified that hairs collected at the crime scene were of Negro origin. They were compared with similar hair samples from Gary's associates, including Malvin Alamichael Crittenden, but no testimony on the results of such comparison was offered. The next four witnesses testified about the collection and analysis of latent fingerprints from the crime scene. One of the prints collected from the door frame leading into Ms. Scheible's bedroom matched Carlton Gary's right thumbprint.

The final witness of the day was prepared to testify that she saw Carlton Gary in the neighborhood on the day of Ms. Scheible's murder. Prior to her testimony before the jury, however, Siemon requested a brief hearing before Judge Followill on the admissibility of her statement. With the jury dismissed, Doris Laufenberg gave her account of how she saw a black man rushing down the street near her home, a man whom she later identified as Carlton Gary. After questioning by Smith and during rigorous cross-examination by Siemon, the defense attorney asked, "A few minutes ago you were reaching into your purse. Were you reaching into your purse to pull out your glasses?"

"No, I was reaching for my nitroglycerine," she replied. After assuring the court that she was fine, questioning continued.

After both sides had completed their examination, Followill approved her testimony. "I don't find that there's any...pretrial taint of the identification," he said. "I believe this is going to be a question for the jury to determine what weight and credit they want to give her. I'm satisfied that there is sufficient evidence...for her to be able to testify as to it."

With the jury back in the courtroom, Ms. Laufenberg, an older widow, testified that during the afternoon of October 21, 1977, she had just returned from the grocery store and was taking her groceries out of the car parked in her driveway, located on 12th Street, approximately three blocks from Ms. Scheible's residence. She noticed a black man coming up the sidewalk from the direction of the Scheible apartment. He was "traveling at quite a fast pace, and he kept looking behind him." Her gaze darted nervously around the courtroom as she spoke. When asked what attracted her attention, Ms. Laufenberg replied, "Well, I guess everybody was pretty edgy back in those days, and we noticed things that we didn't ordinarily notice." Ferne Jackson and Jean Dimenstien had been murdered only weeks before. She described the man as "quite tall," with an afro, a light beard, and dressed in a dark green jogging suit, black turtleneck sweater, a black knit cap, and boots. She went up on the porch of her house and watched him from about twenty feet away as he passed, in total for about two minutes, later in her testimony describing him as having "a very distinctive face, a very high forehead, and wide forehead and an unusual nose." At the time, she was not aware of Ms. Scheible's murder, but heard about it later that afternoon. She thought about notifying the police, but after consideration, "I decided not to do anything about it at that time." Several months passed with more murders by the Strangler. In February 1978, Ms. Laufenberg heard of the attack on Ms. Schwob, who survived. Ms. Schwob "described the clothes that he was wearing, and the same as I have just told you." She called the police and reported to them what she had seen on the afternoon of Ms. Scheible's murder.

More than six and a half years passed. In October 1984, Ms. Laufenberg was contacted by the Columbus police about the tip on the strange man she had reported after the Schwob incident in 1978. Det. Sgt. Mike Sellers, who was part of the investigative team after Gary's arrest, came to her home to ask her if she could identify this man from a photograph. Without in any way suggesting which image to choose, "he just put five of the photographs on the coffee table and said do you recognize the man that you saw pass your house that day?" She replied that she did, and signed and dated the photograph.

"Do you recognize this same person in the Courtroom today?" Bill Smith asked.

"Yes, I do," Ms. Laufenberg replied, and pointed to Carlton Gary. As it was late in the day, court adjourned until the next day.

Court resumed shortly after 9:00 A.M. the following morning, Wednesday, August 13th. Prosecutor Smith announced the state's intention to call another witness who would identify Gary, but unlike Doris Laufenberg's statements, this witness's testimony would not require a due process hearing as there had been no law enforcement or prosecutorial involvement in the identification process. Siemon argued that the publicity surrounding the case, including the release of Gary's photographs, would not have been possible without the cooperation of the police, thus possibly influencing a witness's identification. He called for a hearing on the matter. Judge Followill denied his motion, allowing testimony to proceed.

Sue Nelson, a young lady who was living on Dimon Street diagonally across from Ms. Scheible in September 1977, testified that late one afternoon she had been with a friend in Lakebottom Park, just behind the Scheible residence.* Around dusk, she stated she was frightened by the actions of a black man. She described him as a "camel-colored black man, with a nose that wasn't typical of a black person, I didn't think." He was dressed in a jogging suit and cap and ran toward her, something she interpreted as a threat. She called out to her friend and left the park with him. Asked if the man she saw was in the courtroom, Ms. Nelson pointed to Carlton Gary and replied, "Yes, that's definitely the man."

Two days before Ms. Scheible's murder, she saw the same man again, this time jogging past her apartment as she sat on the porch reading a book. He was dressed in the same clothes, in a jogging suit and hat, and apparently did not see her. Ms. Nelson said she did not know Ms. Scheible personally but frequently saw her in the yard in front of her house and "waved at her almost every day whenever I went by on my ten-speed or walked by." Ms. Nelson later moved to Germany and was living there in 1984 when Gary was arrested. A friend sent her a newspaper clipping of the event, but it did not have a photo of the man charged with the Strangler's crimes.

Ms. Nelson thought no more of it until April 1986, when she was living back in the United States and saw a photo of Gary in the *Atlanta*

---

* Lakebottom (or Lake Bottom) Park is also known as Weracoba Park. See footnote in chapter 6 for the relationship to Ms. Scheible's apartment.

Journal-Constitution. "I thought it was the same man at the time, but wasn't certain until I saw a video tape [on television].... I thought about it for a few days and decided it was time to call the district attorney."

"Now that you've had an occasion to see the defendant in person," Smith asked, "is there any doubt in your mind that this is in fact the same man that you saw sometime in September at Lakebottom Park, jogging, who attracted your attention and that you saw approximately two days before Ms. Scheible's murder?"

"It's the same man," she replied.

Chapter 30

The Trial—Part IV: Murder Details

Bud Siemon was clearly displeased with Sue Nelson's testimony. Calling it "unreliable" and a violation of due process, he demanded that Judge Followill declare a mistrial when the judge differed with him on a point of law in a comment the judge made in the presence of the jury. It illustrated, Siemon said, "the bias that you've got against us." The motion for a mistrial was denied.

The state's next witness was Bill Thurmond, Ms. Martha Thurmond's son. Accompanied by his wife and their son, he had spent the weekend of the 22nd and 23rd of October 1977 with his mother at her residence at 2614 Marion Street in Columbus. They stayed most of the day on Monday, the 24th, leaving at about 3:30 in the afternoon to return home to Tucker, Georgia. Within twelve hours his mother would be dead.

Thurmond described his mother's house as "very secure," with dead bolt locks on the entry doors and additional locks on the outside screen doors. On the back door, she had installed a heavy metal "burglary guard screen." Shown photographs of the house, Thurmond identified a hole in the screen that had been cut after he left Monday afternoon, an evident attempt at entry. The dead bolt lock on the front door, which had been in good working condition when he left, was "damaged." It was apparently through this door, discovered ajar around midday Tuesday by a neighbor, Irene Darden, that the killer made his entry into Ms. Thurmond's house.

Larry Banks, at the time a patrolman with the Columbus Police Department, responded to Ms. Darden's call. On arrival, he "noticed that the dead bolt lock on the front door of the residence had been taken apart and also that the lock had been installed incorrectly and the lock was disassembled and the door opened." It was a "dark, rainy day," and the interior lights in the house were off. Banks and a second officer explored the house with flashlights, finding Ms. Thurmond's body in a back bedroom, covered with blood-stained sheets and a pillow placed over her face. They secured the house and called for additional units.

Frank Simons, the detective who testified earlier about the Scheible murder, described the crime scene. Ms. Thurmond's body was found lying on its back, with "a stocking wrapped around her neck and tied." In addition to evidence of entry attempts at the front and rear doors, it was clear that the victim was fearful of being attacked. In her bedroom, a letter-sized piece of paper with the word "Police" and a phone number was taped to the wall. The back door to the house had no fewer than four locks: two dead bolts, a chain lock, and a lock in the doorknob. The kitchen door likewise had four locks plus a "reinforced screen over the window section."

Dr. Joe Webber, testifying about the victim's autopsy, described "considerable hemorrhaging and bruising of the entire face and head, and the left eye." There was bleeding from both ear canals, consistent with a "fracture of the base of the skull." Such an injury "usually requires a considerable amount of trauma or energy delivered to the head," Webber explained. "It's often seen in head injuries associated with automobile impact, aircraft crashes and so forth." There was bruising in and around the vagina with numerous spermatozoa seen in the vaginal fluid. Ms. Thurmond had suffered "violent sexual intercourse consistent with rape." The cause of death was "ligature strangulation," due to the stocking tied around her neck. Her hyoid bone was broken and there was hemorrhage into the neck muscles.

Three witnesses, including the chief imprint examiner for the state crime laboratory in Atlanta, testified about fingerprint collection and analysis from the scene of Ms. Thurmond's murder. One well-defined latent print collected from the bathroom window screen frame matched the print from Carlton Gary's right middle finger based on multiple points of similarity.

Later in the trial, Charles Oliver would testify.[*] At the time of the trial, he was the track coach at Troy State University in Troy, Alabama. In 1977, however, Oliver had just finished college and was working as a teacher and coach at Columbus High School. He and his wife lived in a duplex at 1159 Tate Drive, just down the street and less than a hundred yards from Martha Thurmond's house on Marion Street. Oliver testified that he could see the Thurmond house from his front door. He had known Carlton Gary since his childhood, as they both grew up in the same neighborhood. Gary's cousin Rudolph David lived in the other half of the duplex. Gary was said to have visited both Oliver and his cousin, sometimes accompanied by Earnestine Flowers. When asked about the specifics of his memory, Oliver stated that he remembered the time well, as his son had been born on October 14, 1977, just a few days before Ms. Thurmond's murder. With this testimony, the prosecution was able to place

---

[*] August 21, 1986.

Gary in the same neighborhood around the same time as the crime he was alleged to have committed.

The prosecution next turned to the murder of Kathleen Woodruff, the Strangler's fifth victim and the third in the series of crimes with which Gary was charged. Tommie Stevens, Ms. Woodruff's maid, described coming to work on the morning of December 28, 1977, and discovering her employer's lifeless body. She contacted Ms. Woodruff's son, George Woodruff Jr., who arrived in a matter of minutes, followed shortly by the police. Called as a witness, Woodruff identified photos of his mother in life, and her body as it was found at the crime scene. He recognized the scarf that had been wrapped tightly around her neck to strangle her.

William Turner, the Columbus patrolman who first responded to the call, described Ms. Woodruff's body as being "covered up to her chest by the bedspread." Dr. Joe Webber, who did an autopsy on the victim's body that afternoon, estimated she had been killed between 1:00 and 4:00 A.M. She was wearing a brown dress but the lower part of the body was otherwise unclothed. There were bruises on her left jaw. The scarf wrapped tightly around her neck was the method of strangulation. Spermatozoa were present in the vaginal fluid, consistent with recent sexual intercourse.

Columbus police officer Bruce Sanborn, who collected evidence from the crime scene, described a possible "scuffle" in the area where Ms. Woodruff's eyeglasses and checkbook were found on the floor. In the bedroom "someone had ransacked a couple of closets" and rifled through a jewelry box. Hidden under an outbuilding behind the house, a pillowcase contained women's hose and undergarments. A sand-like granular substance was found on the floor of the house in several areas; after examination, an expert witness believed it to be a type of seasoning, possibly sausage seasoning or celery salt.

Harold Harris, of the Identification Division of the Columbus police testified about lifting latent fingerprints from a window screen in the rear of the house, which was the presumed entry point of the Strangler. The screen itself had been punctured to lift off its catches, and the window sash showed pry marks. A fingerprint found on the edge of the aluminum window screen frame matched that of Carlton Gary's right fifth finger. As it was after 5:00 P.M. at the end of Harris's testimony and cross-examination, Judge Followill adjourned court, to resume the following day.

On Thursday morning, August 14th, court began with the testimony of Larry Hankerson, a latent fingerprint examiner from the Georgia State Crime Laboratory. In addition to Gary's fingerprint found on the window-screen frame, Hankerson was able to identify Gary's left palm print, found on the inside sill of the same window.

Thus far in the trial, the three burglaries, rapes, and murders with which Gary had been charged, and the evidence supporting them, had been presented to the jury. While Bud Siemon had aggressively cross-examined witnesses, offered numerous objections, and frequently demanded financial support from the court, to an objective observer it would appear that the state had a strong case.

Chapter 31

The Trial—Part V
A Key Witness

Following the fingerprint expert's testimony, Bill Smith called his next witness, Gertrude Miller. Bud Siemon immediately objected, leading the judge to dismiss the jury while the attorneys argued their positions in front of the bench. Without doubt, Ms. Miller was one of the prosecution's key witnesses. She was one of two women who survived attacks attributed to the Strangler, and the only one available to testify, as Ms. Ruth Schwob had died earlier. She was able to give a convincing account and—unlike Ms. Schwob—had gotten a good view of her assailant. It would be in the defense's interest to block or severely limit her testimony. Siemon called for a separate hearing on the matter based on three grounds: the general admissibility of Ms. Miller's testimony based on constitutional grounds, "a strong reason to believe" that she had received "psychiatric counseling," and the assertion that she had been hypnotized in an effort "to try to enhance her ability to recall what had happened." Both sides understood that testimony obtained via or following hypnosis was not admissible. Siemon accused the prosecution of knowingly trying to "deceive the court" and withhold possibly exculpatory evidence from the defense. Prosecutor Smith denied the accusations, stating that Ms. Miller's testimony would not be based on her hypnosis and that the defense had been provided all pertinent documentation. After a long discussion, it was decided that Bud Siemon would be allowed to listen to the tape of Ms. Miller's hypnosis interview, and Judge Followill would withhold a ruling until a later time. The discussions on these matters took up much of the day. As these issues were being sorted out, the court moved on to other witnesses.

Lucy Mangham, a close friend of Strangler victim Ferne Jackson, described taking her home after attending church on the night of September 15, 1977. When Ms. Jackson did not appear at work the next day and could not be reached by phone, a coworker recounted calling the police and obtaining permission from a relative to have them enter her residence. Jesse Thornton, a Columbus patrolman, told of gaining entry to Ms. Jackson's home by jimmying a front living room window. After opening the front door for another officer, the two began to search the house. There was evidence that things were amiss. In one room "there was stuff laying on the floor, papers, articles just scattered all over the floor. There was a pillow on the floor, there was a suitcase that was opened, the drawers had been opened on the dresser, and stuff was pulled out and hanging out of it, and so I knew that, you know, I didn't know what I was going to find," Thornton said. At the end of a hall, in a bedroom, he discovered Ms. Jackson's body on a bed. "The sheets had been pulled up around her head, her gown was pulled up around her waist, I believe," he recalled. "I believe on the pillow there was blood, and there was blood on the sheets and stuff."

Medical Examiner Webber performed an autopsy that evening. Ms. Jackson had been strangled by "a ligature around the neck, three passes of what proved to be a nylon stocking and a sash from a dressing gown combined together to make a single ligature." There were multiple fractures of the hyoid bone. The body had multiple bruises and hemorrhages, a fracture of the sternum, and other signs of trauma. Tears in the vaginal area were consistent with forcible rape, though no spermatozoa were seen on microscopic examination of the vaginal fluid. Dr. Webber estimated that Ms. Jackson was killed between 1:00 and 2:00 A.M. Following Dr. Webber's testimony, three witnesses testified regarding a latent palm print lifted from a door facing Ms. Jackson's dining room. The print matched Carlton Gary's left palm.

The state's next witnesses told of the circumstances of Jean Dimenstien's death. Elizabeth Sherman, a friend of the victim, spoke of leaving Ms. Dimenstien's house on 21st Street about 9:45 P.M. on the evening of September 24, 1977.* Around 10:00 A.M. the next morning, Ms. Dimenstien's sister-in-law arrived at her house to discover all the outside lights on, her car missing and the carport door open and hanging off its hinges. She immediately called the police. William Ellison, the officer who responded to the call, noted the hinge pins had been removed from the door to gain entry. The interior of the house was in disarray: "The contents of a lady's pocketbook had been turned over." In a back bedroom, "all the contents of the dresser drawers had been rummaged through and thrown on the floor." In the front bedroom, "I saw on the bed all the sheets and everything were piled up in a pile," Ellison said, "and...a right foot of a white individual sticking out from under the covers." Further explaining, "I tried to arouse the person by calling, then I shook the foot a couple of

---

* The name of 21st Street was later changed to Cross Country Hill Street. The house numbering remained the same.

times, got no response, and then I moved the sheets back from the head area, at which time there was a pillow over the head. Then when I moved the pillow I realized without any doubt the person was dead."

Crime scene investigators described Ms. Dimenstien's body as lying on its back, a stocking wrapped tightly around the neck. A pink pajama top was pushed up over her breasts, with the bottom completely removed from her left leg but remaining on the right leg below the knee. There was blood in the bed around the victim's pubic area. The intruder had evidently gained entry by the carport door.

Dr. Joe Webber, who did Ms. Dimenstien's autopsy later that afternoon, described "considerable trauma to the head," especially on the left side, evidence of strangulation with multiple fractures of the hyoid bone, and "extensive hemorrhage" and lacerations in the vaginal area. Numerous spermatozoa were found in the vaginal fluid. Though the time of death could not be determined with certainty, Dr. Webber estimated that Ms. Dimenstien was killed early on the morning of the 25th.

After an overnight recess, the trial resumed the next morning with the jury absent and a contentious debate in front of Judge Followill on possible testimony from Gertrude Miller. Since the discussion on the issue the previous morning, Bud Siemon had listened to the tape of Dr. Stewart Wiggins's attempt to hypnotize Ms. Miller. All parties agreed that the tape was of less than optimal quality, with some parts garbled or unclear. Bill Smith pointed out that the definition of a hypnotic state was ill-defined, and thus it was unclear if, in fact, Ms. Miller was under hypnosis at that time. Siemon expressed concern that there were discrepancies between what she said then, and what she may have told police in other interviews. He suggested that the court hold a hearing with the individuals who were present at Ms. Miller's October 1977 interview, and that experts be consulted to see if the tape quality could be "improved." He again accused the state of withholding information vital to his client's defense. With no clear resolution of the disagreements and over Siemon's objections, Judge Followill allowed the state to proceed with Ms. Miller's testimony.

With the jury back in the courtroom, Ms. Miller began her testimony. She was a short, frail seventy-three-year-old who was assisted to the witness stand by a bailiff. White-haired, wearing glasses, and dressed in a pink blouse with a dark jacket, she spoke clearly, describing her ordeal without hesitation. She had gone to bed around 11:30 P.M. and was awakened in the early morning hours of September 11, 1977, by a person "on top of me" in her bed. He had removed three pairs of stocking from her dresser, using them to tie her hands. Turning her over in the bed, he "raped me front and back, both," afterwards striking her on the head with a board. Of importance, she testified that "when he was raping me, he turned on the [small reading] light so he could see better." She had a good view of his face from more than one angle and was able to describe him as a clean-shaven young black male. When asked if she recognized "the person who attacked you" in the courtroom, Ms. Miller pointed to Carlton Gary.

In the investigation that followed, Ms. Miller was shown "hundreds" of suspect photos by the police, but was unable to make an identification. Years passed. By May 1984 she had moved in with her brother and saw a video of Carlton Gary on television taken at the time of his arrest. "When I saw him, I said, oh, that's the man," and contacted police. On cross-examination, Siemon pressed Ms. Miller about inconsistencies in her testimony and various statements she had made to police investigators.

A neighbor, Elizabeth Bell, testified next how, at about 10:00 to 10:30 the next morning, she had found Ms. Miller in a state of apparent confusion. Discovering the back door open, she entered the house to find Ms. Miller leaning against her bathroom door and unable to say anything except "beat, beat." The Columbus Rescue Squad was summoned, and she was taken to St. Francis Hospital. Det. Frank Simons was called by the emergency responders, who described Ms. Miller as being in a "bloodied and beaten condition." At the scene, Detective Simons found evidence of an "apparent struggle" in Ms. Miller's bedroom, and "a bed that was heavily bloodstained." In the center of the bed there were "articles of women's underclothing tied in a knot, as well as a pair of pantyhose rolled up." "Additional pantyhose tied in a knot" were found in the bathroom area. The bedroom window was open and the screen was removed, the intruder's apparent site of entry.

The final witness referable to Ms. Miller's attack was Dr. Anderson Wasden III, a staff physician at St. Francis Hospital at that time. Ms. Miller had been admitted to the hospital by a neurosurgeon due to her head trauma; Dr. Wasden was requested to see her for possible sexual assault. She told him that "she had been hit on the head, tied up and raped by a black male." He noted blood coming from her left ear and a small vaginal laceration consistent with "forced sexual intercourse."

Though the interpretation of its importance rested with the jury, Ms. Miller's testimony and her identification of Carton Gary as her assailant appeared to add powerful additional support to the state's case.

Chapter 32

The Trial—Part VI
Burglaries and Murders

The state's next witness was William Swift, whose house was burglarized on the evening of December 20, 1977, while he and his wife were out at a Christmas party. The Swift house, one of the places Carlton Gary admitted burglarizing, was located at 1710 Buena Vista Road, "almost directly across the street, just two doors down" from the residence of Kathleen Woodruff, who was murdered by the Strangler only seven days later. Some currency, a few pieces of jewelry, and a small handgun were stolen.

Virginia Illges testified next, describing the two burglaries at her home at 2021 Brookside Drive, the first during the night of December 31, 1977, and the second during the early morning hours of February 11, 1978. Ms. Illges and her husband slept in separate upstairs bedrooms. During the first break-in, her pocketbook, containing cash and car keys, was taken from her bedroom while she slept. Her husband's trousers, containing his wallet and cash, were stolen from his bedroom without waking him. Their car, a new Cadillac, was missing as well but was recovered less than twenty-four hours later, abandoned in south Columbus. Interestingly, several days later, a maid cleaning a downstairs bedroom discovered the empty pocketbook, the missing trousers, and an empty Coca-Cola bottle under a bed.* Prior to the second burglary, the Illgeses had an alarm installed, which was triggered at 5:15 A.M. on February 11th. The burglar fled. Ms. Illges's description of the burglar's sites of entry matched the account Gary had given to police officers as they rode around the Wynnton area on the night of his arrest.

Dr. Fred Burdette, the next-door neighbor of Ms. Ruth Schwob, described being awakened by an alarm going off at approximately 5:45 A.M. on the morning of February 11th. The alarm, installed for fear of the Strangler, had been triggered by Ms. Schwob. It was a prearranged signal for Dr. Burdette to call the police. Instead, he called Ms. Schwob. When

---

* These strange findings produced speculation that the burglar had hidden under the bed for a period of time and consumed the soft drink while there. No evidence of this possibility was ever produced.

no one answered after letting it ring ten times, he instructed his wife to call the police and got dressed to go to Ms. Schwob's. He arrived at the same time as Richard Gaines, the Columbus patrolman who responded to the call. Walking around the house, the two discovered a kitchen window was "a bit ajar." Climbing in through the window, Sergeant Gaines began exploring the darkened house using only his flashlight as illumination. In a back bedroom he found Ms. Schwob sitting on the edge of a bed.

> She had a stocking wrapped around her neck; it was hanging down between her legs; also saw laying on the floor was a screwdriver; then went over to where she was and when she saw me coming she said, "I thought you were him coming back." And then she said, "He's still here, he's still in the house." And I went over and checked the...stocking that was wrapped around her neck to make sure it was not tight, and it was loose.

By this time, a second officer had arrived. Together they checked the house, but the Strangler had escaped.

The next day, Sunday morning, around 11:30 A.M., Judy Borom, Ms. Mildred Borom's daughter-in-law, accompanied by her three children, stopped by to pay a visit to Ms. Borom on their way home from church. She testified about what happened next. Ms. Borom lived at 1612 Forest Avenue, near both the Illgeses and Ruth Schwob. Judy's husband, Perry Borom, had last seen his mother when he stopped by her house at about 4:00 P.M. two days earlier. She parked her vehicle in the parking area behind the house and rang the rear doorbell. She could hear the television playing in Ms. Borom's bedroom. When no one answered, she sent her son around to the front of the house to look in the living room window. Meanwhile, she peeked in the bathroom window but saw no one. At that point, Judy said, "I heard my son scream, 'Mama! Mama! Come here!' And now, I was close enough to the corner of the house that I looked around the corner and I saw a white screen from one of the windows lying on the ground. And, so, I immediately thought of this man sitting right over here and...," turning her eyes and nodding toward Carlton Gary as she spoke.

Bud Siemon immediately leaped up, exclaiming, "What? What? Your honor, we've got a motion."

"Well, of somebody...," Judy interjected from the witness stand. Judge Followill dismissed the jury.

"Your honor," Siemon said, "blatant, intentional attempt to prejudice this trial. We move for a mistrial."

"What words...?" Followill began, as Siemon continued, "She's got no idea at all who committed this crime, none whatsoever." A brief discussion followed.

Followill asked the witness if she wanted to make a response to Siemon's accusations. "Well, I will say that I..., I was wrong in looking over there, that I was..., when I said, I immediately thought of the Strangler, that is all I meant," Ms. Borom responded. Followill denied Siemon's motion, stating that he would instruct the jury to ignore Ms. Judy Borom's remarks referring to Gary.

With the jury back in the courtroom, the trial resumed. Johnny Harris, one of the police officers who responded to the scene, described gaining access to the house by kicking in the back door—with Ms. Judy Borom's permission. Inside, the body of Ms. Mildred Borom was found in a hallway leading to her bedroom. She lay on her back, her gown pulled up over her face, and then a dress draped over her. There was evidence that she struggled with her attacker in a fight that started in the bedroom and ended in the hall. It appeared that the Strangler had gained entry through the front door and possibly exited this same way. A bit of a hallway run was found caught under the closed door.

Dr. Joe Webber, who performed Ms. Borom's autopsy, was at the crime scene and "observed the body there and the house itself. The house was in disarray," he testified. "Lamps were turned over and bed clothing was strewn about the bedroom. The body had a ligature around the neck, which I personally removed. The ligature this time was tightly woven cord or sash cord that is commonly used to hold window weights or operate Venetian blinds and is very dense, hard, thick cord." The autopsy revealed a fractured hyoid bone and hemorrhage into the neck from strangulation. There were bruises on the victim's chest and "a broken fingernail on the left thumb, possibly indicating or consistent with a struggle, hand-to-hand struggle with an assailant." Vaginal fluid contained "abundant spermatozoa." Webber said he could not be certain of the exact time of death, only that it had occurred in the thirty-six hours before the autopsy, an estimate he narrowed to "approximately thirty to thirty-six hours" prior in later testimony. The significance of this time frame suggested, as the prosecution was trying to demonstrate, that the second burglary of the Illges home, the attack on Ms. Ruth Schwob, and the strangulation murder of Ms. Mildred

Borom were likely to have been committed by the same person, presumably Carlton Gary.

It was near the end of the day, and Judge Followill dismissed the jury for the night. It was Friday evening, with court scheduled to resume on Monday, August 18th. In the jury's absence and prior to the formal adjournment, Bill Smith said he had two things to bring before the court. First, he requested that the judge consider allowing the jury to see where the Strangler's crimes took place. He proposed a simple ride-by, with the jury in a van, but no attempt to see the interiors of the victim's homes. As the often-proximate location of the murders and burglaries attributed to the Strangler were important to the prosecution's narrative, this would help reinforce the case he was presenting in court. Smith did not ask for an immediate decision, suggesting instead that the idea be considered over the weekend.

This second item was an observation designed to rebut Siemon's claims that Gary was impaired to the point that he could not effectively participate in his defense. "I would just like the record to reflect—it's often reflected the illness or incapacity of the defendant—that since Monday [August 11th] his appearance has improved," Smith said. "He's obviously fully dressed better today. He has on a suit, coat and tie. He has participated with his counsel, consulted with him regularly, taken notes, and obviously participated in his defense." The prosecutor's comments were clearly designed to undermine the possible allegation that Gary was incompetent at the time of his trial, something that the defense might use as grounds to request a new trial. Siemon responded that he would "be the first to admit that I've seen a great improvement in [Gary] over the last three weeks." He attributed this to the assertion that "the pattern of solitary confinement is being broken."

Chapter 33

The Trial—Part VII
A Bite Mark and a Stolen Gun

The second week of testimony, and the fourth week of the trial, began on Monday morning, August 18th. Six of the seven murders attributed to the Strangler had been presented to the jury, leaving only that of Ms. Janet Cofer. The state's first witness was her son, Mike Cofer. A former high school football coach, he was working an interim job in Manchester, Georgia, close to Columbus, while his family lived in Dallas, near Atlanta. As a matter of convenience, he stayed with his mother during the week, going home on weekends. When unpacking his bag, Mike realized that he had left part of his clothes at his house in Dallas. Breaking with his usual routine, he decided to go home on Wednesday night, April 19, 1978, and return to his job and Columbus the next day. During his absence that night, the Strangler struck, murdering his mother.

Vivian Tyler, a friend of Ms. Cofer, stated that she had last seen her about 9:15 P.M. on Wednesday evening as they were both leaving choir practice. Ms. Grace Sutton, Ms. Cofer's next-door neighbor on Steam Mill Road in April 1978, testified that her husband collected antique vehicles. A particular one, a 1929 Ford pickup truck painted to resemble a firetruck, was at the time parked in her carport facing Ms. Cofer's driveway. This was apparently the same "old firetruck" that Gary described to police officers in his conversations in the hours and days that immediately followed his arrest in May 1984. Gary said that he and Michael Crittenden had broken into the house next door to the firetruck and that Michael had assaulted the woman who lived there. Jack Hendrix, the principal at Dimon Elementary School where Ms. Cofer taught kindergarten and first grade, recounted how he went to her house out of concern when she did not report to work and could not be reached by phone on the morning of April 20th. There he found a damaged window screen and called police. Sally Mitchell, a Columbus police youth services officer, gained entry through a living room window.* Mitchell, with two other officers who had arrived at the scene, found Ms. Cofer's body in one of the bedrooms.

Bruce Sanborn, a detective sergeant with the Columbus police at the time, described the crime scene. Ms. Cofer was lying on one of two twin beds. She was nude "with the exception of an undergarment that had been pulled up." A pillow covered her face. Looking under the pillow, Sanborn saw "what appeared to be a nylon stocking around her neck" as well as "some small bruises about her face and about her body." It appeared that someone had rummaged through a chest of drawers. In the kitchen, the top of a coffee canister lay on the counter. The canister itself was found in the front yard, where it appeared that what "looked like coffee" had been strewn about, presumably to deter tracking dogs.

Dr. Joe Webber performed an autopsy on Ms. Cofer's body later that afternoon. He described "a ligature, a nylon or silk stocking" wrapped "two throws around the neck, very tight." The cricoid cartilage, the uppermost cartilage of the trachea, was fractured, with hemorrhage into the adjacent muscles of the neck. There was "contusion or bruising of the upper end of the vagina...indicative of trauma." No spermatozoa were found on microscopic examination. What appeared to be "tooth marks" were found on the victim's left breast, an issue that would become important later. The estimated time of Ms. Cofer's death was between 6:00 and 7:00 A.M. on the morning of the 20th.

With the jury out of the courtroom for a midmorning recess, Bud Siemon entered a motion requesting funds for "a forensic odontologist" to further assess the "tooth marks" mentioned by Dr. Webber. "It's an extremely critical piece of evidence, because we know that whoever murdered that woman left those teeth marks," he explained. In response, Bill Smith noted, "Your Honor, we have learned in the interim that [Gary] had had dental repair work done between the time the murder was committed, and the time of his arrest. And therefore any comparison, we felt like, would have been invalid." Siemon objected forcefully, but Judge Followill denied the motion.

Next, the state's case moved to the complicated series of events that led to Carlton Gary's arrest in May 1984. The first to testify was Nellie Sanderson, the sister of Callye East, with whom she was living in 1977. She described waking up on the morning of October 8th to discover that

---

* Mitchell was not married in 1978. She testified at the 1986 trial under her married name, Sally Culberson.

their house at 1427 Eberhart Avenue had been burglarized. Her son, Henry Sanderson, and his wife were in town for a family event and were staying with his mother and aunt. During the night a burglar had entered the house through a kitchen window, crept into Mr. Sanderson's room, where the intruder took his trousers and car keys, and then left without being detected, having stolen his car. On the witness stand, Mr. Sanderson testified that, in addition to having his pants and wallet stolen, when his vehicle, a 1975 Toyota, was recovered the next day, he discovered that a bank bag containing receipts and cash, some credit cards, and a .22 caliber Ruger automatic pistol had been taken from the car as well. The box in which the Ruger was purchased was left in the car and listed the pistol's serial number. He was shown both the box and a .22 caliber Ruger pistol, serial number 13-70073. He identified it as the gun stolen in the burglary.[†]

Aaron Sanders, a self-employed drywall contractor from Kalamazoo, Michigan, was sworn as a witness and identified the same pistol as the one he was given by his mother, Lucille Gary Sanders, in October 1981. As required by Michigan law at the time, he registered the pistol with the local police and was given a card to show this had been done. This document was entered into evidence. Sanders said that he had been told that Carlton Gary was his first cousin but had never met him.

Lucille Sanders, Aaron's mother, who lived in Indiana, testified that she had received the pistol she gave her son from her brother, Jim Gary. She could not recall exactly when she acquired the weapon. On questioning, she said she had seen Carlton Gary only once, when he visited her brother and his father, Willie Frank Gary, who was living in Indiana. She could not remember the date, but said Carlton was young at the time.

Jim Gary, the final link in the chain of custody, was Carlton Gary's paternal uncle. He lived in Russell County, Alabama, just outside of Phenix City and across the Chattahoochee River from Columbus. When shown the Ruger, he testified that it looked like the one he had purchased from his nephew, Carlton Gary, for twenty or twenty-five dollars. Being uncertain as to whether Gary had acquired the gun legitimately, he said that he took it to the local sheriff and was told it was not stolen. Shortly

---

[†] It was a call from Mr. Sanderson in the spring of 1984 that helped renew interest the stolen gun. At that time, there were concerns that he was having memory issues. His testimony in court in 1986 might confirm this: He was unsure of the model of his stolen car. He could not recall when the car was found by police. He could not recall whether his missing pants were ever found.

thereafter, apparently in the summer of 1978, he saw a picture of a similar gun on television with a request to notify the police if anyone had information on the pistol. Soon after the television story appeared, Carlton returned to his uncle's and said he wanted to get the gun back, but did not have money to pay for it. Gary's first thought was that Carlton wanted "to sell the gun again and make him a few extra bucks." Carlton told him the gun was "hot." Gary lied to his nephew, saying that he no longer had it. He later passed it on to his sister, Lucille Sanders. It was Jim Gary's identification of his nephew as the source of the stolen gun, followed by the matching of Carlton Gary's fingerprints with those found at several of the murders attributed to the Strangler, that broke the cold case.

Bruce Sanborn, who was part of the Strangler Task Force, reinvestigated the burglary at the home of Callye East and Nellie Sanderson in the summer of 1978. By that time, it had been several months since the Strangler's last murder, and interest had turned to some of the unsolved burglaries in the Wynnton area, hoping to discover a missing lead or clue. As this crime occurred only three houses away from the site of the Scheible murder, it deserved a closer look, Sanborn said. A gun similar to the stolen Ruger was photographed and the information, including the serial number, sent to law enforcement agencies, pawnshops, and the news media. Patricia Hardy, the librarian for the *Columbus Ledger-Enquirer* newspapers, read for the record the article about the stolen gun that appeared in the July 24, 1978, issues. Despite the publicity, no useful information was obtained. At that time, the fate of the pistol seemed to be another dead end for the investigation. This would change with the murder of Patrolman Michael Bowen in March 1984 and renewed interest in its whereabouts.

It was past midday. With the jury dismissed for lunch, Bill Smith and Bud Siemon argued before Judge Followill the state's request for the jury to tour the sites of the burglaries and murders attributed to the Strangler. Smith proposed that "it would be very helpful and very beneficial to the jury to see where the offenses occurred and to see the relationship of one scene to another." Siemon, in turn, pointed out that during the competency hearing the judge had refused to allow the jury to see Gary's cell. He was uneasy as to what the jury might see on a tour and would have no opportunity to rebut subjective opinions that might be detrimental to the defense's case. Followill said he felt the jury could make "reasonable deductions and inferences" from viewing the map on display in the courtroom. He denied the motion.

Chapter 34

The Trial—Part VIII
Malvin Alamichael Crittenden

The prosecution next turned to presenting the particulars of Carlton Gary's capture in Albany, Georgia, on May 3, 1984. Joe Monzie and James Paulk testified about the details of the arrest in room 254 of the Holiday Inn. Robert Windham, the supervisor in charge if the identification and lab section of the Albany Police Department, identified the loaded .38 caliber Colt revolver that had been found on the nightstand in the room. Charlie Lee Cochran, a detective with the Albany police, described advising Gary of his Miranda rights. He had been ordered not to interrogate Gary, and did not attempt to have him waive his rights against self-incrimination or the presence of a lawyer if he chose to make a statement.

Mike Sellers, one of the Columbus officers who rode back from Albany to Columbus with Gary on the night of his arrest, testified next. What Gary revealed during this journey and his subsequent interrogation that evening and beyond midnight into the next morning were at the heart of the state's case. Sellers's testimony and cross-examination lasted for the remainder of the day and resumed the following morning, more than two hours in total. He described taking custody of Gary in Albany and advising him once again of his rights. He told of the ride back to Columbus when Gary spoke in detail about the burglary of the East/Sanderson residence and the two burglaries of the Illges home. At police headquarters the conversations continued, with Gary referring to break-ins at the Woodruff and Scheible residences, admitting he had been present but blaming the murders of both women on Malvin Alamichael Crittenden. As the conversation progressed, with Gary providing more and more information on the crimes attributed to the Strangler, Sellers described how Gary seemed eager to "show us" the scenes. Bill Smith asked him, "Did you suggest that he show you these houses, or did he suggest that to you?"

"No, sir. That was his idea. It was at his suggestion," Sellers replied. For approximately two hours, Gary, accompanied by officers Sellers, Boren, and Rowe, was driven about Columbus's Wynnton district. Without prompting, he pointed out the Illges home ("the castle") and the nearby residences of Mildred Borom and Ruth Schwob, sharing details of each crime. For example, he pointed out to the officers where he had hidden from police when fleeing the Illges home after he tripped an alarm during the second burglary. Gary identified the homes of murder victims Florence Scheible, Jean Dimenstien, Martha Thurmond, and Kathleen Woodruff. He showed familiarity with the details of the burglaries of the East/Sanderson and Swift homes.

In the hours that followed his arrest on May 3, 1984, Carlton Gary told police officers, "I did the burglaries and Michael killed the old ladies," referring to Malvin Alamichael Crittenden. It was a statement that the prosecution contended was part of a pattern in which Gary attempted to shift the blame for his alleged crimes to other individuals. To rebut Gary's accusations, Crittenden appeared as a witness for the state. Crittenden, a well-spoken black man who had lived in Columbus for most of his life, was thirty-six years old at the time of the trial, about the same age as Gary. He wore a short beard and a purple suit with wide lapels and a tie that matched his pocket handkerchief. "Mike" (or "Michael"), as he was usually called, had known Gary during their pre-teenage years and had reconnected with him in 1978. He had started, but not completed, his college education, had been fired from more than one job, and had a history of some minor run-ins with the law. Between May or June and October of 1978, he and Gary committed a series of robberies of "fast-food places" and restaurants in Florida, South Carolina, and elsewhere. Crittenden said he would wait "two or three blocks away" in a get-away car while Gary committed the robberies. Their close relationship ended when Crittenden decided he wanted to quit what they were doing. Testimony established that he had never been formally charged with these robberies, and neither had he been offered immunity or any reward for testifying in the trial.[*]

Prosecutor Smith asked Crittenden if he ever committed any "house burglaries" with Gary in 1977 or 1978, to which he answered, "No, sir." Naming each victim and/or burglary individually, Smith asked if he had, "alone or with the defendant, Carlton Gary," ever broken into the homes of, or raped or strangled, Gertrude Miller, Ferne Jackson, Jean

---

[*] To be clear, the police did not ignore Gary's attempt to implicate Crittenden following his arrest in Albany, Georgia, in early May 1984. Immediately thereafter, Crittenden was taken into custody, brought to Columbus police headquarters, and interviewed at length. Finding no reason to charge or detain him, he was released and continued to cooperate with police throughout the investigation.

Dimenstien, Callye East, Nellie Sanderson, Florence Scheible, Kathleen Woodruff, Ruth Schwob, Abraham or Virginia Illges, Mildred Borom, or Janet Cofer. To each question, the answer was a uniform "No, sir." The next five witnesses for the state testified that Mike Crittenden's fingerprints did not match any latent prints found at the scene of crimes attributed to the Strangler, confirming his testimony in a negative sense.

The remainder of the day was devoted to the technically difficult subject matter of genetic markers found in blood and semen. In his opening statement, Bill Smith advised the jury that the state would present evidence on chemical markers that humans secrete in their bodily fluids. The secretion of these markers can, in many cases, allow the determination of an individual's blood type based on analysis of his or her semen or vaginal fluid. Only about eighty percent of persons secrete these markers. Their presence in a sample of body fluid in a case of rape, for example, might be used as positive evidence to *exclude* a man as a suspect in the crime if markers that did not match his blood type were found. On the other hand, failure to detect such markers could have multiple explanations and *would not exclude* the same person.

With the jury out of the courtroom, the attempt by the state to introduce such evidence began with Bud Siemon attacking the scientific methods used to detect and analyze these genetic markers, referring to them as "inherently unreliable." In addition to requesting funds for the defense to hire its own experts, he asked for a hearing "to establish the reliability of this type of testing before it can be admitted in front of the jury." After a prolonged discussion relative to the case law on the subject, Judge Followill agreed to hear from the state's first witness, a forensic serologist, prior to making any decision. John G. Wegel, an employee of the Georgia Bureau of Investigation, Division of Forensic Sciences, took the witness stand. Wegel had a Bachelor of Science degree from Georgia Tech and a Master of Science degree in forensic chemistry from the University of Pittsburgh. He explained in detail the basic methodology of testing, the potential results, and the factors that could influence testing results. After examination and cross-examination by the attorneys, the judge ruled that Wegel could testify as an expert, and "that these tests are generally acceptable procedures in the scientific community, and...reliable and valid to the point that a jury should be able to listen to them and draw its own conclusions as to the weight and credit they will give them."

With the jury present, Connie Pickens, a forensic serologist with the Georgia State Crime Laboratory in Atlanta, testified next for the state.

Based on her examination of Carlton Gary's blood and saliva, she had determined that he had International Blood Group Type O, and was in the eighty percent of the population that were "secretors." Next, John Wegel, who had testified earlier in the absence of the jury, was placed back on the witness stand to discuss his findings on the analysis of blood and fluid specimens collected from the scenes of the Strangler's murders. He had personally received and examined evidence from the Scheible, Thurmond, Jackson, Borom, and Cofer murders. Excluding the Cofer case, where the material submitted was not found to contain seminal fluid, his results indicated that Gary could not be excluded as "the donor of the seminal fluid" in the other four rapes. Wegel stated that he did not receive specimens from the Dimenstien case. Finally, Linda Tillman, who had worked as a forensic serologist at the state crime laboratory, testified that semen found in the vaginal fluid of Kathleen Woodruff did not exclude Gary as her rapist.

As it was late in the day, court adjourned until the following morning, when the prosecution planned to present testimony regarding Carlton Gary's crimes in New York.

Chapter 35

The Trial—Part IX
Similar Crimes in New York

The state's presentation next turned to the crimes that Carlton Gary had committed, or was accused of committing, in New York and South Carolina. The importance of this was the demonstration of a similar pattern of criminal behavior and—when accused—of Gary's attempts to deflect blame to an alleged accomplice. The first witness was Robert Westervelt, who, in April 1970, was employed as a crime scene investigator for the Albany, New York, Police Department. On the 14th of that month, he and another officer photographed and collected fingerprints from a room in Albany's Wellington Hotel where eighty-three-year-old Nellie Farmer had been raped and strangled. Westervelt described the modest room of the elderly retiree, whose partially covered body lay face down on the floor at the foot of her bed: "The room basically in general was ransacked," Westervelt said. "It was all messed up. Stuff laying all over the place, and on the foot of the bed was a large steamer trunk, open, some of the stuff was pulled out of that and thrown around." A photograph entered into evidence by the prosecution showed Ms. Farmer's body "with some kind of a housecoat or something over her neck." Her perineal area was bloody, suggesting sexual assault. Charlie Moss, a latent print examiner from the Georgia State Crime Laboratory, testified that a fingerprint found on the steamer trunk matched that of Gary's right middle finger.

Dr. Leon Feldman, at the time the coroner's physician* in Albany County, New York, attended the autopsy of Ms. Farmer's body on the afternoon of the discovery of her death. Fractures of the hyoid bone and cricoid cartilage and bleeding into the adjacent muscles of the neck indicated that strangulation was the cause of her death. There were lacerations of the vagina and anal ring consistent with forcible sexual intercourse.

Retired Albany, New York, detective Anthony Sidoti testified next. Sidoti had given testimony earlier in the trial in the absence of the jury as Judge Followill considered the admission of similar crimes for which Gary

---

* The "coroner's physician" position is roughly equivalent to the position of medical examiner in Georgia.

was not on trial. On July 21, 1970, he arrested Gary, who was at the time an inmate at the Albany County jail, on a charge of first-degree murder in Ms. Farmer's death. Sidoti identified Gary as the person he knew as Carl Michaels, the alias Gary was using at the time. Gary was advised of his rights and agreed to give a statement to the police. The statement was transcribed by a typist as he gave it, after which Gary read and signed it in the presence of witnesses.

Sidoti read the statement for the court. It was a long and detailed narrative of how Gary and a man he knew as "Pop" had been committing burglaries as a source of income. His usual role, Gary (or "Michaels") said, was to act as "chickie" or lookout man, as Pop committed the burglaries. He admitted to being in Nellie Farmer's room, but only after Pop had gone in first and apparently killed the woman. In his statement, Gary said that after being shown mugshots, he identified Pop as John Lee Mitchell. Based on Gary's statement, Mitchell was arrested and subsequently tried for the murder of Nellie Farmer. He was acquitted despite Gary's testimony against him.

The state called John Lee Mitchell as the next witness. Richard Hyatt, who was covering the trial for the Columbus newspapers, described the moment when the two men first saw each other in the courtroom. "Their eyes met. Mitchell said that Carlton Gary was that man. The prosecutor was moving on to another question, but Mitchell and Gary continued to stare. This moment wasn't lost on two men who seemed to be playing optic games across the courtroom."[218] Mitchell said that he and Gary had first met in 1969 at a nightclub in Albany. He described them as having "a very casual relationship" and that he "barely even knew" Gary. Mitchell denied completely Ms. Farmer's murder and the events of April 14, 1970, as described in Gary's statement. He spent approximately a year in jail prior to his trial and was confined near Gary. Mitchell had asked him why he tried to blame Farmer's murder on him. The gist of Gary's reply, Mitchell said, was, "It's better him than me."

Jean Frost testified next. On January 2, 1977, she was living in an apartment in Syracuse, New York. It was her fifty-fifth birthday and she had been out to dinner with her mother. Sometime during the late hours of January 2nd or the early hours of January 3rd, something awakened her. It was dark, but she saw a shadow on her bathroom door. She described the events that followed:

So I lay there very quietly, because I didn't know what else to do, and as he came close enough to touch me I tried to shove him aside and run, and I screamed. And he said you shouldn't have struggled, and he smashed my face, ripped off my nightgown and stuffed it down my throat so that I couldn't scream. And after that I was unconscious for I don't know how long.

On further questioning by Bill Smith, Ms. Frost said she had lost consciousness when "he strangled me." Sometime later she woke up and for a moment could not remember exactly what had happened. She said she was bleeding from "my vagina." Her living room "was all torn up," and it appeared that she had been robbed. She called the operator and asked for assistance, afterwards spending several days in the hospital, where she required surgery for her wounds.[†] Ms. Frost could not give the race of her attacker, only that he was male based on his voice. She recalled, "I think he was surprised that I struggled, because he—just before he smashed me—these were the words he said to me, 'You shouldn't have struggled.'" Later, Ms. Frost realized that she had been robbed of "some money, some costume jewelry, and a watch." It was a gold pendant Kelbert watch that she had left on her dining room table when she returned home on the night of the 2nd after her birthday dinner. When shown the watch, which the state had entered into evidence, she identified it as the one that was stolen that night.

Steven Thompson, a Syracuse police officer, arrived at Ms. Frost's apartment shortly after 3:00 A.M. at about the same time as Louis Handlen, another Syracuse officer. Frost greeted them in a bloody nightgown, then collapsed on the floor. An open window next to a patio appeared to be the burglar's site of entry. There had been recent snowfall in the hours prior to the incident. Thompson described a "fresh set of footprints leading from the area of the window" in the snow. He was clear that there was "just one" set of tracks. Leaving Ms. Frost with the other officer, Thompson followed the footprints for several hundred yards before turning over tracking to other officers who had responded to the scene. The trail was eventually lost about half a mile away in a congested area. Thompson said, "I asked [Ms. Frost] who had done this to her, and she

---

[†] Dr. Renate Chevli, a specialist in obstetrics and gynecology, testified later in the trial that Ms. Frost was "severely hemorrhaging from the vagina" and required blood transfusions and emergency surgery to repair a "very traumatic" vaginal laceration.

told us a black male with a mustache. I asked her if she had seen anything, anybody else, and she said no. She was quite disoriented."

While Officer Thompson was pursuing the footprints in the snow, Officer Handlen was administering first aid to Ms. Frost while waiting on the arrival of the ambulance. "The victim was laying on the floor. She was wearing a nightgown that was covered with blood. Her neck was red and appeared to be swollen. I didn't believe she was going to live." When asked if she was able to say who attacked her, Handlen replied, "She was conscious, at this time she stated to me that she had been strangled and raped by a black man with a mustache."

Sgt. Raymond D. Grinnals of the Syracuse Police Department testified next. He identified Gary as the man he had questioned at Syracuse police headquarters on the night of January 4, 1977, roughly thirty-six hours after the attack on Ms. Frost. Earlier that day, Carlton Gary and another man named Dudley Harris went to a local bank in an effort to exchange some coins for paper money. Bank personnel were suspicious and notified the police. Several days earlier there had been a burglary at the residence of William Howland in which some coins, some clothes, and a police scanner were stolen. Howland was able to identify the coins as his. Gary was arrested and taken to the police station where he was asked to empty his pockets. He had two watches in his possession, one of which was the gold Kelbert watch stolen from Jean Frost. Grinnals was shown a mug shot of Gary taken at the time of his arrest. He had a moustache. He had been initially charged with the possession of stolen property, but his possession of the watch taken from Ms. Frost indicated more serious charges might be appropriate.

Under the threat of being charged with the burglary and rape of Jean Frost, and after being advised of his Miranda rights, Gary elected to give Syracuse police a statement regarding those crimes. Sgt. David Fix, a Syracuse police officer, read Gary's statement from the witness stand. In another detailed account, Gary said that on the night of January 2, 1977, he and a man named Dudley Harris were cruising around Syracuse after getting out of a movie shortly before midnight. Harris decided to try to burglarize an apartment building and asked Gary to watch the car while he did. The break-in took place around 2:30 A.M. on January 3rd. According to Gary, Dudley said that he got only "chump change" but gave Gary the Kelbert watch which he had in his possession when he was arrested. The statement continued, "Later that day on the 12:00 news I learned that a woman had been hurt in the apartment where Dudley had been. I wished to state that at no time did I enter this woman's apartment. Dudley was the only one who did. I did not know that he had hurt a woman." The statement was signed and dated by Carlton Gary and Sgt. David Fixx. According to Fixx, Harris went to jail for perjury, but no one was tried for the attack on Ms. Frost. Gary pleaded guilty to the possession of stolen property, had his parole revoked, and was sent back to prison.

Chapter 36

The Trial—Part X
The State Rests Its Case

The prosecution was nearing the end of its case and was now presenting witnesses to buttress and fill in blank spaces in their narrative. On the afternoon of August 20th and continuing the following morning, three police officers and a former employee of the Po' Folks restaurant in Gaffney, South Carolina, testified about the events of the evening of February 15, 1979, and the following day. Patrolman Richard Weaver, upon seeing an employee fleeing the restaurant, drove into the parking lot just as a black male, later identified as Gary, emerged from the back door of the restaurant with a money bag and a pistol. Tracking dogs were available, and Gary—who identified himself to police as Michael David—was captured several hours later. Gary (or "David") said that he was only acting as a lookout, but it was, in fact, Malvin Crittenden who had robbed the restaurant but had fled just before Weaver arrived. The police did not believe his story, and furthermore, this robbery was similar to others committed by a lone black male who had become known as the "Steak House Bandit." Fingerprints revealed Gary's true identity the following day, leading to his decision to plead guilty to a series of robberies. He would remain in prison in South Carolina until his escape and return to Columbus in March 1984.

Sheila Dean, the mother of three of Carlton Gary's children, testified next. He was sixteen and living in Gainesville, Florida, when their first child, a girl, was born in August 1967. Two other sons with Sheila came later, only one of whom survived. Gary moved to New York in the spring of 1968, and Sheila soon followed. In November or December 1969, they moved to Albany, New York, where Gary was arrested following the rape and murder of Nellie Farmer a few months later. He went to prison after admitting to the robbery in the case; Sheila stayed in Albany until 1981 before moving back to Gainesville. She next saw Gary in Gainesville in late April 1984, days before his arrest. She confirmed that in addition to using his given name, he also used the aliases of Michael Davis and Michael Christy.

Maurice J. Sheedy, a senior parole officer with the New York State Division of Parole, testified that Gary entered the New York prison system in March 1971 after having spent about eight and a half months in jail in Albany following his charges in the Nellie Farmer case. Other than some brief periods spent on parole, he remained incarcerated until August 22, 1977, when he escaped from the Onondaga County Correctional Facility located near Syracuse.* Picking up the thread, Louis J. Racona, at the time a "permanent" resident of New York's Auburn Correctional Facility, testified that he and Gary escaped the Onondaga prison on August 22, 1977, by sawing through two bars of a second-floor window and jumping out to the ground about twenty feet below. In the process, Gary twisted his ankle but was able to make it with Racona to the village of DeWitt on the outskirts of Syracuse by riding on two stolen ten-speed bicycles. There they split up. Racona, who was arrested later and sent back to prison, said he had not seen Gary since then.

After his escape from the New York prison, Carlton Gary returned to Columbus, arriving near the end of August or the first of September 1977. He initially stayed with an elderly relative, Alma Williams, at 1027 Fisk Street in the Wynnton area before moving to 3231 Old Buena Vista Road in early October. On November 11, 1977, he moved to 2826 Ninth Street, where he lived until early August 1978. These addresses were significant in that they were located in reasonably close proximity to the seven murders attributed to the Strangler as well as to the attacks on Gertrude Miller and Ruth Schwob, the burglaries of the Swift and Illges residences, and the sites where the stolen vehicles of victims Jackson and Dimenstien had been abandoned. The prosecution's next three witnesses testified as to Gary's whereabouts during the time frame of the murders and attacks. Dolly Crittenden, the mother of Malvin Crittenden, the man Gary accused of committing the Strangler's rapes and murders, lived next door to Alma Williams. She spoke of Gary's demeanor when he first arrived back in Columbus. His injured ankle was apparently still bothering him at the time. Referring to 1977, she said that "about the end of the summer or the first of the fall, Carlton came over there hopping at Mrs. Alma's house and

---

* Although Gary was either incarcerated or on parole from April 1970 until his escape from prison in August 1977, Sheedy's testimony did not provide specific details other than to say he was supposedly under supervision the entire time. After being sentenced to ten years in prison for the Farmer robbery, Gary was released on parole in March 1975, after which he moved to Syracuse, New York. He was back in prison in July 1975 but released a year later, again on parole. Gary went back to prison in early 1977 after the attack on Jean Frost. (A cold-case discovery in 2007 would dramatically alter the significance of this timeline.)

wouldn't allow no windows to be opened, no doors, and I stopped going over there to see about her because, in a way, I was real afraid of him." Ennis Williams, Alma Williams's son, who lived in Florida at the time, testified that he placed a collect call to his aged mother to check on her health. Gary answered the phone and refused to accept the call. This event led to Gary's moving to Old Buena Vista Road.

The next two witnesses, Benny Blankenship, of the state crime laboratory in Columbus, and Myron Scholberg, a retired FBI special agent and forensic scientist specializing in the field of hairs and fibers, testified about the analysis of hair samples found at the scenes of the murders. Hairs collected from each of the seven murder scenes were found to be "Negroid in type." While there were some similarities and some differences between the hair samples collected and those from Carlton Gary, there was no clear match. At the same time, there were no findings that would *exclude* Gary as the source of the crime scene hairs.

Through the end of the court's day and continuing the following morning, several witnesses gave evidence of Gary's residences during the time of the murders. For more than half the time of the hiatus between the Thurmond murder and the robbery of the Swift home and the Woodruff murder a week later, Gary was employed at Golden's Foundry under the alias of Michael Anthony David, working the night shift from 8:00 P.M. to 4:00 A.M. Although not specifically stated by either witnesses or the prosecutor, the implicit observation could be made that during this time frame Gary was otherwise occupied during the usual hours when the Strangler attacked his victims.

Michael Anthony David, a cousin of Carlton Gary, was shown the employment application from the foundry where Gary was employed for approximately five weeks, and a rental application for 5737 Spencer Lane, a house in east Columbus where Gary moved in November 1978. Both were in the name of Michael David, with the date of birth, November 26, 1949, the birthday of the witness, and signed with his forged signature. For whatever reason, Gary had attempted to adopt the identity of his cousin. When the real Michael David became aware that his cousin was using his name and date of birth, he asked Gary the reason. "Well, he said he thought it might help him get a better job or something like that," David stated. It is unclear from the record if David (or others) knew at the time that Gary was a prison escapee.

Two deputies assigned to the Muscogee County jail testified about Gary's escape attempt discovered on December 29, 1985. "Two days earlier on the 27th," Deputy Marvin Nance said, "a couple of jailers had reported that they had heard loud noises and some type of strange behavior coming from Carlton, loud television, some scratching, sounding like some beating." Bud Siemon interrupted to object to the testimony "on the grounds that Carlton Gary has been held illegally under illegal conditions of confinement. And that it would violate due process to hold him like that and then present testimony of behavior that we would contend would result from the unconstitutional confinement." Judge Followill allowed the testimony to proceed.

Gary was removed from his cell while deputies inspected it. When it was evident that something was amiss, the deputy warden was called and the inspection continued. It was discovered that the light had been manipulated and one of the bulbs was not illuminated. A floor drain had a piece of concrete block and loosened mortar inside. Gary had been given special privileges, which allowed him to hang art and photographs on his cell wall as well as being provided with a television and "stereo radio." Deputy Warden Michael Land testified that hidden behind a collection of family photos and a birthday greeting card above his sink, Gary had managed to cut a large hole in the concrete blocks. A second hole was at one end of his bed, hidden by his television and mattress.

Gary was moved to another cell. Siemon used his cross-examination questions to condemn the conditions under which his client was being held. The deputy warden admitted that between May 1984 and August 1986, Gary had lost about thirty-five pounds and that his outdoor exercise had been curtailed. The reasons behind the latter were lack of manpower, Gary's history of escapes from other jails, and the inability to "provide for his safety if someone comes around there and wants to take a pot shot at him or something."

The state's final witness, Earnestine Flowers, had been scheduled to testify on Friday, August 22nd. Despite having been personally served with subpoenas and reminded to be in court, she did not show up. Over the weekend, sheriff's deputies were sent to pick her up and hold her in jail until she was called to testify. When court resumed on Monday, August 25th, Flowers was the day's first witness, and the last that the state would call before resting its case. Ms. Flowers had grown up in the same neighborhood as Carlton Gary and was apparently surprised when he called her on returning to Columbus after his escape from the prison in New York. She described their relationship as a very casual one, which seemed to contrast with her reluctance to testify. When she first saw Gary, he had a cast on his leg, but said she had no additional information. Flowers was instrumental in Gary's getting a job at the foundry where he worked in November and December 1978. She worked as a Muscogee County sheriff's deputy from January 1978 to January 1980, but denied seeing Gary after he went to work at the foundry in November 1977. Even though Gary told police officers he had use of her car, a 1975 Datsun 280Z, Flowers denied loaning it to him, stating the only time she recalled his ever driving it was to the car dealership for brake repairs.

Following Flowers's testimony, the state rested its case. Rather than dismiss her, Judge Followill asked, "I'm curious about why you didn't appear in response to your subpoena." She began by replying, "First of all, Your Honor, I was not given a subpoena," then going on to say that she had, in fact, been given more than one subpoena while providing a list of excuses as to why she had not shown up. When sheriff's deputies attempted to locate her, her husband said he could not reach her and did not know where she was. This led to her being brought in to jail the day before her testimony. After listening to her excuses, Followill said, "I find you have obstructed justice, upset the orderly processes of this court, and I am going to find you in willful contempt." He sentenced her to twenty-four hours in jail, with credit for time served, allowing her to leave without further consequences.

Prior to presenting the defense's case, Bud Siemon objected to the eyewitness identifications of his client by Gertrude Miller, Sue Nelson, and Doris Laufenberg, asking Judge Followill for a hearing on the admissibility of their testimony. He objected to Gary's being referred to as the Steak House Bandit during witness testimony, asking the court to instruct the jury to disregard this nickname. He again requested funds to hire experts in the fields of blood type analysis, hair comparison, and fingerprints, plus a "forensic odontologist," all to examine and possibly refute testimony presented by the state's experts in those fields. Finally, as the witnesses presented by the prosecution had said negative things about the character and actions of his client, he requested "funds to bring in witnesses to testify in mitigation as to the character of Carlton Gary." Except for advising the jury to ignore the Steak House Bandit sobriquet, Followill denied the motions.

The prosecution had presented a strong case in favor of the guilt of Gary. It was now Siemon's turn to present contrasting arguments designed to induce doubts in their minds.

Chapter 37

The Trial—Part XI
The Defense Presents Its Case

In sharp contrast to the presentation of the state's case, which had lasted ten days with 135 witnesses and more than two hundred exhibits, the defense's presentation took approximately two hours, with six witnesses and only five exhibits.[219] Siemon's first witness was Ronnie Jones, director of the task force organized in late December 1977. Jones generally described the structure and functioning of the task force, including records of contacts made, a total of about 16,000 "field interviews" before he resigned in October 1978. He confirmed that tracking dogs were used following the murders of Thurmond, Woodruff, and Cofer. It was brought out on cross-examination that the Strangler was evidently aware of the tracking dogs, as pepper or other pungent substances were left at some crime scenes.

J. B. Hicks, who at the time was deputy commander of the detective division of the Columbus Police Department, admitted being aware of the beating and rapes of two elderly black women in the "thirty to sixty days" prior to the attack on Gertrude Miller. Hicks and members of the task force were aware that "Negroid hairs" and been found at the scene of the Strangler's murders and that the suspected perpetrator was black.

Siemon's third witness was Jerome Livas, at the time serving a life sentence in the Georgia prison system for the murder of Beatrice Brier. In October 1977, while under arrest for the assault of Ms. Brier—with whom he was living at the time—Livas was questioned and signed a confession admitting to the rape of Gertrude Miller and the murders of Ferne Jackson and Jean Dimenstien. He later recanted his confession and denied any involvement in the crimes. Dressed in a nondescript starched white short-sleeve shirt and black pants on the witness stand, he appeared passive and a bit bewildered. It had previously become public knowledge that Livas was illiterate and of limited intellectual capacity. Following his arrest, he remained in jail during the Strangler's subsequent murders, making his "confession" even more suspect. Cross-examination revealed that Livas, as an early suspect in the crimes, had been taken out of jail and driven to the sites of the Miller, Jackson, and Dimenstien attacks by two police officers.

Specific details of the crimes were revealed to Livas at that time. A short while later, two other police officers who were working on separate cases took Livas out of jail a second time and again showed him the sites of the attacks. This time he showed familiarity with the details. This was interpreted as evidence that he was the perpetrator. Livas signed a confession. Because he could not read, it was unclear if he truly knew or understood what he was signing. Bill Smith asked, "Do you remember telling me that the reason that you signed this statement was that you had never been in any trouble before and you thought they would let you go home if you signed it?"

"Yes, sir," Livas replied. He was never formally charged with the Miller, Jackson, or Thurmond crimes. As a further indication of his confused state, when Siemon asked on redirect examination if he had killed Beatrice Brier, Livas denied this as well. Following Livas's testimony, Ronald Lynn was called to the stand. In the fall of 1977, he was a detective with the Columbus Police Department assigned to the homicide unit. When shown a copy of Livas's confession, Lynn confirmed that it reflected accurately what Livas had told him and another detective. Although not stated specifically, his testimony, juxtaposed with that of Livas, clearly implied that Columbus police fabricated Livas's confession in an attempt to frame him for crimes he did not commit.

Siemon's final witness was Richard Smith, one of the Columbus detectives who interviewed Gary in Greenville, South Carolina, in March 1979 following Gary's arrest while robbing the Po' Folks restaurant in Gaffney. Gary was already facing a long prison sentence in that state; the purpose of the interview was to clear five unsolved armed robberies that had occurred in Columbus between April and October 1978. Gary spoke with the detectives in the presence of, and over the objections of, his attorney. He "freely spoke of his successes as regards the armed robberies, in fact was very proud of his accomplishment," Smith said on cross-examination. With that, Siemon ended the defense's case. With the jury dismissed, the remainder of the day was spent with the judge and attorneys for both sides reviewing procedures and the charge that would be given to the jury before their deliberations.

Chapter 38

The Trial—Part XII
Closing Arguments and a Verdict

With both sides having presented their cases, the time had arrived for closing arguments, an attempt for the attorneys on each side to summarize their cases, to emphasize supporting testimony or evidence, and to weave a final coherent narrative before the jury began its deliberations. Bud Siemon would speak first. There was no doubt that his position was a difficult one. Fingerprints provided positive evidence of Gary's presence at all three scenes of the crimes with which he was charged. There appeared to be a clear pattern found in the modus operandi of these crimes, which also matched others for which he was not charged. There was the eyewitness identification by Gertrude Miller. Perhaps most incriminating were Gary's own statements and admissions that while he might have participated in the burglaries of the Strangler's victims, an accomplice was responsible for the rapes and murders. His strategy of blaming these acts on someone else had been effectively unmasked by its repetitive use. It would be Siemon's task to create enough uncertainty to convince the jury that the state had not proven its case beyond a reasonable doubt, that perhaps there were other plausible explanations and/or other plausible suspects.

Speaking with passion and conviction and often raising his voice as he addressed the jury, Siemon began with his strongest argument, the confession of Jerome Livas. In that statement, Livas allegedly knew the details of the attack and rape of Gertrude Miller and the rapes and murders of Ferne Jackson and Jean Dimenstien. Siemon addressed the jurors:

> There's only two possible theories for that, ladies and gentlemen.... He was either the person who committed these crimes, or he had this information pumped into him by the police, and that the police were trying to frame him for the attack[s].... Those were the only two possible theories. One of those two things happened. Did he commit those crimes? Do you think he's the person that was able to commit those crimes? That [he] was able to get into these neighborhoods and get in and commit these horrible crimes and escape without being detected? A man that can't read or write, a man...you watched...on the stand

testifying? You can make your own evaluation of how intelligent that person was, whether or not he had the ability to commit those crimes and get away with it. Or do you think the police decided he was a good suspect? Do you think the police gave him the information that he needed, that information that we know he couldn't have gotten out of newspapers, ladies and gentlemen, because he couldn't read? Do you think that which one of these theories is more plausible? Do you believe that he committed the crimes, or do you believe that he was locked up in jail, that the evidence was molded to fit him, and that he was going to be the suspect, he was going to be the person on trial for the attack on Gertrude Miller, and the murder[s] of Mrs. Jackson and Miss Dimenstien, until the killings kept going on?

Siemon went on to compare the statements made by Gary after his arrest to Livas's confession, referring to them as "suspect" and inconsistent. In total, Gary talked to police for fifteen and a half hours, but Mike Sellers's written account "could be read in thirty minutes." "You know he was saying something," Siemon said. "He was probably telling them whatever he thought they'd like to hear so that they would turn him loose. He was probably trying to talk his way out of trouble."

In his opening statement at the beginning of the trial, Siemon described Gary as "a career criminal," going on to say, "The one thing about his crimes, though, the ones they have caught him on, the ones they've convicted him of, is that nobody's ever been hurt." He again echoed this theme in his closing argument, saying that he "wouldn't be surprised" if Carlton had in fact burglarized the Illges or Swift houses, "but there was nobody hurt in those burglaries."

The testimony of the eyewitnesses who identified Gary was "unreliable," Siemon said, expressing a belief that they saw the defendant's image on television. As to fingerprint evidence, he suggested that the police may have planted it. "Do you believe they could have planted it? I mean I know...it's hard to believe the police will do that kind of thing. It's hard to believe that police would do what they did to Jerome Livas, but they did and you know they did it. Can you find, beyond a reasonable doubt, that the same police department that didn't try to frame Jerome Livas didn't try to frame Carlton Gary?" The results of both hair and body-fluid analysis were unreliable and did not implicate the defendant, Siemon asserted.

In summary, the case against Carlton Gary was a circumstantial one, Siemon said. The only piece of possibly incriminating evidence the state possessed was Gary's fingerprints, but those could have been planted by the police. "I would suggest to you that in [this] circumstantial evidence case, that the evidence is insufficient to convict Carlton Gary." A reporter for the *Enquirer* commented that "Carlton Gary's entire defense case took less time than the prosecution's opening statement to the jury two weeks ago," about an hour and a half in all.[220]

Bill Smith began the state's closing argument by observing, "In trying cases for sixteen years, I've never seen a defense lawyer in a trial come before a jury and not say to the jury, 'Members of the jury, my client is not guilty.' Now, he did say that the state hadn't proved him guilty and how they are not going to prove him guilty and what have you, but never, in his opening statement to you or in his closing argument, did he say to you, 'Members of the jury, my client is not guilty.'" Referring to the state's evidence, Smith advised the jury that while expert testimony concluded the foreign hairs found at the scene of the crimes did not implicate Gary, neither did they exclude him. The assertion that no one had been hurt in the crimes Gary "had been convicted of or been associated with...would come as great news to Miss Nellie Farmer in Albany, New York if she were alive today," or to Jean Frost, whose watch was found in Gary's pocket after she was raped and strangled. "No one's been hurt in the crimes?" Smith asked rhetorically.

"The real thrust of the defense in this case is that the defendant was framed by the Columbus Police Department," Smith continued. If such were the case, it would mean that witnesses such as Mike Sellers, Doris Laufenberg, Gertrude Miller, and the fingerprint experts from Columbus and Atlanta "committed perjury." By extension, that would mean that the district attorney's office would be involved as well. The weight of the objective evidence excluded this possibility; "How do you fake...fingerprints?" Smith asked. Even though much of the state's case was based on circumstantial evidence, it "can be just as strong or stronger than direct evidence; often the law doesn't distinguish between them."

Smith spoke with purpose and conviction, frequently gesturing with his hands as he spoke, and often pointing at Gary when referring to the defendant. He spoke of the sadness of the Strangler's murders, citing a photograph taken at Martha Thurmond's home as an example. It was a crime scene image of her bedroom. "She's lying dead in the bed, her body covered, we now know strangled and raped, and on an eight by ten piece

of notebook paper taped to her wall, right above her bed, is 322-8811....
That is the number of the Columbus Police Department."

The greater portion of Smith's presentation focused on a systematic review of the evidence presented and how, when considered as a whole, it left little doubt that Carlton Gary was guilty of the crimes with which he was charged. Assisted by a large map of the Wynnton area and a timeline showing Gary's residence addresses, Smith pointed out the proximity and times between specific crimes and where Gary was living at the time. A large chart emphasized the commonalities between the burglaries of the Swift, Illges, and East/Sanderson homes and the attacks and/or rapes and murders of Nellie Farmer, Jean Frost, Gertrude Miller, Ferne Jackson, Jean Dimenstien, Florence Scheible, Martha Thurmond, Kathleen Woodruff, Ruth Schwob, Mildred Borom, and Janet Cofer. He reminded the jury of Gary's consistent attempts to shift blame for his crimes to an alleged accomplice such as Theopolis Joe Preston, Malvin Alamichael Crittenden, John Lee Mitchell, or Dudley Harris.

In the case of Jerome Livas, Smith pointed out that he could not have committed the three burglaries, rapes, and murders with which Carlton Gary was charged as Livas was in the county jail at the time. He continued,

> Perhaps there was some over-zealousness. Perhaps there was some improper police practices in one group of detectives inter-viewing him, and then another one when taking him [to the crime scenes] that night. But the important thing is that he wasn't charged. The system had almost failed but it worked be-cause he was never arrested. [Defense counsel Siemon] phrased it, perhaps inadvertently, but he said Jerome Livas was arrested on these charges and was in the Muscogee County jail when he was interviewed. The evidence is to the contrary; he was in the county jail for the murder of his girlfriend that he got in a fight with.

As a final point, Smith pointed out that the defense had called no alibi witnesses to explain the alleged circumstantial evidence or how or why Gary's fingerprints were found at the crime scenes of the rapes and murders with which he was charged. The jury's conviction of Gary would not rest on absolute proof, but rather proof "beyond a reasonable doubt" and "not a mere possibility that the defendant might be innocent." He requested that the jury find Gary guilty of each of the nine counts with which he was charged.

With the closing arguments completed and the jury out of the court-room for a brief recess, Siemon announced that he wished to make "several motions for a mistrial." He accused prosecutor Smith of "numerous mis-statements of fact," further alleging that such had happened "a multitude" of times in other capital cases in the Chattahoochee Judicial Circuit. Due process had been violated, Siemon said, which was grounds for a mistrial. Secondly, "for years" the court had refused to grant the defense funds to interview witnesses, thus weakening the defense's case. Finally, Siemon expressed umbrage that Smith "argued that he had never before seen a case where the defense counsel failed to tell the jury that he thought his client was not guilty of the charges." Describing it as "a totally improper argu-ment," it, too, was grounds for a mistrial. Followill denied each of Sie-mon's motions.

For most of the next hour, Judge Followill charged the jury prior to their beginning deliberations. He explained in detail the crimes with which Carlton Gary was charged. He explained that the burden of proof was on the state, and, conversely, "There is no burden of proof upon the defendant whatever." For a conviction, he continued, "the state, however, is not required to prove the guilt of the accused beyond all doubt, or to a mathematical certainty. Moral and reasonable certainty is all that can be expected in a legal investigation." He reminded the jurors that they were, "by law, the sole and exclusive judges of the credibility or the believability of the witnesses, and it is for you to determine what witness or witnesses you will believe, and those which you will not believe, if there are some you do not believe." Followill discussed evidence, and, in particular, the jury's duty to decide on the validity of circumstantial evidence. He re-minded the jury that their verdict must be unanimous.

The judge's charge completed, the jury retired to elect a foreperson and begin their deliberations. The indictments and evidence in the case were delivered to them at 4:48 P.M. Exactly one hour later at 5:48 P.M., they knocked to indicate they had reached a verdict. The foreman deliv-ered the verdict to the judge, who, after reviewing it, handed it to the clerk to read aloud. She began, "We, the jury, find the defendant guilty of the murder of Florence Gerche Scheible...," continuing that the panel had de-termined guilt in each case for the murder, rape, and burglary of Florence Scheible, Martha Thurmond, and Kathleen Woodruff. As required by law, Judge Followill polled the jury individually, confirming that the ver-dict had been reached "freely and voluntarily" and reaffirming that it re-mained each juror's verdict.

Followill directed the sheriff to take charge of the prisoner. Gary, wearing dark glasses and with a bundle of folders and papers in hand, waved at someone in the audience, giving a thumbs-up sign as he was escorted by deputies from the courtroom. He had been charged with and convicted of the capital crimes of rape and murder of three victims. Under Georgia law, in capital cases, a determination of guilt and the appropriate punishment required separate trials by the same jury. The next day, August 27th, would determine Carlton Gary's fate.

Chapter 39

The Trial—Part XIII
Punishment

With the verdicts of guilty on all counts delivered, it was now up to the jury to decide on the appropriate punishment. The panel began hearing the arguments of the prosecution and defense shortly after 10:30 A.M. the following day. Judge Followill advised the panel that both sides had a right to submit additional evidence "in aggravation or in extenuation and mitigation of the punishment to be imposed." The state announced its intention to introduce evidence of Gary's prior convictions. The defense had nothing new. Bill Smith would speak first.

The prosecutor began by reminding the jury that they were "acting as the conscience of the community." In his position, Smith was speaking for the State of Georgia, the laws of which, under very specific circumstances, allow death as a punishment for certain heinous crimes. Murder as a crime would only warrant the state seeking the death penalty if it were accompanied by aggravating circumstances, including other felonies such as rape. The presence of these other factors did not require a sentence of death; life imprisonment was another option. The final decision was that of the jury. Smith reminded the jury that during their selection in Griffin, all had said that they would be willing to consider objectively the death penalty in case of a conviction.

Factors to be taken into consideration in determining punishment would include what the jury had learned about the defendant during the trial, what they learned about his crimes, and how they felt about "the degree and certainty of the proof of his guilt." As to Gary himself, Smith said, "I think it's reasonable and logical for you to conclude that this is a person of at least average if not above average intelligence." As to Gary's character, Smith reminded the jury that the defendant's own lawyer described him as a "career criminal," pointing out that much of his adult life had been spent either in prison or on parole for his crimes. He pointed out that Gary was "prone to escape" and, when not imprisoned, engaged in a life of crime. "It means, members of the jury, that if you give him a life sentence, is it not logical to conclude that he'll try to escape again?" Smith spoke again of the violent nature of Gary's crimes, of how his victims,

Scheible, Thurmond, and Woodruff, had been "brutally beaten in addition to the rape and murder." As to degree of proof that Gary committed the three murders, Smith asked the jury to consider "the personal signature of the man in the form of his fingerprints in each of these three residences."

In arguing for the death penalty, the prosecutor spoke of "retribution"—not "revenge"—as an appropriate sentence for the nature and viciousness of crimes committed. Many would regard the imposition of such a sentence as a potential deterrence for similar future crimes. Smith asked the jury to consider, "Is a person who's been proven guilty beyond a reasonable doubt of committing the acts which resulted in the scenes depicted in those photographs capable of any kind of rehabilitation? Look at his prior history, this stack of criminal records. Is [he] capable of any kind of rehabilitation?"

In closing, Smith reminded the jury that if they chose to impose the death penalty, the responsibility for that lay not on them, but on Carlton Gary. "He imposed the death sentence on himself—assuming you do vote to impose it—when he, after burglarizing the home of Mrs. Scheible and raping Mrs. Scheible, he strangled the life out of her with one of her stockings, one of her own hose or stockings. He is responsible for his own death sentence." As his final statement, Smith called for justice, not revenge. "You don't see any family members sitting out here on the front row demanding vengeance, demanding their pound of flesh. All they want, all I ask you for on behalf of the state of Georgia, is justice."

After a break for lunch, Siemon stood before the jury. Acknowledging that members of the panel had said that they "would consider the death penalty in a case...if you felt that the facts and the circumstances of this particular case justified it," he reminded them that they also agreed to consider alternatives. "And that's what I'm up here to talk to you about this afternoon, is asking you to bring back a sentence of life imprisonment on Carlton Gary." Apparently still stung by Smith's statement in his closing argument that "he couldn't recall ever seeing a defense lawyer not tell the jury that he thought that his client was innocent," Siemon said his personal opinion did not matter. "My role is to defend my client as zealously and as adequately as I possibly can. That's what I've tried to do. And my opinions in this matter just don't count, it's your opinions that count."

Siemon referred to the standard of "reasonable doubt," assuring the jurors that they did not have to impose a death sentence "if you have any question at all whether or not he was the person that did these crimes." He referred once again to the Livas case, implying that the conduct of the police then could cast doubt on their current statements made in Gary's case. He discounted the reliability of the eyewitness testimony of Laufenberg, Nelson, and Miller, terming it "just unbelievable." The fingerprint evidence, Siemon said, was also subject to suspicion: "There are no circumstances in this case that prove when the fingerprints were left." Gary was a burglar, he admitted, saying, "We don't know whether there are other houses in the Wynnton neighborhood where murders, where killings didn't occur, that may or may not have Carlton Gary's fingerprints in them." As with fingerprints, Siemon discounted the significance of the "blood evidence," stating there was "a very real possibility" it could exclude Gary, a conjecture that appeared to be in contrast to trial testimony. He discounted the hair evidence as well since no match was made with samples taken from his client.

Changing tone somewhat, Siemon began to use the word "kill" when referring to the death penalty, as in, "I would urge you not to kill Carlton Gary because of these armed robberies and the fact that he's pointed guns at people before, because he hasn't killed anybody." Stating "We all feel sorry for the families of the victims," he then asked the jurors to "consider Carlton Gary's family, too," referring to them as "innocent victims." "If you vote to kill him, those people are going to suffer."

The final portion of Siemon's argument took on a religious tone, quoting the biblical commandment of "Thou shalt not kill." He quoted Jesus's admonition to "turn the other cheek,"[*] and after equating Smith's reference to retribution with revenge, he reminded jurors that vengeance belongs to the Lord.[†] He spoke of God's power "to cleanse all manner of sin and sickness," implying that Gary "is not beyond the power of some rehabilitation." He spoke of Jesus and Judgment Day, suggesting that a death sentence for Gary would violate biblical directives. At the end, Siemon referred to Bill Smith's request for "justice," asking instead for "mercy" on behalf of Carlton Gary.

Following the closing arguments, Judge Followill charged the jurors, reviewing with them the standards and procedures they must follow in arriving at a sentence for the accused. Deliberations began at 3:04 P.M. At 6:05 P.M., the foreman sent word that the panel had reached a verdict. Back in the courtroom, the written verdict was passed to the judge, who

---

[*] Matthew 5:38–39 (KJV).

[†] Romans 12:19: "Dearly beloved, avenge not yourselves, but rather give place unto wrath: for it is written, Vengeance is mine; I will repay, saith the Lord" (KJV).

approved it, then handed it to the clerk to read. In each of the three cases of murder, the jury recommended the death penalty. As required, the judge polled the jurors, each of whom affirmed the verdict.

Turning toward the defense table, Judge Followill asked the deputies to bring Gary in front of the bench. Gary rose, dressed this time in prison garb, a distinctive change from the suit and tie he had worn daily since the second day of the trial. "I am about to pass a sentence on you Mr. Gary. Is there anything that you wish to say?"

A reporter for the *Columbus Enquirer* described the scene:

The words in the death sentence were emotionless, but the strained expressions on the faces of the jury told a different story. Some looked away. Some held hands to their lips. Some were seeing through reddened eyes. This nine-man, three-woman panel was sentencing Carlton Gary to die.

When Clerk Johnny Womack had announced the death penalty Wednesday evening on each of the three counts of murder, Judge Kenneth Followill ordered Gary brought forward to the bench. Surrounded by officers, Gary stood there—hands on either hip, his mouth chewing gum at an uneven clip—while the judge repeated the sentences.

Gary shifted from one foot to the other as the judge said the convicted Stocking Strangler, "shall be electrocuted no sooner than noon on the 3rd of October and no later than noon on the 10th of October...." Gary opened his mouth as if to speak but declined comment when asked if he had anything to say. He left with a smile and a wave to family members seated on the third row behind the defense table.[221]

It should have been, as a reporter described it when paraphrasing a comment by the sister-in-law of one of the Strangler's victims, "A period at the end of a long sentence."[222] Instead, it would be the beginning of yet another phase in the saga, a period that would last some thirty-two years.

The body of Mary "Ferne" Jackson, a fifty-nine-year-old widow and
Director of Education for the Columbus Health Department, was
discovered on the morning of September 16, 1977. At the time, she was
the Strangler's first known murder victim. *Courtesy of Tim Chitwood*

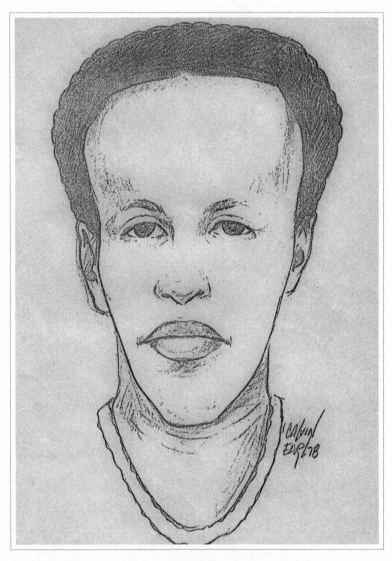

Gertrude Miller was attacked and left for dead by the Strangler, but survived and was later able to testify in court. Her eyewitness description of her assailant to a police sketch artist produced this drawing which was widely circulated by police.
Courtesy of Mike Sellers

Kathleen Woodruff, the seventy-four-year-old widow of famed University of Georgia coach and industrialist George Woodruff, was strangled with a scarf emblazoned with the University of Georgia seal. *Evidence photo from 1986 trial*

William Henry Hance, a serial killer and soldier stationed at
Columbus's Fort Benning, attempted to cover his crimes by attributing
them to the Forces of Evil, a non-existent white-supremacist group
allegedly active in the city during the time of the Strangler's murders.
Courtesy of William Winn

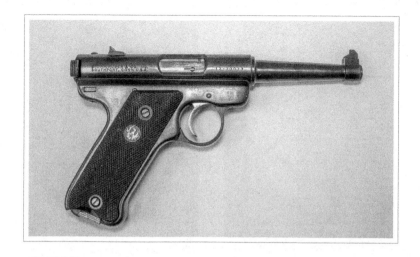

```
04/11/84 10:29 COLT 0000 NLET 0122
AM.GA1060100
08:31 04/11/84 01092
08:31 04/11/84 01197 GA
TXT (AP,GA1060100)
REQUEST NATIONAL BROADCAST


REQUEST FOR NATION WIDE BROADCAST

FROM: COLUMBUS POLICE DEPT, BUREAU OF
INVESTIGATIVE SERVICES, COLUMBUS, GEORGIA

REQUEST ANY INFORMATION ON DEPT THAT HAS
SUPPOSEDLY RECOVERED A STOLEN RUGER 22 CAL
SEMI-AUTO PISTOL WITH SERIAL NUMBER 13-70073.
PISTOL WAS STOLEN FROM COLUMBUS, GA AND INVOLVED
IN HOMICIDE CASE. OWNER REPORTS BEING CONTACTED
BY AN UNKNOWN POLICE DEPT. IF YOU HAVE RECOVERED
SAID WEAPON PLEASE NOTIFY COLUMBUS GEORGIA POLICE
DEPT, GA.1060100.

AUTH/SGT M SELLERS                          OPR/DM
```

In early April 1984, Henry Sanderson, whose pistol (above) had been stolen in 1977, called to ask about the missing gun. Years earlier, Columbus police had searched for the weapon, thinking it might have a connection to the Strangler case. In response to Sanderson's call, a new inquiry searching for the gun was sent out to law enforcement agencies nationwide. This began a chain of events that led to Carlton Gary's capture in May 1984. *Courtesy of Mike Sellers*

Florence Scheible　　　　　　　Martha Thurmond

Kathleen Woodruff

The seven women whose deaths were attributed to the Strangler between September 1977 and April 1978 all lived in a relatively small area of the city of Columbus. *Courtesy of Julia Slater*

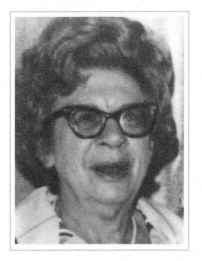

Jean Dimenstein

Mildred Borom

Ferne Jackson

Janet Cofer

Columbus Police Department

P.O. Box 1866 • 937 First Avenue
Columbus, Georgia 31994 - 3699
(404) 324-0211

INFORMATION CONCERNING: CARLTON GARY B/M

ALIAS':   MICHAEL DAVID, MICHAEL DAVIS, CARL MICHAELS, CARLTON MICHAELS,
               MICKEY DAVIS, MICKEY DAVID.

PHYSICAL DESCRIPTION: BLACK MALE 6'1½" tall, 193 pounds, Medium Complexion,
                        Medium build.

DATES OF BIRTH USED: 9-24-50, 11-24-49, 4-30-58,

SOCIAL SECURITY NUMBERS USED: 112-54-8264, 264-93-8460

IMPORTANT ADDRESSES: MOTHER'S ADDRESSES: FORMER: 2824 COLORADO ST.
        MOTHER'S NAME: CAROLYN DAVID;   PRESENT: 2909 BUENA VISTA RD.

        SISTER: MIRIAM WHITE   PRESENT: 2909 BUENA VISTA RD.

        COUSIN: BELETHA TURNER   PRESENT: 4647 ILLINI DRIVE

        COUSIN: SHASTA THOMAS   PRESENT: 4647 ILLINI DRIVE

        COUSIN: CHRISTINE GARY   PRESENT: 921 LAWYERS LANE APT # 3.

        COUSIN: DELLA GRAY   PRESENT: 921 LAWYERS LANE APT # 3.

    *CARLTON GARY'S ADDRESS BEFORE GOING TO PRISON IN 1979: 5357 SPENCER LANE.

CARLTON GARY IS <u>ARMED</u> AND <u>EXTREMELY DANGEROUS</u>, <u>WILL RESIST ARREST</u>.

    VEHICLES USED IN LAST 4 WEEKS:

    1983 FORD LTD BURGANDY IN COLOR BEARING ALA. TAG 43F-6852.
    LATE MODEL TOYOTA BLUE IN COLOR BEARING GA TAG BYJ 926 (AUGUSTA, GA.)
    LATE MODEL VAN BLUE IN COLOR TAG NUMBER UNKNOWN (PROBABLY GA. TAG)
    Yellow or Beige Volvo

                                THIS MEMO EFFECTIVE AS OF: 4-30-84.

The search for the missing pistol eventually led investigators back to Columbus and a connection to Carlton Gary, at the time a South Carolina prison escapee. He was identified as a suspect in the Strangler murders when his fingerprints from prison files matched latent prints found at several Strangler murder scenes. *Courtesy of Mike Sellers*

Carlton Gary used a number of aliases during his criminal career. After he was identified as a likely suspect in the Strangler killings, he became the focus of an intense manhunt. On April 18, 1984, Gary was arrested in Columbus on a minor drug charge but carried no identification and gave his name as Michael Anthony David. He was released on a cash bond and promptly disappeared. *Courtesy of Mike Sellers*

Carlton Gary is escorted into Columbus Police Headquarters by Detective Michael Sellers following Gary's arrest in Albany, Georgia, on May 3, 1984. Media representatives and photographers were waiting for a first glimpse of the accused "Stocking Strangler."
Courtesy of Mike Sellers

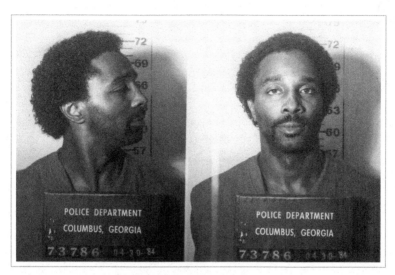

Carlton Gary was arrested at a Holiday Inn in Albany, Georgia, on May 3, 1984 and returned to Columbus that same evening. This is his initial mugshot. Note that the date of "4-30-84" is in error.
Courtesy of Julia Slater

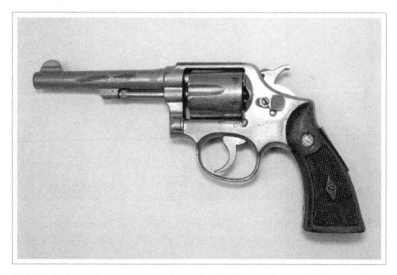

When Carlton Gary was arrested in an Albany, Georgia, Holiday Inn, he had with him a chrome-plated .38 caliber revolver with its serial number ground off located just out of reach on a small stand between the beds in his room. *Evidence photo from 1986 trial*

In late December 1985 during the pre-trial phase of his detention, it was discovered that Carlton Gary was in the process of attempting to escape from the Muscogee County jail. Concealed behind cardboard taped above his sink, he had managed to surreptitiously open a hole in the wall of his cell. Afterwards he was moved to more secure quarters and placed under closer observation. *Evidence photo from 1986 trial*

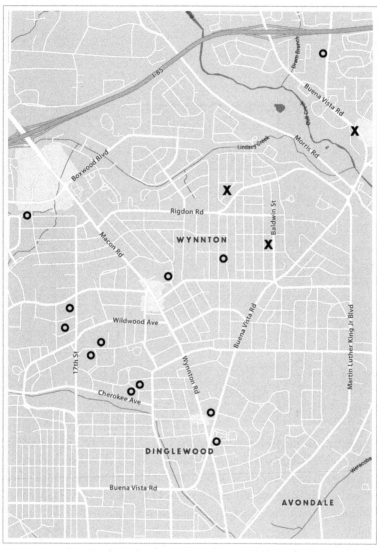

The Strangler's crimes were limited to a relatively small area of the city of Columbus, Georgia. During the September 1977 through April 1978 crime spree, Carlton Gary lived in or near the neighborhoods of the victims, an important commonality pointed out at his trial. Crime scenes are noted with O's and Gary's residences with X's.

Courtesy of Jim Burt; ©Google Maps

	ATTEMPTED / FORCED ENTRY	RAPE	MURDER OR ATTEMPTED MURDER	MURDER VICTIM COVERED	METHOD OF ATTACK STRANGULATION	LOCALE (WYNNTON AREA)	CLOSE PROXIMITY OF CRIMES & GARY'S RESIDENCES	GARY ADMITTING PRESENCE
FARMER (4-24-70)	X	X	X	X	X		X	X
FROST (1-3-77)	X	X	X		X		X	X
MILLER (9-11-77)	X	X	X		X	X	X	
JACKSON (9-16-77)	X	X	X	X	X	X	X	
DIMENSTEIN (9-25-77)	X	X	X	X	X	X	X	X
EAST (10-8-77)	X					X	X	X
SCHEIBLE (10-21-77)		X	X	X	X	X	X	X
THURMOND (10-25-77)	X	X	X	X	X	X	X	X
SWIFT (12-20-77)	X					X	X	X
WOODRUFF (12-28-77)	X	X	X	X	X	X	X	X
ILLGES (1-1-78)	X					X	X	X
ILLGES (2-11-78)	X					X	X	X
SCHWOB (2-11-78)	X		X		X	X	X	X
BOROM (2-12-78)	X	X	X	X	X	X	X	X
COFER (4-20-78)	X	X	X	X	X		X	X

The victims of the Columbus Stocking Strangler and the manner and details of their deaths had many similarities. Although Carlton Gary was charged with only three of the murders and associated crimes, others for which he was the prime suspect but not charged displayed a common pattern with them. *Courtesy of Julia Slater*

	STATEMENT	STATEMENT NAMES CO-CONSPIRATOR	STATEMENT BLAMES VIOLENCE ON CO-CONSPIRATOR
FARMER (4-14-70)	X	X	X
FROST (1-3-77)	X	X	X
MILLER (9-11-77)			
JACKSON (9-16-77)			
DIMENSTEIN (9-25-77)	X	X	X
EAST (10-8-77)	X	X	
SCHEIBLE (10-21-77)	X	X	X
THURMOND (10-25-77)	X	X	X
SWIFT (12-20-77)	X	X	
WOODRUFF (12-28-77)	X	X	X
ILLGES (1-1-78)	X	X	
ILLGES (2-11-78)	X	X	
SCHWOB (2-11-78)	X	X	X
BOROM (2-12-78)	X	X	X
COFER (4-20-78)	X	X	X

During his criminal career, when apprehended or charged with a crime, Carlton Gary commonly attempted to shift the blame to an accomplice or co-conspirator. *Courtesy of Julia Slater*

William J. Smith was the district attorney in charge of prosecuting Carlton Gary's murder case. He later served as a Superior Court judge. *Courtesy of Judge William J. Smith*

August F. ("Bud") Siemon was Carlton Gary's lead attorney from August 1984 through his conviction and initial appeals of Gary's case. *Courtesy of Judge William J. Smith*

The prosecution team in August 1986 following Carlton Gary's conviction. In the foreground, seated, from left to right: Ricky Boren, Doug Pullen, Charlie Rowe. Standing from left to right: Lem Miller, Al Miller, Bill Smith, Jim Warren, Mike Sellers.
Courtesy of Judge William J. Smith

Carlton Gary's scheduled execution on December 16, 2009 was cancelled at the last minute by the Georgia Supreme Court in order to pursue DNA testing not available at the time of his conviction nearly twenty-three years earlier. The newspaper headlines are from the 16th and 17th of the month respectively.

Part III

Thirty-Two Years

Chapter 40

Reaction

No one realistically expected Carlton Gary's death sentence to be carried out in October 1986, some six-odd weeks after his conviction. In Georgia, appeals were mandatory in all such cases. Among those familiar with the process, the consensus for the date was several years at the earliest, but only then if his conviction and sentencing were upheld, uncertain possibilities at best.

Almost immediately after the sentencing, reporters fanned out seeking comments and opinions about the trial and its outcome. Reactions varied widely. Gary's family members who attended the trial appeared to react with both sorrow and anger. On the other side, the stepdaughter of one of the Strangler's victims responded by saying, "I feel like it's a real personal question and I have no comment." Another relative, the grandson of a victim, said, "I'm relieved that it's over, firstly, and that he's caught, for the sake of everybody else. Now you can, more or less, continue with your life and hope the rest works out good."[223] Members of the jury, tracked down after their return to Griffin and Spalding County, were "tight-lipped." One juror, interviewed as he stood outside his business, said, "No comment. We just decided we would leave it all behind at court."[224]

Former police chief Curtis McClung expressed his approval. "I was very pleased to see the jury reach a guilty verdict. It was clear he was guilty, and I'm pleased to see the case finally draw to a close. Fingerprints at the scene of the crime are awfully difficult to explain away." He described Siemon's contention that police may have planted the fingerprints as "ridiculous," commenting that the appeals "will go on for years." The Rev. Arthur Threatt, who attended the trial on behalf of a group of African Methodist Episcopal churches, said, "I expected him to be found guilty. I thought they would have deliberated a little longer."[225]

As might be expected, Bruce Harvey and Gary Parker, Bud Siemon's former co-counsels, felt the trial should have turned out differently. "I am not surprised, given the lack of resources the defense had," Harvey said, declaring that without court-supplied funding "it was impossible to prepare an adequate defense or challenge evidence presented by the prosecution." More directly, "There is very little real evidence to convict him of the crimes of murder," he asserted. Gary Parker thought "the fact that the jury deliberated only an hour suggests that its members were weary. I think these folks are away from home and are ready to go home." Appeals were certain, both agreed.[226] Anticipating such actions, Siemon's comments to reporters were more muted: "It's our contention that the state did not present an overwhelming case."[227]

Bill Smith and his team from the Office of the District Attorney were clearly pleased. The *Ledger*'s reporter described the scene as Smith spoke to the press:

"We were trying this case for the people of Columbus and Muscogee County," [Smith] said in a crowded news conference after the sentence had been pronounced. "Maybe it was an added burden I carried myself, but I wanted to prove—beyond a shadow of a doubt—to black and white, men and women, young and old, that this was the man. I think a one-hour verdict and this sentence should answer any questions."

That atmosphere is also why Smith revealed that the State had turned down last May a defense offer to plea bargain. Defense attorney August "Bud" Siemon had offered a guilty plea in exchange for a life sentence. "If anybody deserved the death penalty it was this man," Smith said. Around Smith were the men credited with putting together his case: First Assistant District Attorney Doug Pullen, District Attorney Investigator Al Miller, and Columbus Police Officers Mike Sellers, Ricky Boren and Charlie Rowe.[228]

With the immediacy of the trial and sentencing fading rapidly into the past, the following weeks saw a series of thoughtful literary postmortems of the events that had taken place over the preceding nine years. A long, unsigned editorial in the *Ledger-Enquirer* on the weekend after the trial spoke of the fear the Strangler had caused: "For the women he attacked and their families, Gary forever changed reality in ghastly and permanent ways. But he also succeeded in irreversibly altering the community, and his baleful influence reached into the lives of people whose names he will never know." The author spoke of the episode's damage to race relations in Columbus, citing the attempt by the Ku Klux Klan to inject themselves into the search. The reputation of the police force suffered as well, despite massive efforts to apprehend the killer. For the city at large, the outcome was not a positive one: "Columbus had the unhappy experience of being in the national spotlight, not for any of the reasons residents like to think make the city special, but because seven women had been brutally slain here. The stories out-of-town reporters went back and wrote ranged from discerning and sensitive to downright awful." On a positive note, "The trial has also been an ordeal for the community, but in a sense it has also been a release. There is an almost palpable feeling that something has been put behind us."[229]

In the same issue, an opinion piece by Tom Kunkel, the executive editor of the *Ledger-Enquirer* newspapers, bemoaned the trial's lasting damage to racial harmony. Carlton Gary had become a symbol, Kunkel wrote.

> His imprisonment and trial became a collection point for long-simmering resentment of all kinds toward the white establishment.... I imagine that ultimately, the number of blacks who honestly felt Gary was an innocent scapegoat probably diminished as the evidence in these specific crimes, and of his career as a professional criminal, accumulated. Yet for some, I believe the sense nagged that Gary's conviction and arrest were stage-managed by a white-run police department, court and, yes, the press, in order to write a final chapter in this most unpleasant story. These blacks—those who believe in their souls that Carlton Gary was used—will harbor resentment toward white Columbus for a long time. And yet those blacks who believe he was in fact guilty of the heinous crimes he was accused of will feel equally betrayed—by a man who had so much talent, and yet fell so far. For many years to come, then, Carlton Gary will have divided black and black, and black and white. Such will be the most longstanding, and most pernicious, legacy of the Stocking Stranglings.

In a letter to the editor, a black man, Walter E. Gould, who stated that he had attended Gary's trial daily, expressed doubt about Gary's guilt and questioned the honesty of the police and prosecution in the case. He suggested that racial bias was possible and that "the death penalty is for blacks only, since they make up a majority of the ones on death row from Columbus. It seems that everyone else can cop a plea and receive a life sentence."[230] Responding to Gould, James H. Cannington wrote that he "read with disgust" Gould's "bleeding heart letter." "His statement that the death penalty is for blacks only is an outrage and an affront to every decent, law-abiding citizen everywhere. It simply isn't true, and to make such a statement is irresponsible and a disservice."[231] Such disparities of opinion seemed unlikely to fade quickly.

On Wednesday, September 3rd, a week after his sentencing, Gary was transferred by Sheriff Gene Hodge and two deputies to the Georgia Diagnostic and Classification Center in Jackson, Georgia, the site of the state's death row and executions. "It was a quiet ride," Hodge said.[232]

Rushing to meet a thirty-day deadline, on September 25th Bud Siemon filed a two-page document with the Muscogee County Superior Court Clerk's Office requesting a new trial for Carlton Gary on the grounds that the verdicts were "contrary to law," "contrary to the evidence presented," and "strongly against the weight of the evidence." The hearing date was set for October 8th. The hearing before Judge Followill, which lasted about forty-five minutes, began with Siemon stating he was not ready to proceed, alleging that he had not been given copies of the trial transcripts and other required documents. Speaking firmly, Followill replied that Siemon had indeed been provided with all the required documents, and given the fact that Gary was sentenced to death, an appeal was already mandatory under Georgia court rules. Siemon's motion was denied. Prosecutor Bill Smith was quoted as saying Siemon's complaints were "another attempt to delay...first the trial and now the appeal."[233]

Early November found the clerks in the office of the Muscogee County Superior Court packing nearly two and a half years of records spanning the period from Gary's arrest in May 1984 through his appeal for a new trial before Judge Followill a few weeks earlier. The records, including a stack of trial and hearing transcripts some six feet in height, were to be sent to the Georgia Supreme Court for formal review as part of the appeal process.[234] In the meanwhile, Gary remained on death row at the state prison in Jackson.

Chapter 41

Appeals and Appeals and...

From the perspective of the legal system, Carlton Gary's conviction and sentencing were *faits accomplis*. While subject to review and challenge, it would be necessary to show some grievous error to undo them. During the trial every effort was made to shield the jury from outside influence through their sequestration and the banning of news and media reports. The judge had imposed a gag order on the attorneys and other court officials. With the verdict now in place, these restrictions were lifted, at least in theory. As appeals were certain and their judgment and actions would be under attack, on a practical basis, the judge, prosecutors, and members of law enforcement who had a role in Gary's apprehension and trial were limited in what they could say. Any comment, however benign, might be seized upon as evidence of preexisting bias. Gary's defenders on the other hand, both those who believed in his innocence and those hired or appointed to challenge the outcome of the trial, were free to speak their minds. And they did so. As the appeals process took shape, the weeks and months following the end of the trial saw allegations offered as facts, half-truths presented without contradiction, and suggestions of dark conspiracies among those responsible for Gary's arrest, conviction, and sentencing.

The struggle that would now take place had moved to a more public arena, with decisions to be made by judges and members of the parole board. While held to a high standard of objectivity, such individuals were human as well, and often owed their positions to contested elections or politically inspired appointment. They were free to read newspaper commentary and editorials, listen to broadcast media, and receive letters and other communications from those with a vested interest in the outcome of Gary's appeals. In short, there was a possibility, however remote, that their decisions could be influenced. With Gary facing a sentence of death, there was nothing to be lost—and perhaps much to be gained—in trying.

Two days before Christmas, Bud Siemon filed a twenty-nine-page brief with the Georgia Supreme Court requesting a new trial for Carlton Gary. The twenty "enumerations of error" alleged included the lack of state funding that prevented the defense from hiring expert witnesses and "made it impossible to introduce mitigating evidence in the death-penalty phase of the trial." "The total absence of any assistance given the complexity of the case made it impossible to construct any meaningful defense," the brief stated. Gary's twenty-six months of solitary confinement violated his rights. He was "tried while he was mentally incompetent." Jury selection was characterized by "overt racial tactics" on the part of the prosecution and judge. There were significant differences in the racial makeup of the jury pools in Muscogee County and those in Spalding County from which jurors were chosen. The state responded to Siemon's allegations with a 119-page brief, setting the stage for a hearing before the court.[235]

The Georgia Supreme Court heard arguments on January 21, 1987. Once again, Siemon spoke for the defense and Bill Smith for the state before six justices. Referring to the criminal justice system as "trial by combat," Siemon said that it is presumed "that both sides have fair access to the necessary tools that it takes to go into the arena." The lack of state-provided funds prevented this. Smith argued that the state had fulfilled its obligations, that the scientific evidence presented was neither novel nor controversial, and that the defense had the opportunity to interview the state's witnesses before trial. The conditions of Gary's confinement were dictated by security and his history of escapes. His cell was "as comfortable as possible without sacrificing the very real need for prison security." With regard to the racial makeup of the jury pools, there was only a 6.3 percent difference in the black/white ratio of Muscogee and Spalding Counties, well within the court's guidelines.[236] It would be several months before the Supreme Court issued its ruling.

In the meantime, Gary sought and received permission from a federal judge to file civil suits for damages against the Columbus newspapers and the Muscogee County jail. Judge Robert Elliot refused, however, to assign a federally paid attorney to represent Gary in the suits. In early April, Gary sued Muscogee County sheriff Gene Hodge and chief jailer Richard Miles, listing "dozens of complaints." These included denying visits from his children, allowing him to be "viewed by female jail personnel while performing private bodily functions," being kept in a "dimly lit cell" with "unsanitary conditions" for more than a year, etc. He sought payments of $1.5 million from each man. In a separate suit demanding $2 million each from the *Columbus Ledger-Enquirer* newspapers and reporter Richard Hyatt, Gary alleged that Hyatt's April 13, 1986, profile violated his "personal zone of privacy," sought to deprive him of his right to a fair trial, and exposed him to "hatred, shame, obloquy, degradation, disgrace and to induce evil opinions."[237,238]

In June, the Georgia Supreme Court ruled, sending Gary's case back to the Muscogee County Superior Court with two instructions: a new "competent counsel" was to be appointed to represent the defendant, and a hearing held "which shall be conducted to determine if for any reason, including lack of funds, the defendant failed to receive effective assistance of counsel." If the latter were found to be true, a new trial would be granted. Otherwise, the court would consider what further actions, if necessary, should be taken. As Judge Kenneth Followill would appoint the new counsel and preside over the hearing, over the following days Bud Siemon filed motions objecting to the appointment of another attorney and asking (once again) for Judge Followill's removal from the case alleging bias and a lack of "fitness to judge." Both demands were rejected. In mid-August, Followill appointed local attorney H. Haywood Turner III to represent Gary, citing his experience in defending indigent clients charged with serious crimes. A hearing scheduled for September was put off until November 16th to allow time for Turner to familiarize himself with Gary's complex case. Siemon was instructed to turn over his transcripts and related files to Turner, who would be assisted by a second court-appointed attorney, Peter Hoffman.

The appointment of a new attorney for Gary set off a dispute as to who would be allowed to represent him. Bud Siemon insisted that he was Gary's counsel and should be allowed to represent his interest even in a hearing where his performance in defending his client was being examined. Siemon questioned Turner's competency and, citing attorney-client privilege, refused to turn over the trial and hearing transcripts as directed by Followill. Instead, Siemon suggested that Turner get the clerk of court to copy the thousands of pages of documents for him. Furthermore, Siemon said, he no longer had the documents, having turned them over to Atlanta attorney Frank L. Derrickson, who would represent Gary in the upcoming hearing.[239] When threatened with contempt of court and a possible fine or jail time, Siemon reluctantly delivered the transcripts to the court on the afternoon of November 6th, just five minutes before the court-appointed deadline to do so. The issues were heard in a hearing on November 12th.[240]

Siemon pleaded that he should remain as Gary's co-counsel with Derrickson, a conflict pointed out by Assistant District Attorney Doug Pullen, who responded for the state. Followill removed Siemon from the case and ordered him to leave the courtroom. Derrickson "immediately questioned Turner's competency and honesty by accusing him of fraud and perjury." Placed on the witness stand, Turner denied the accusations. Followill denied motions for a hearing on racial bias in jury selection, a further request for funds, and a request "for a hearing on defense claims that District Attorney Bill Smith practices racial discrimination by seeking to impose the death penalty exclusively on poor black defendants."[241]

The hearing resumed on Monday, November 16th. Followill, disputing Derrickson's contention that Haywood Turner was "using Gary's case to learn about capital punishment defense," ruled that Turner, Hoffman, and Derrickson would have to work together to defend Gary. Siemon was called to testify as to the issue of adequacy of Gary's defense, but Gary refused to waive attorney-client privilege, effectively barring Siemon from testifying on the issue. Doug Pullen commented that Gary "cannot have it both ways, saying 'My counsel was ineffective but I'm going to muzzle my counsel.'" Followill gave attorneys twenty-five days to submits briefs on the issue of the adequacy of counsel in Gary's August 1986 trial, now nearly fifteen months in the past. He would review the testimony and evidence and would submit his ruling at a later date.[242]

Weeks passed. In early January 1988, Frank Derrickson submitted another series of motions to the court. He requested funds in support of Gary's defense. He asked for hearings on the previous denial of funds as well as "racial factors" that led to his client's conviction. Once again, he called for Judge Followill to remove himself from the case. Followill denied the requests. For more than a year, news of the case disappeared from the headlines.[243]

On June 12, 1989, nearly two years after the Georgia Supreme Court referred the case back to the Muscogee County Superior Court, Judge Followill issued his long-awaited ruling on the "effectiveness of the assistance rendered the defendant by his counsel." Followill's twenty-nine-page order was detailed and thorough, pointing out that "the Supreme Court had directed the trial court to determine if 'for any reason, including lack of funds, the defendant failed to receive effective assistance of counsel.'" Followill emphasized the word "any." The third anniversary of Carlton Gary's trial, conviction, and sentencing was only months away. It was evident that the judge wanted to bring closure for these issues—if such were possible—and obvious that he was sensitive to the long delay in the production of his order. He wrote,

> Should it seem that the trial court has taken a great deal of time
> in rendering its decision on this not-so-limited issue, it should

be noted that it was ordered to decide the effectiveness issue from <u>any</u> standpoint, not solely as to the funding question. This involved a re-examination of the entire record which the Supreme Court has before it, consisting of literally dozens of oral and written motions supported by hundreds of pages of briefs and followed by rulings thereon, more than thirteen thousand pages of transcripts contained in sixty or more volumes representing approximately twelve forty-hour weeks of in-court time, and additional countless legal pads filled with the trial judge's own notes on every facet of the proceedings and his independent research conducted without the benefit of a law assistant. No doubt the Supreme Court will agree that a case of this magnitude demands an excess of care and an abundance of deliberation.

As his operating premises, Followill focused on two areas, the "possibility of ineffective assistance of counsel based on a lack of funding," and the same "arising from any other source or from conduct of the defendant's trial counsel." In an orderly and carefully reasoned manner, he found that Gary's attorney had adequate opportunity to investigate the state's evidence, interview experts in the fields of blood and body fluids, fingerprint and hair analysis, and mental issues. "This court is convinced and finds as a matter of fact," Followill wrote, "that this defendant willfully, purposefully and knowingly attempted and did successfully evade appropriate testing by state mental health experts. His condition from a mental standpoint never rose to the level of a significant issue in the trial of the case." As to funding issues, Followill found that "the defendant has completely and totally failed to demonstrate any harm or prejudice to him to any degree." Addressing the issue of ineffective counsel, the judge wrote,

> It is now apparent that the course of conduct of the defendant's trial counsel throughout as carefully observed by this court was a deliberately planned attempt to create an impression of ineffective assistance, laying the blame solely upon the court's failure to provide funding, and to pave the way for that issue to be raised by way of appeal and habeas corpus. There is no doubt that such course received Carlton Gary's full acquiescence.

In an at-times contentious hearing before the Georgia Supreme Court on September 12, 1989, defense attorneys Bud Siemon and Frank Derrickson accused Judge Followill and prosecutor Smith of "rigging" the case against Carlton Gary by "consistently withholding the money they needed to prepare a defense." Doug Pullen*, arguing for the state, echoed Followill's contention that the defense's allegations were a deliberate strategy to force a new trial. "These lawyers are experienced capital-case litigants who know what they are doing. The defendant is an intelligent man who knows what he's doing," Pullen said. A ruling from the court was said to be expected in a matter of months.[244]

On March 6, 1990, the Georgia Supreme Court issued a final ruling in the case of *Gary v. State*. After addressing each of the major issues that had been raised in posttrial appeals, six justices of the court unanimously found that "after reviewing the record, including the proceedings on remand, we conclude that the sentences of death were not imposed under the influence of passion, prejudice, or other arbitrary factor. The sentences of death are not excessive or disproportionate to sentences imposed in similar cases, considering both the crime and the defendant." The court refused a motion to reconsider its decision later in the month.

On October 1, 1990, the United States Supreme Court refused to review Carlton Gary's conviction and sentencing, thus confirming the decisions of the lower courts.[†] The appeals would continue as Gary remained on death row.

---

* District Attorney and Prosecutor Bill Smith announced in January 1988 that he would run for the office of superior court judge in the Chattahoochee County Judicial Circuit. He won the election handily and took office in January 1989. Douglas Pullen was then elected to the position of district attorney at that time, a position he would hold until 1995.

† The proper term is that the US Supreme Court "refused to grant a writ of certiorari." This is an order to the lower court(s) to send the record of the case to the Supreme Court for review, most commonly when the issues on which the appeal is based have constitutional significance.

Chapter 42

Semen and a Bite Mold

The US Supreme Court's rejection of Gary's case notwithstanding, in 1991 he filed, via a new set of attorneys, a habeas corpus petition in Butts County Superior Court against Albert Thomas, the warden of the Georgia Diagnostic and Classification Center prison where he remained on death row. Gary's defense team was now led by Algenon Marbley, who at the time was in private practice with a law firm in Columbus, Ohio.* A commentary in the *Atlanta Journal-Constitution* noted that for many reasons, including both those of reputation and lack of financial reward, few attorneys wanted to undertake death row appeal cases.

> The search for a lawyer for Gary went statewide, but from Savannah to Atlanta to Augusta, the reply was the same: no Georgia attorney would represent the man known as the "Columbus Strangler." "Every lawyer I called said the case was too high profile, that clients would fire them if they agreed to represent Mr. Gary," says Mike Mears, director of the Multi-County Public Defenders Office, an agency funded by the State Bar Association that defends capital cases at the trial stage.† "Here's a guy who was facing death and the only chance he has is a good

---

* Algenon L. Marbley, an African American attorney originally from North Carolina, was nominated for a federal judgeship by President Bill Clinton in 1997 and confirmed for that position by the US Senate that same year. As of 2021 he is chief judge of the United States District Court for the Southern District of Ohio. From this point forward in Gary's appeals, representation of the state's case transitioned from the local district attorney to the office of the Georgia State Attorney General represented by Senior Assistant Attorney General Susan Boleyn.

† In a strange twist, Michael Mears, who was mayor of the Georgia city of Decatur from 1985 to 1993, and described as "a leading death penalty defense lawyer," arranged to have artwork from five of Georgia's death row inmates displayed at the Decatur Arts Festival in May 1992. According to the *Atlanta Journal-Constitution* (5 May 1992), "Carlton Gary, also known as the 'Stocking Strangler' after being convicted of the burglary, rape and murder of three elderly Columbus women in 1977–78, will have paintings for sale. Gary is responsible for the mural hanging in the visitor's room of the state prison, Mr. Mears said."

attorney, and not one Georgia lawyer stepped forward. It's downright embarrassing to the legal profession," says Mears.[245]

During an initial hearing before Judge Daniel Coursey of the Dekalb County Superior Court, Gary's attorneys "submitted numerous affidavits and other documents, totaling ninety-three exhibits, in support of his claims." In this and a series of subsequent hearings, Judge Kenneth Followill, former prosecutor and then-judge Bill Smith, and Gary's former defense attorney Frank Derrickson were called to testify for the state. In January and March of 1993, the court narrowed the myriad of claims to five: that the prosecution did not turn over exculpatory material to the defense, that the court's denial of funds deprived Gary his due process rights, that Derrickson gave ineffective counsel on Gary's appeal, that Georgia's Unified Appeal Procedure[‡] also violated Gary's due process rights, and that the death penalty represented "cruel and unusual punishment." In a brief summary, Judge Coursey denied Gary's claims on November 13, 1995. Gary applied to the Georgia Supreme Court for a certificate of probable cause to appeal. The court denied his application; subsequently, Gary's petition for a writ of certiorari with the United States Supreme Court was denied on May 27, 1997.

In November 1997, Gary's new court-appointed attorneys filed a new habeas corpus petition in US District Court for the Middle District of Georgia.[§] Under lead attorney John R. ("Jack") Martin, the twenty-nine claims were similar to those filed in the state courts system. This appeal would consume most of the next seven years. In a number of hearings that followed, two matters became prominent, the issue of serologic testing, and a dental mold made of Carlton Gary's teeth in reference to the murder of Janet Cofer. In March 2000, Gary's attorneys requested and received funds to hire a forensic serologist to review and analyze the notes and work papers of John G. Wegel, the state crime-laboratory serologist who had testified about Gary's secretor/non-secretor status at his 1986 trial. In a November 2000 hearing, Wegel testified that the donor of the semen specimens he examined was from a weak or non-secretor. Roger Morrison, the defense's newly hired expert, testified that based on examination of

---

‡ The Unified Appeal Procedure is a set of rules under Georgia law that lists the requirements for appeals in death penalty cases. It is designed to ensure that all appropriate legal issues are examined and that errors are minimized during the appeals process.
§ *Gary v. Schofield*, 336 F. Supp. 2d 1337.

Gary's sputum, he was a normal secretor. In rebuttal, Wegel countered Morrison's conclusions by stating that secretion levels in the sputum may differ from those in semen, and that in the eighteen years between the rapes and the then-current time, secretory levels can vary. The tests, despite the defense's arguments, did not exclude Gary as the donor of the semen from the victims. The court denied a defense request for additional funds to collect and analyze Gary's semen.

In early 2001, David Rose, a journalist who was at the time writing a book on the Gary case, asked Jack Martin, on behalf of his law firm, Martin Brothers, PC, to appoint him as a paralegal investigator for the firm. This allowed Rose, a death penalty opponent and professed believer in Gary's innocence, access to Gary on death row. According to Rose, shortly thereafter he and Martin devised a plan to surreptitiously obtain a semen specimen from their client and have it analyzed by their own experts. As described in detail in his 2007 book,[*] in late March, Rose set up an appointment with Gary under the pretense of working on other issues related to his appeal.[246] Avoiding the eyes of the guards, during a morning session he slipped Gary an envelope containing "paper and ClingWrap." Returning from a break for lunch, Gary passed the envelope containing his alleged semen specimen back to Rose and then collected some hair samples ("complete with roots") that he plucked from his head. Back at his hotel later that evening, Rose dried the specimen, noting that "the unmistakable pungent stink of semen filled the room." The specimen was then sent to a serologist in California who determined that Gary was "not a low-level secretor." The defense filed a motion with the court in May 2001 again requesting independent testing of Gary's semen. The request was denied. At this point, the possibility of evaluating DNA evidence had not been formally requested by the defense. Such testing was not available at the time of Gary's trial but subsequently had been approved as a valid scientific method by the Georgia Supreme Court.

At Gary's 1986 trial, the Muscogee County medical examiner, Dr. Joe Webber, had testified that the postmortem examination of Ms. Janet Cofer's body revealed what appeared to be "tooth marks" on the victim's left breast. Ms. Cofer, the Strangler's last victim, was murdered on April 20, 1978, and was not one of the deaths with which Gary was charged.

---

[*] See the next chapter for more on David Rose's book *The Big Eddy Club*. In his book, Rose reveals that the cost of the testing was paid for by *Vanity Fair* magazine, where Rose was a contributing editor (*The Big Eddy Club* (2007 ed.), xvii).

The issue was an important one, however, as her murder was one of the similar crimes and, to quote Bud Siemon at trial, "It's an extremely critical piece of evidence, because we know that whoever murdered that woman left those teeth marks." The prosecution was aware of this and had a mold made of the bite mark on Ms. Cofer's breast.[††] In preparation for trial, they consulted an odontologist, but after discovering that Gary had restorative dental work between the time of Cofer's murder and his arrest six years later, they determined that an accurate comparison would be impossible. Siemon's request at the time for funds to hire a "forensic odontologist" was denied. The issue had been raised before in the appeals process and not felt to be of value to either side. This time the district court chose to pursue it, responding to the defense counsel's allegation that the prosecution intentionally withheld the mold as exculpatory evidence.

The bite mold was last said to be in the possession of the coroner, Don Kilgore, who had died in 2000. The district court subpoenaed the coroner's widow, Karen Kilgore, and his two stepdaughters, demanding that they appear in court with the bite mold. None of the family members could produce the mold. Kilgore's widow said that "she had seen the exemplar at one of her husband's offices but could not recall which one." His son-in-law, appearing voluntarily for his wife, said he "may have seen" the mold, but was familiar with it from Kilgore's description. One of the stepdaughters said Mr. Kilgore had shown it to her son, who was then subpoenaed. He testified that he had seen the mold "at his grandfather's house in a box" but did not know what had become of it. With the mold apparently lost, on September 28, 2004, the district court denied Gary's petition for habeas corpus relief on the merits of the case.

With the rejection of Gary's claims by the federal district court, his attorneys initiated an appeal to the next highest court in the federal system, the US Eleventh Circuit Court of Appeals. As this process was getting underway, James L. Dunnavant, Don Kilgore's successor as the Muscogee County coroner, discovered the missing bite mold in the bottom drawer of a cabinet in his office. This was duly reported to the court, which sent the matter back to the district court for a hearing. In the ensuing testimony, it was established that on April 20, 1978, when Dr. Joe Webber discovered the presumed "tooth marks" on Ms. Janet Cofer's body while doing the autopsy, he consulted with a local odontologist, Dr. Carlos Galbreath. Using a rubber-like gel and a syringe, Dr. Galbreath made an

---

[††] The mold is referred to in court records as "an exemplar."

impression of the bite marks, which was then stored in the coroner's office. Following Carlton Gary's arrest in May 1984, the Columbus Police Department took possession of the mold as part of their investigation.

The prosecutors took the mold and dental x-rays of Gary's teeth taken while he was in prison in South Carolina to a forensic dentist, Dr. Thomas David, of Atlanta. The x-rays had been taken prior to subsequent Gary's dental work, which included capping and a false tooth. After his examination, Dr. David concluded that no reliable comparison could be made between the bite mold and the pre-repair x-rays. As Gary had undergone dental work between the time of the murder and his arrest more than six years later, any comparison would be speculative. Accepting Dr. David's opinion, the prosecutors returned the mold to the coroner's office after deciding not to introduce this evidence at trial. Having seen the autopsy report, Gary's attorneys were aware of the bite mark but did not know a mold had been made of it, or that prosecution attorneys had consulted Dr. David. The court ruled,

> Even if Gary had access to the exemplar at trial, he could only have shown that the bite marks were inconclusive; because of the intervening dental work, any bite mark comparison would neither identify nor exclude him as the perpetrator of the Cofer crime. The jury, in fact, actually heard evidence that the bite marks were inconclusive. Dr. Webber, the state's pathologist, testified that the marks neither conclusively proved or disproved that Gary was the perpetrator. Taken in context with the other evidence, including Gary's confession that he was at the Cofer residence when she was murdered, there exists no "reasonable probability" that the admission of an inconclusive bite mark exemplar would have changed the outcome of the proceeding.[247]

The Eleventh District Court of Appeals considered the issues raised by the defense, including allegations that in addition to the bite-mark mold, the prosecution had withheld other, potentially exculpatory evidence from defense attorneys. In upholding the lower courts' decisions, the justices wrote,

> In conducting our Brady analysis, we are mindful that we must consider the cumulative impact of the suppressed evidence. That is, we need to consider the cumulative effect of the bite mark exemplar, and the expert testimony its disclosure may have

engendered, in conjunction with all other exculpatory evidence the prosecution did not disclose. Even when we do so, we cannot say that the combined effect of this evidence undermines confidence in the jury's verdicts at the conclusion of the guilt or penalty phases of the trial. In this regard we mention once again the probative evidence that linked Gary to the crimes in this case. Specifically, Gary confessed that he was present at, or had knowledge of, eight of the nine 1977–78 rape/murders portrayed to the jury. Although he tried to blame these crimes on a boyhood friend, Malvin A. Crittenden, the police found no evidence to corroborate his assertion. Nor were the police able to locate anyone else who may have been with Gary on these occasions. While the hair evidence was inconclusive—Gary was neither included nor excluded from the class of potential perpetrators—his fingerprints were found to match latent prints found at four of the crime scenes. In sum, considering all the evidence the state withheld from the defense, allegedly in violation of the Brady rule, we could not say that confidence in the jury's verdicts following the guilt or penalty phase of the trial is undermined, for there is no reasonable probability that the verdicts would have been different had the jury received the evidence at issue.[248],‡‡

The court issued its opinion on February 12, 2009. Nearly twenty-five years had passed since Gary's arrest, more than twenty-two of which he had spent on death row.

---

‡‡ The terms "Brady analysis" and "Brady rule" derive from the landmark 1963 US Supreme Court decision in the case of *Brady v. Maryland* (373 US 83) that held prosecutors are required to disclose materially exculpatory evidence in their possession to the defense, including evidence that would go towards negating a defendant's guilt, that would reduce a defendant's potential sentence, or would have bearing on the credibility of a witness. Importantly, the defendant bears the burden of proof that the evidence in question is both material and favorable. In other words, the defendant must prove that there is a "reasonable probability" that the outcome of the trial would have been different if the evidence had been disclosed by the prosecution.

Chapter 43

The Big Eddy Club

Beginning shortly after his arrest and continuing through most of his incarceration, Carlton Gary maintained an active correspondence with a number of people, most often seeking support or denying his guilt for the crimes with which he was charged. On May 22, 1984, for example, just two and a half weeks after his arrest, Gary wrote a female friend in Greenville, South Carolina, explaining why he had suddenly left and requesting that she raise money to fight his legal woes. Denying that he had ever killed or raped anyone, he attributed his situation to an "attempt by the Georgia Rednecks to place the blame on me." He confidently predicted that he soon would be released. In 1991, Gary began a correspondence with a woman named Debra, who had been introduced to him by a church group. Interviewed later, she said that through his letters, "she felt an instant connection to him." For several years they corresponded, finally meeting in person. Even though Gary remained on death row, they married in 1996, thereafter talking frequently by phone or during personal visits.[249],*

Between 1996 and 2007, Gary sent more than two dozen letters to a Columbus resident, "Carrie," a volunteer at a local community ministry whose work focused on support for those in need, on racial justice, and on similar programs for the marginalized and downtrodden citizens of the area.† Gary's letters, written in a flowing left-slanted style, reflect both intelligence and a firm desire to convince the recipient of his innocence.

---

* This was apparently not Gary's first marriage. While in prison in New York under the alias of Carlton Michaels, Gary married Nancy J. Page on June 29, 1974. In August 1976, while Gary was free on parole, his wife contacted his parole officer and "told him to have Carlton start divorce proceedings." The following month, Gary met with someone from Legal Aid about the divorce. Whether or not this divorce was completed is unknown. In January 1977, Gary (as "Carlton Michaels") was rearrested following the burglary of Jean Frost. This information was gleaned from the investigation of Gary's past by Muscogee County prosecutors after his arrest in 1984.

† "Carrie" is used as a pseudonym to preserve the anonymity of this individual.

Almost uniformly, they begin with a blessing and word of thanks and are signed "Mike." He wrote of his religious beliefs, occasionally including holiday cards and apparently receiving letters from Carrie in return. There are frequent references to his wife, Debra, as well as to "our son" and "our daughter." The union was, in the words of a journalist, "unconventional at best." Gary's newly found status as a family man appeared out of character based on his acknowledged past, fathering by his own estimate fourteen other children whom, for practical purposes, he had abandoned.

In 2004, Gary began writing to Carrie about the details of his case and of how he was being denied justice due to conspiracies on the part of law enforcement and the judiciary. He mentioned David Rose, who had championed his cause, and referred to "The Big Eddy Club" and other theories on his case that mimicked those that Rose would later include in his book of the same name. At some point, the letters stopped. Gary had requested assistance from Carrie's husband, a person of some influence in the local legal community. In a written note that accompanied the sheaf of letters, Carrie speculated that Gary quit writing because her husband "couldn't help him." She described Gary as "truly the most educated and articulate person I have written in prison." And in a final note, she wrote, "Ferne Jackson was my mentor when she died. I have never believed that this man killed her."

Filed in among the letters Gary sent to Carrie was an article from *The Observer Magazine* that appeared in London, England, on June 13, 2004. It was by David Rose, the British journalist. Titled "Terminate with Extreme Prejudice," the opening page displayed a photo of Gary in handcuffs and a jail uniform. The subtext below the title read, "His fingerprints didn't fit. His blood type didn't match. The bite marks belonged to another man. But 26 years after seven elderly women were savagely murdered in Columbus, Georgia, Carlton Gary is still on death row. David Rose investigates the strange case of the Stocking Strangler." Rose, whose name was highlighted in bold print, worked as a contributing editor at *Vanity Fair*. The title, a quasi-military term allegedly used as an instruction to murder or assassinate someone, suggested the tone of the article. A footnote stated that Rose's book, *The Big Eddy Club*, "will be published next year by HarperCollins." Filled with innuendo attacking the police, the judiciary, and the legal system in general, Rose quoted Gary Parker, one of Carlton Gary's former lawyers, who stated that his client was the victim of a "legal lynching." Nowhere in the article does Rose substantiate the allegations regarding fingerprints, blood type, or bite mark. Referring to "fresh evidence, some of it unearthed by me," Rose bemoans the fact that a judge refused to consider it based on "procedural grounds." He questioned the honesty and integrity of Columbus police officer Michael Sellers and implied that the then-current federal district judge was a racist because of events attributed to his great-grandfather nearly a century earlier.

Rose's decision to write about Carlton Gary's case came in part from his interest in the death penalty in the American South. He was aware of Gary's situation, and was further introduced to him by Wendy Murphy, who contacted Rose by letter in late 1997. Murphy, an English dental hygienist who maintained an active correspondence with Gary, lived in Norfolk, a coastal county in East Anglia some hundred miles or so north and east of London. Despite the vast distance between their places of abode, she visited him in prison on a number of occasions. After reviewing the material she gave him, Rose began to explore the possibility of a book on Gary, initially visiting him in 1998. In his book, Rose related, "One of the first things [Gary] told me was about the Big Eddy Club. 'All those crackers who run Columbus and its legal system belong to it,' he said, going on to list the families of most of the strangling victims, together with members of the legal establishment who had helped convict him, and who, he claimed, were members or regular visitors."[250] These included prosecutor Bill Smith and Judge Kenneth Followill. From this seed, and its implication of conspiracy, the book's title was born.

It would be nearly three years before Rose's book was released in print. Published by The New Press in the United States in June 2007 under the title *The Big Eddy Club*, and in the United Kingdom by HarperCollins a few months earlier under the title *Violation: Race, Justice and Serial Murder in the Deep South*, the editions generated an assortment of reviews, mostly positive, on both sides of the Atlantic. A second paperback edition with a new afterword section was released in the United States in 2011. While purporting to be an account of the trial and (in)justice delivered to Carlton Gary, Rose's book uses Gary's case to expound on his preconceived notion that the legal system of the American South is fundamentally biased against persons of color. While the book is well-written and engaging, Rose conveniently ignores details and facts that do not fit his narrative, engages in ad hominem attacks against members of law enforcement and the legal profession who disagree with him, and implies a vast, if undocumented, conspiracy involving police, prosecutors, and all levels of the judiciary. In glaring examples of confirmation bias, he referenced events of the nineteenth and early twentieth centuries in support of his theses while questioning the honesty, integrity, and motivations of those charged with upholding the law. Lest he be accused of bias, it is only when the reader has completed approximately ninety percent of the book that Rose reveals he served as an active member of Gary's defense team.

In England, the March 10, 2007, *Observer* under the headline "A clear-cut case of trial and error," referred to the book as "a dazzlingly reported, supremely elegant book of scholarly confidence." The *Times* of the same day was similarly effusive in its review, titled "White man's justice, Dixie-style." An April 15, 2007, review in the *Sunday Times* opined that "David Rose has done a meticulous job that as good as exonerates the man from the crimes he is alleged to have committed. Whether his book will convince the white folks of Columbus is another matter. The black folks, meanwhile, have been convinced for years. *Violation* is about as good a piece of investigative reporting as you're ever likely to get." The American response was more muted. In May 2007, *Publishers Weekly* described *The Big Eddy Club* as an "ineptly titled tome," "an engrossing blend of true crime, legal drama and acute exposé of racial antagonism." With less than enthusiastic endorsement, the review notes, "The author harps unconvincingly on the 'Southern rape complex' and insinuates more than he demonstrates about the role of Columbus's Big Eddy Club of white movers and shakers." During the same month, Don O'Briant penned a similarly lukewarm review for the *Atlanta Journal-Constitution*.[251] On examining the published reviews, it is clear that their authors were not aware of—or chose to ignore—the full range of evidence and facts that led to Gary's arrest, conviction, and sentence of death.

In Columbus, *The Big Eddy Club* was an instant best seller. "They're flying off the shelves," an employee of Barnes & Noble booksellers said to an inquirer.[252] The assessment of, and reactions to, the book varied widely, however, often in relationship to the reader's personal knowledge of the victims, the case, or those individuals directly involved in its prosecution or defense. Mark Shelnutt, a Columbus lawyer who had begun his practice as an assistant district attorney in 1988, was appalled by the book's insinuations of conspiracy and corruption on the part of the police and the judiciary. With access to court transcripts, he carefully compared Rose's allegations to the hard facts and evidence presented at trial and on appeal through the time the book was published. His assessment of Rose's scholarship was devastating. Referring to the author in a book review of *The Big Eddy Club* given at St. Luke Methodist Church in Columbus on August 22, 2007, Shelnutt said,

He has to get the reader to look at the case through the angry eyes of prejudice, interweaving accounts of terrible abuses as long as 150 years ago all through it to frame your view of the case. Now, for Mr. Rose, this isn't just an exercise in history...but it's the very ammunition he needs to lead you away from the damaging mountain of evidence, to support the only premise under which Carlton Gary could be innocent, and that is that everyone in the system from the everyday police officer, to the investigator, the detectives, to the Chief of the Police, the D[istrict] A[ttorney], the judges, not only in Columbus, but in other states: Michigan, New York, South Carolina, the Attorney General of the State of Georgia, the Georgia Supreme Court, the US District Court, the [US] 11th Circuit Court of Appeals and even the Supreme Court of the United States have all participated in or sanctioned this conspiracy. And that the conspiracy to frame Gary would have to have started...in 1977, despite the fact that his name had never been included in any report of literally hundreds, if not thousands, of the suspects that were investigated at the height of the stranglings, and [it] didn't even surface until 1984. He must do all of this because—make no mistake about it—the goal is one thing: see the sentence imposed under law by that Spalding County jury who heard the case is never carried out, and more importantly, work to abolish the death penalty. Now, on that type of mission...Mr. Rose has shown that the truth will not interfere or stop him.[253]

Two of the leading targets of Rose's vitriol were Bill Smith, who prosecuted Gary's case, and Mike Sellers, the Columbus police officer who initially identified Gary as the prime suspect in the Strangler investigation. Sellers's notes on Gary's admissions following his arrest played a vital role in his conviction. Both men were accused of lying and the fabrication of evidence. When asked for his comments, Bill Smith referred to Rose's dismissive treatment of the William Henry Hance case, which rated a single brief paragraph in *The Big Eddy Club*. Rose implied that Gary was prosecuted because of his race and the fact that the crimes with which he was accused targeted prominent white women. Hance, a second serial killer active in Columbus during the same time period as the Strangler, targeted black prostitutes, victims at the other end of the social scale. Yet the case was pursued with the same intensity as that of Gary and resulted in the same sentence. Mike Sellers was more direct in his condemnation of Gary's book. "He misquoted me and fabricated what I said," Sellers replied. "I deeply resent that he came to Columbus and accused every white officer of a deep-seated hatred of blacks. Nothing could be further from the truth."[254]

While the controversy over Rose's book swirled through Columbus during the summer of 2007, in Syracuse, New York, cold case detectives were pursuing leads in a rape and murder that occurred on Friday, June 27, 1975. On that evening, Marion Fisher, a forty-year-old physical education teacher at a local high school sent her two children to a neighbor's house for the night and went out to dinner with her husband, Jack, to celebrate their wedding anniversary. After the meal, the two retired to the bar area of the restaurant for drinks in the company of another couple. At some point, the Fishers began to argue. According to later reports, the dispute "escalated to the point where Marion slammed down her drink and announced that despite the late hour and the over a mile distance, she was walking home." With that she left the bar. Jack Fisher and the other couple unsuccessfully searched for her but, finding nothing, went home. The next day, when his wife had not returned, Jack Fisher contacted the police. At about 9:20 that morning a caddie arriving for work at a nearby country club discovered Ms. Fisher's body behind a row of bushes near the entrance. "Mrs. Fisher's bra and blouse were pushed up around her shoulders and her slacks and panties were shoved down around her ankles." "Evidence at the crime scene strongly indicated that she had been raped and strangled to death by someone using her own stockings." As the most obvious suspect, Jack Fisher was arrested. He was unable to say what happened to his wife; he admitted that he had been drinking and "maybe he blacked out and hurt Marion." Although police were convinced that Jack murdered his wife, there was insufficient evidence to charge him with the crime.[255,256,257]

More than thirty years passed. In 2007, Syracuse's Cold Case Task Force decided to reexamine the Fisher killing. At the time, a police officer familiar with the case said, "We know the husband did it, we just can't prove it." In examining the archived evidence from the crime, material for DNA testing was identified. A suitable profile was developed and entered into a national DNA database maintained by the Federal Bureau of

Investigation.‡ Within weeks, a conclusive match was made with the DNA of Carlton Gary, who had been free on parole in Syracuse, New York, at the time of the murder. Because Gary was in a Georgia prison on death row, Onondaga County district attorney William Fitzpatrick elected not to prosecute him for this murder in New York.[258]

In his ten-page afterword to the new edition of *The Big Eddy Club* in January 2011, David Rose went into detail updating information on Gary's case and insisting that DNA testing should be done to show his innocence. He recounted that prior to the Georgia Supreme Court's December 2009 ruling to stay Gary's execution, he had—at the suggestion of the case's defense attorneys—sent copies of the book to the justices "as an exhibit" in an effort to influence their decision. Although the 2007 DNA evidence linking Gary to the rape and murder of Marion Fisher was unambiguous and widely covered in the press at that time, Rose failed to mention it in his update.[259]

---

‡ The Combined DNA Index System (CODIS) is the United States national DNA database created and maintained by the Federal Bureau of Investigation. It is a national system of computer databases designed by the FBI to store DNA profiles from individuals as well as crime scene evidence. Any DNA profile developed from the evidence in a case with no suspects can then be searched against the databases, with possible investigative leads developed from any matching profiles in the database. Carlton Gary's DNA profile was added to the database in 2005.

Chapter 44

"Judge Signs Warrant for Execution"[260]

The summary of the US Eleventh Circuit Court of Appeal's February 2009 decision was brief and to the point:

> Twenty-two years ago, in the Superior Court of Muscogee County, Georgia, twelve jurors unanimously found Carlton Gary guilty of three counts of murder, rape and burglary. As a result of the murder convictions, Gary was sentenced to death. Since then, he has pursued every possible legal avenue available to him to obtain a new trial. In all, his convictions and death sentences have been reviewed on at least ten separate occasions. In each instance, he has been denied relief.... We find no merit in the issues presented and therefore affirm.

A headline on the front page of the next day's *Ledger-Enquirer* read, "Stocking Strangler Denied a New Trial." Accompanying the news article was a brief insert with Gary's photo and the heading "Who Is the Stocking Strangler?" The crimes for which he was convicted occurred more than three decades earlier, so far in the past that the paper now found it necessary to remind its readers of who this person was and why his case rated front-page coverage.[261]

Months passed. On November 30, 2009, the US Supreme Court declined to hear Gary's appeal for the third time, setting the stage for his execution. Again, the Columbus newspaper carried a list of crimes for which he had been convicted as well as those he was thought to have committed. This time, Marion Fisher's name was added to the list.[262] Three days later, Muscogee Superior Court judge Robert Johnston signed an order for Gary's execution by lethal injection during the week of December 16th through 23rd. The Georgia Department of Corrections, the agency responsible for choosing the exact time, designated December 16 at 7:00 P.M.

On the following Monday, December 7, 2009, defense attorney Jack Martin filed a motion in Muscogee County Superior Court requesting that Gary's execution be halted and DNA testing done "to determine his guilt or innocence once and for all." "A cloud has hung over the Carlton Gary case for decades," Martin said. "This is the classic circumstance where DNA testing can conclusively answer the question as to whether Carlton Gary committed these awful crimes." Martin's motion appeared to be born out of desperation. Given the other evidence in the case, it might logically appear that DNA testing would be more likely than not to weigh toward Gary's guilt, not innocence. But even then, it would delay his execution, and the defense had nothing to lose by requesting it. Martin's motion said "that prosecutors had told Gary's lawyers that semen evidence from the case no longer existed," but the preceding week "he and Aimee Maxwell, executive director of the Georgia Innocence Project, found semen evidence collected from the victims that had been stored in the property room of the Columbus Police Department," implying this was a discovery of new evidence.[263]

Since 2003, Georgia law allowed post-conviction DNA testing provided it "would raise a reasonable probability that the petitioner would have been acquitted if the results of DNA testing had been available at the time of conviction, in light of all the evidence in the case."[264] District Attorney Julia Slater, responding for the state, called Martin's motion a delaying tactic, noting he "was given access to this same material in the Columbus Police Department in 2001," but in his motion "failed to explain why he did not seek DNA testing from this court or file an extraordinary motion for a new trial at that time." Noting that "numerous state and federal courts have reviewed the sufficiency of the evidence to support the defendant's convictions and death sentences during the last twenty-three years," Slater said such testing would not meet the "reasonable probability" standard in Georgia law. Judge Robert Johnston denied the defense's motion.

With Gary's execution scheduled to take place in one week, Jack Martin announced that he was filing an appeal with the Georgia Supreme Court and a petition to the State Board of Pardons and Paroles, the two entities that now had the power to halt or delay the execution.[265,266] At the same time, Martin filed a motion with the US District Court seeking funds to have experts testify before the Board of Pardons and Paroles. Judge Clay Land denied his request, noting that the same two witnesses had earlier testified in the case in federal court. "A clemency hearing before a parole board is not the place to 'relitigate issues that have been already considered extensively and thoroughly by the state and federal courts,'" Land said.

Over the weekend, a press release from the Georgia Department of Corrections revealed that Gary had declined the "special last meal inmates may request before they are executed." If he chose to eat that evening, he would be served the same meal as other inmates on death row: a grilled cheeseburger, oven-browned potatoes, baked beans, coleslaw, cookies, and a grape beverage.

On Monday, December 14th, the Georgia Board of Pardons and Paroles held a seven-hour hearing on Gary's case. The defense presented about three hours of testimony including presentations from Gary's wife and her daughter; Dr. Thomas David, the forensic odontologist; Roger Morrison, the blood work expert; and Jim Covington, a former GBI agent who testified on a shoeprint attributed to the Strangler found at Ms. Ruth Schwob's home, and on crime scene fingerprints. The hearing was closed to the public and the press, but board members were said to be "intently focused on the testimony, taking notes and asking questions." As of early Tuesday morning, the board had not issued its ruling.[267]

On Wednesday morning, December 16th, the bold-print heading on the *Ledger-Enquirer* front page read "Execution Set for Tonight," just above a large courtroom photo of Carlton Gary dressed in a suit with matching vest, gesturing to someone off-camera from behind his signature dark glasses. Late the preceding afternoon, the Board of Pardons and Paroles had denied Gary's request for a stay of execution. Two appeals were still pending before the Georgia Supreme Court, one from a Muscogee County Superior Court denial, and the other of a denial from the Butts County Superior Court where Gary was awaiting his fate on death row. The news reporting now had taken on a sense of finality. The article just under Gary's photo was titled "Details emerge about Gary's suicide attempts, lavish attire." Under Georgia's Open Records Act, the *Ledger-Enquirer* had obtained the right to inspect jail records that included details of Gary's alleged suicide attempt, his escape attempts, and the personal belongings his mother had picked up from the Columbus jail a week after his conviction. These included three suits—two with vests, five ties, three pairs of shoes, and four handkerchiefs. Witness reports from the jail recorded that on March 15, 1985, Gary "hurled racial slurs at...two white deputies, and threatened to kill them and their mothers."[268] All this did not matter now. Within a matter of hours, Carlton Gary would be dead. Or so it seemed...

To the amazement of many, the headline on the *Ledger-Enquirer* of December 17th read, "Court Stays Gary's Execution." At 2:00 P.M. the preceding afternoon, a delegation of members of Columbus's law enforcement and judicial officers left the Columbus Public Safety Building en route to the prison in Jackson, Georgia, where Gary was to be executed. Among the group were Ricky Boren and Charlie Rowe, now Columbus police chief and assistant police chief, respectively, Maj. Lem Miller, Det. Sgt. Mike Sellers, and former police chief Curtis McClung, all of whom had been actively involved in the case decades earlier.* Julia Slater, the current district attorney, was to represent the prosecution team that won Gary's conviction. Shortly after 3:00 P.M., less than four hours prior to the scheduled execution, word came down that the Georgia Supreme Court, by a five to two margin, had ordered the Muscogee County Superior Court to hold a hearing on DNA testing. The Supreme Court's order was specific in rejecting Judge Johnston's ruling, stating that Gary "demonstrated that he complied with the requirements" of the 2003 law allowing post-conviction testing, and "that the trial court erred in failing to order a hearing on the motion." The Columbus delegation turned around and drove back to the city.[269]

At the prison, Gary's attorney Jack Martin held what he thought was to be a final meeting with his client, who by that time had been moved to a cell closer to the execution chamber. It was a "sad" meeting, Martin said. Gary seemed "resigned in a sense." With news of the Supreme Court's order, Gary's wife, whom he married while on death row in 1996 and with whom he had never lived, said her prayers had been answered. State NAACP president Edward DuBose termed the court's ruling "common sense" and said he believed that Gary did not commit the stranglings. "I say to District Attorney Julia Slater and Judge Johnston, who signed the death warrant, that evidence and life means something," DuBose said. Former district attorney Bill Smith had no comment.[270]

The Georgia Supreme Court had not overturned Gary's conviction, and neither had it ordered a new trial. The primary reason that the case was sent back to the Muscogee County Superior Court was to hold a hearing on the issue of DNA testing. It was now a few days before Christmas. Judge Johnston said that the hearing would likely take place early in the new year. Carlton Gary had once again been granted a reprieve. How long it would last and its eventual outcome remained unknown.

---

* Mike Sellers left the Columbus Police Department in 1987 to accept a job with the Gwinnett County (Georgia) Police Department.

Chapter 45

Is Carlton Gary Telling the Truth?

Judge Johnston set Gary's court-ordered hearing on the DNA issue for February 1, 2010. In addition to hearing arguments as to whether the request for testing met the "reasonable probability" standard, he also wanted to hear contentions on "whether the petitioner's motion for DNA testing was filed for the purpose of delay." In preparation for the hearing, defense attorney Jack Martin, District Attorney Julia Slater, and the defense's DNA consultant, Boise State University professor Greg Hampikian spent several hours examining boxes of evidence at the Columbus Police Department. Hampikian, the director of the Idaho Innocence Project, told a reporter, "We spent the day here and looked through a substantial amount of evidence, and there are excellent, well-preserved slides that were taken from the rape victims, that have a very high probability of producing a profile of the perpetrator. It's very similar to many other cases I've done in Georgia, including several exonerations with the Georgia Innocence Project, and actually several cases where guilt was validated."[271]

The scheduled February 1st hearing lasted only four minutes, time enough for Martin to request a three-week continuance until February 22nd. Behind the scenes, District Attorney Slater had made an offer to Martin to allow DNA testing, but this was refused prior to the hearing. As she would note later, it was the state's position that the jury had heard sufficient evidence in Gary's 1986 trial to convict him in three of the seven serial killings. But "an agreement to which both the prosecution and defense agreed [would reduce] the potential for future appeals based on how the tests were conducted."[272] The obstruction this time, however, was Gary himself. He refused to grant his permission for the testing.

On February 16th, Judge Johnston abruptly resigned, citing poor health.* Gary's case was transferred to Superior Court judge Frank J. Jordan Jr. Four days later, District Attorney Slater announced that both the

---

* Judge Robert Johnston III died in March 2011, some thirteen months after stepping down from the bench, and after a long period of declining health. He was sixty-two years of age.

prosecution and defense had reached an agreement to have four semen samples from three of the Strangler's victims analyzed by the GBI Division of Forensic Sciences at the state crime laboratory. Specimens were available from Jean Dimenstien, Kathleen Woodruff, and Martha Thurmond. If the state laboratory were unable to satisfactorily complete the analysis, both sides agreed that further testing would be done by the Bode Technology Group in Lorton, Virginia, with whom the GBI had established a working relationship. Slater said that victims' relatives had been consulted prior to signing the agreement, and that she was confident that the results of the tests would not challenge Gary's conviction. "The evidence against Mr. Gary even without positive DNA tests is overwhelming," Slater said. "The conviction in this case is solid and Gary's guilt is inescapable."[273]

As an agreement for testing had been reached, the hearing planned for the 22nd was cancelled. But problems arose. In an impromptu press conference held in front of the Columbus Government Center that day, Debra Gary, Carlton's wife, announced that Gary had not signed the consent agreement reached by the attorneys, and that his current defense team, headed by Jack Martin, was "not representing him according to his wishes."[274] Gary Parker, the attorney who obtained and witnessed Gary's signature, disputed Ms. Gary's claims. After an additional delay of more than four weeks, another hearing to settle the issues was held on March 23rd. In the six minutes the hearing lasted, it was confirmed that Gary had now agreed to DNA testing. Debra Gary said her husband "had no choice but to agree to proceed with the tests because he was told [Judge] Jordan had a 'death warrant' ready to sign if Gary did not agree." District Attorney Slater confidently predicted the results of the testing would be available "within a month."[275]

By mid-May, two months later, the laboratory had not reported on their analysis. By late August, five months after all parties agreed to DNA testing, a spokesman for the Georgia Bureau of Investigation said the crime lab had completed its testing "months ago," and that the evidence was being transferred to the Bode Technology laboratory in Virginia. Both defense and prosecution attorneys refused further comment.

On Monday, December 13, 2010, almost exactly one year after Carlton Gary received a stay of execution from the Georgia Supreme Court, attorneys from the prosecution and defense in the case held what a reporter described as "dueling news conferences" to announce the results of the DNA testing. A grim-faced Julia Slater, flanked by two equally grim-appearing assistant district attorneys, announced that DNA collected in the death of Jean Dimenstien matched that of Carlton Gary. Despite efforts by both the Georgia and Virginia laboratories, no DNA profile could be developed on evidence collected from Kathleen Woodruff. The most stunning finding, though, one that had the potential to change much of what had been assumed, revealed that male DNA recovered from Martha Thurmond's body did not match that of Gary and was assumed to be that of another man whose identity remained unknown. Even with this unexpected setback, Slater said, "I will say that we continue to believe that Carlton Gary committed all of the murders, rapes and burglaries." Evidence from the Dimenstien case "proved Gary was the Strangler, so he no longer could claim he was being 'framed' for the killings." Slater said Susan Boleyn, a former senior assistant state attorney general, had been called in to assist as a special prosecutor in the case. A "status conference" was scheduled the following week "to determine how to proceed."[276]

On the other side, Jack Martin, accompanied by DNA consultant Greg Hampikian, said "the results in the Thurmond case show Gary should get a new trial." He planned to file a motion to that end. Semen found on Ms. Thurmond's body was tested in the GBI laboratory, yielding two DNA profiles, one belonging to the victim and the other to an unknown male. Hampikian said "the semen from the Thurmond case could have come from a consensual male partner, but no evidence indicates the victim had one." Referring to Gary, "It was an absolute exclusion," Martin said. "There's no way it's him." Based on the Thurmond result, both men agreed that "the rapist, if he's still alive, may be at large."[277] "We now know for a scientific fact from DNA tests not available at the time of his trial that Mr. Gary did not commit the Thurmond murder.... It is obvious he deserves a new trial and the real perpetrator of the Thurmond murder needs to be found and brought to justice," Martin said.[278]

The revelation that DNA from the semen of an unidentified male was found in association with one of the Strangler's victims sent shock waves throughout the community. Pointing out that the DNA results implicated Gary in a murder for which he *had not been* charged, yet suggested he was not the perpetrator of a murder for which he *had been* convicted, an editorial headline in the *Ledger-Enquirer* asked, "Think Gary case was convoluted enough already?"[279] Behind the bold public statements made about the new findings, in truth, both sides' cases had been both strengthened and weakened. From the perspective of the prosecution, Gary had been convicted and sentenced to death based on three cases of rape and murder. If the evidence augured against the state's theory in the

Thurmond case, the convictions and sentences were still valid for the murders of Jackson and Scheible. Furthermore, as Gary's DNA was found in the Dimenstien murder and rape, obtaining an indictment and conviction could likely be accomplished without difficulty. There were two significant problems, however. First, an aura of doubt had been cast upon the theory that Gary was *the* Stocking Strangler, that no one else was involved. How could that be reconciled with the presence of unknown male DNA in semen found at Ms. Thurmond's crime scene? Second, the crimes attributed to Gary had occurred more than three decades earlier. Vital witnesses, for example the two Columbus survivors of the Strangler's attacks, Gertrude Miller and Ruth Schwob, were now deceased. Miller's identification of Gary had been an important part of the state's case. And the terror, horror, and fear of those eight months in 1977 and 1978 during the Strangler's reign of terror was now the distant memory of an earlier generation. Juries could be more sympathetic to the defense's arguments of racism and police malfeasance in a push to find and convict the murderer.

For the defense, while the association of Gary's DNA with the murder of Jean Dimenstien was a setback, the Thurmond DNA results were a godsend. It opened a fissure in the narrative that Carlton Gary acted alone, perhaps one so significant that a jury might find that he was not guilty based on the necessary standard of "beyond a reasonable doubt." The details of Thurmond's murder were noteworthy. According to reports at the time, her murder took place between 1:00 and 4:00 A.M. on the morning of Tuesday, October 25, 1977. Her son and his family had spent the preceding weekend with her, leaving about 3:30 P.M. on Monday afternoon, the 24th. She had talked with a relative on the phone about 9:30 P.M. that night, potentially less than four hours before her death. Although disputed by defense attorneys, Gary had admitted being at Ms. Thurmond's house on the night of her murder; in confirmation, a latent fingerprint found there was identified as being his. The testimony of Charles Oliver, who lived near Ms. Thurmond, was able to place Gary in the neighborhood around the time of the murder. Gary's statements to police officers shortly after his arrest clearly indicated that it was Michael Crittenden who raped and murdered Ms. Thurmond. Although the idea of a secret lover as the source of the unknown DNA had been mentioned, the timeline of the events surrounding her murder would appear to make that possibility unlikely. Carlton Gary was a known liar, that had been established. But could it be that this time he had been telling the truth? Was Crittenden the murderer?

Chapter 46

Delays and DNA

The Georgia Supreme Court's December 2009 decision to send Carlton Gary's case back to Judge Robert Johnston and the Muscogee County Superior Court marked the beginning of a period of eight years when progress in the case ground to a relative halt. This is not to say that nothing happened. On the contrary, there were motions and hearings with attempts to introduce new evidence and redefine old. Matters vital to the case that had been previously considered by other courts were brought up and reconsidered once again. Statements were given to the press by both the prosecution and defense, and speculation swirled as to the meaning and significance of the DNA from the unknown male identified in the Thurmond murder. All considered, however, for most of this time, the matter remained mired in the court of Judge Frank Jordan, who took over the case on Judge Johnston's unexpected retirement. Little else changed: Carlton Gary remained on death row, and the sentence imposed by the jury in August 1986 remained in force.

The goal of the state during these years was to defend the validity of the outcome of Gary's original trial and sentence, including evidence and testimony that supported his involvement in "other crimes" that showed a pattern of "criminal intent" but for which he was not charged. As frequently pointed out by Jack Martin and the defense team, the Thurmond DNA finding called into question whether there was a single "Strangler," or if the crimes were committed by more than one person. From the perspective of the defense, the ideal outcome would be to raise enough doubts about Gary's conviction to warrant the court ordering a new trial. Anything that could be found to call into question evidence or testimony presented at Gary's original trial was fair game. For many reasons, including fading memories and deceased witnesses, even if Gary were convicted once again, obtaining a sentence of death at a subsequent trial would likely be far more difficult.[*]

---

[*] According to former prosecutor Bill Smith, Malvin Alamichael Crittenden's DNA was tested with his permission and found not to match the profile of the unknown male DNA obtained from the Thurmond specimen. This information was shared with defense attorneys but was never entered into evidence.

In pursuit of this goal, in late 2010 Martin requested compensation through the US District Court for work on a motion for a new trial. Judge Clay Land denied the request, noting that federal compensation was available for Gary's appeals but not for "the commencement of new judicial proceedings." Land denied a reconsideration of the request in January 2011. Martin announced that he would appeal the issue to the US Eleventh Circuit Court of Appeals.

In April, David Rose, who was back in Columbus promoting the release of the softcover edition of *The Big Eddy Club*, wrote an opinion piece for the *Ledger-Enquirer* excoriating the prosecutors and legal system that brought Carlton Gary to justice, while promoting an upcoming talk to be given at the local Barnes & Noble bookstore.[280] Responding to Rose's article, journalist Richard Hyatt noted in his column, "Once again, Rose injects the idea that another individual might have been involved. Gary used this ploy in similar cases—something Rose failed to mention. Nor did he mention that he has worked for Gary's defense team." Responding to Rose's call for a new trial, Hyatt wrote,

> The prospect of a new trial is ominous since so many witnesses are dead. Even if he were found guilty, the clock would start ticking on a second appeal. This one has taken twenty-five years. Gary, fifty-nine, would live out his days on Death Row.
>
> Carlton Gary understands the system. He has been in and out of jail since he was nineteen years old and has spent only thirty months feeling the warmth of sunshine on his face. He knows how to play the game, and this should be his last time at bat.[281]

Meanwhile, in the Muscogee County Superior Court of Judge Jordan, defense attorneys requested permission to subpoena evidence relating to the September 1977 rape of Gertrude Miller. Ms. Miller, now deceased, was the one witness who identified Carlton Gary as her rapist. If DNA testing on this material suggested a male other than Gary, it would seriously damage the state's case. Hospitalized after the attack, vaginal swabs had been taken as part of a rape examination. Also, items of clothing collected at the crime scene were stored in the evidence room of the Columbus Police Department. In her response opposing the testing, District Attorney Slater noted that Ms. Miller's vaginal exam did not take place until two days after her rape, lessening the probability of obtaining a useful result. Importantly, Slater pointed out that "it is apparent that such testing will not produce evidence which would create a 'reasonable probability' that defendant would be acquitted and would only result in further unnecessary delay in these proceedings."[282] Rejecting her argument, Judge Jordan granted the motion to proceed with DNA testing on evidence from the Miller case in late August 2011.

On investigation, defense attorneys discovered that no evidence from the 1977 rape examination could be found at Columbus's St. Francis Hospital. Other garments, however, such as those she wore to the hospital and others gathered from the crime scene, were being held by the Columbus police. From these, three items containing stains that might yield DNA evidence were submitted to the GBI laboratory: a white sleeping gown, a white slip, and underwear. In November, the lab reported that "chemical examination of stains on the clothing...fails to reveal the presence of seminal fluid."[283] Judge Jordan then ordered that additional testing be done by the Bode Technology Group in Virginia.

In March 2012, Jack Martin announced that the Virginia laboratory had discovered male DNA on Gertrude Miller's gown. Critically, the DNA was reported not to match that of Carlton Gary. "Gertrude Miller was the sole witness to identify the defendant and was one of the essential pillars of the state's case," Martin said. "We've contended for years she was mistaken and now we know for certain she was." The finding, the details of which were not made public, was a potentially devastating blow to the prosecution. Asked for a comment from the state, Slater replied that she was limited in what she could say, but "eagerly anticipates discussing in court the results of DNA testing, responding to the rhetoric from Mr. Gary's defense team and again showing why the jury's decision in this case must be upheld." To this, Martin replied, "I'm similarly eagerly anticipating how the state can possibly make this new evidence go away."[284] On July 9, 2012, Jack Martin filed a motion in Muscogee County Superior Court seeking a new trial for his client.

Months passed without action on Gary's case. In September 2012, the Sunday edition of the *Daily Mail*, an English newspaper, carried a feature article by David Rose titled, "No fingerprints and a dodgy confession in a Ku Klux Klan stronghold: The shocking Death Row injustice of 'The Stocking Strangler.'" Next to Rose's byline was the sentence, "The man who first saved Carlton Gary from execution in 2009." Illustrated with a photo of Gary on the night of his arrest and two stock photos of robed Klansmen and a burning cross, Rose took personal credit for "unearthing a cast of the killer's teeth" and influencing the Georgia Supreme Court decision to stay Gary's execution: "For weeks, [Gary's] lawyers vainly tried to get a stay while the samples were tested. Finally, on December 16, 2009, after I filed a 'friend of the court' brief enclosing copies of my book as exhibits, the Georgia Supreme Court halted the execution three hours before Gary was due to die." While framing himself as a hero, the author once again depicted the legal establishment of Columbus as corrupt, implying that Gary's race and the influence of the Klan had bearing on his conviction.[285]

More than a year elapsed before Gary's case made the headlines once more.[†] This time, the story was not about the defendant, but rather about the current judge in the case, Frank J. Jordan Jr. The November 21, 2013, front-page headline of the *Ledger-Enquirer* carried the headline, "State AG Seeks Judge's Recusal in Gary Case." The timing was significant in that Jordan was scheduled to hear arguments on December 3, 2013, on the motion for a new trial originally filed by Jack Martin nearly a year and a half earlier. The delay in addressing this motion was not explained. The recusal request came from the fact that the judge had a copy of the book *The Big Eddy Club* in his office.

> The recusal motion filed...by Senior Assistant Attorney General Sabrina Graham says Rose's book constitutes "an extrajudicial source of information" the judge should not have, as his decision must be based solely on the evidence presented in court. The book's display in Jordan's office on the Columbus Government Center's 10th floor also creates the impression he is not impartial...."Additionally, the existence of this book in [Jordan's] personal library indicates this book was either purchased by the court, which would mean it had an interest in learning about Mr.

[†] Although not covered by the press, the sluggishness of the appeals process had become a significant issue. In anticipation of evidentiary hearings to be scheduled by Judge Jordan, in September 2013 the state filed a motion asking the court "to take judicial notice of prior findings of fact made by state and federal courts" in reviewing the defense's Extraordinary Motion for a New Trial, specifically citing the bite mark and shoeprint issues. The motion was accompanied and supported by 140 pages of excerpts from previous hearings documenting that these matters had been examined and found not to have merit as bases of appeal. Judge Jordan denied the motion, in the process allowing testimony on such in subsequent hearings. This ruling materially delayed a final decision on the motion for a new trial.

Rose's extrajudicial investigation, or this book was given to the court by a party with an interest in Gary's case. Also, the prominent display of this book in the Court's chambers, which is clearly an extrajudicial source of information, creates the appearance of partiality.[286]

Acting with unusual speed, three days after its filing, Judge Jordan rejected the attorney general's motion to recuse himself. The action was filed after someone told Assistant Attorney General Graham in a November 8th meeting in Columbus that the judge had a copy of Rose's book in his chambers. As Ms. Graham had not seen it personally, Jordan termed the basis for the motion as "hearsay," and hence "legally insufficient and an improper basis for recusal." Additionally, as the case had been reassigned to him from Judge Johnston more than three years earlier, the motion for recusal was "untimely."

While these events were taking place, another potentially more surprising revelation had come to light. The male DNA profile from the Thurmond case "that showed someone other than convicted Stocking Strangler Carlton Gary committed one of the heinous Columbus serial killings of 1977–78 was wrong," according to documents filed with the court on November 21st. Defense attorney Martin called the discovery "shocking." Once again, the case had taken a totally unexpected turn.[287]

Chapter 47

Yet Another Surreal Twist
in the Continuing Saga

Referring to the latest surprise in the post-conviction appeals process as "yet another surreal twist in the continuing saga of convicted 'Stocking Strangler' Carlton Gary," a front-page *Ledger-Enquirer* article by Tim Chitwood on January 5, 2014, revealed more information on the series of events that had recently come to light. In Atlanta on Wednesday, April 11, 2011, nearly three years prior, a dispute that began with a Facebook feud led to a shooting incident in the city's Morningside neighborhood east of Piedmont Park. Shortly before 1:00 P.M. that afternoon, William Paul Garey, a resident of Greenland Drive, called police to say that he thought someone had just hurled an explosive device through a window of his home. Witnesses described a man in camouflage seen leaving the immediate area. Police called in a SWAT team and sealed off the area, in the process locking down three nearby public schools. Further investigation revealed that instead of an explosive, someone had fired "multiple shots" from a high-powered rifle through the window. Garey was home at the time, but not injured. He told police that he had been involved in an online feud via the social networking site with a man named Christopher Michael Lloyd, who lived on nearby Kings Court and against whom he had previously obtained a restraining order. Tracking dogs were brought in, and Lloyd, dressed in camouflage, was arrested shortly thereafter near the intersection of Amsterdam and North Highland Avenues. After appropriate investigation, charges of aggravated assault were filed against Lloyd. He, in turn, was subsequently diagnosed with schizophrenia and sent to a "mental health facility" in Savannah.[288]

When investigating the crime scene, Atlanta police found a BB pistol behind Garey's house that had been dropped there by Lloyd. This was sent to the GBI crime lab for DNA testing. To the surprise of all, DNA found on the gun matched the same unknown male profile as that found on the Martha Thurmond evidence. There was one problem, however. Christopher Lloyd was thirty years old and had not been born at the time of the Thurmond murder. Jack Martin traveled to Savannah to interview Lloyd, who told him "he regularly kept the pistol in a 1970s-era surplus Army flak jacket he bought." This raised the possibility that "the jacket once belonged to a soldier stationed at Fort Benning in the 1970s, who may have been involved in the stranglings." Confident that the evidence would help his client get a new trial, Martin filed a motion mentioning the Lloyd case on July 6, 2012, but asked that it be sealed from public disclosure. Three days later he filed a motion for a new trial.[289]

Jack Martin's theories aside, the second discovery of the unknown male DNA in two incidents that occurred thirty-four years apart led the state crime laboratory to look at its own processes seeking a possible testing error. In a GBI report dated November 14, 2013, after an exhaustive investigation, the laboratory reported that "a quality control sample," a specimen of semen from a known source used to test and verify the DNA analysis equipment, had either been mixed up with or contaminated the Thurmond sample, leading to a spurious result. Such semen samples were anonymously donated by laboratory employees or their spouses. Because they had no criminal significance, they had not been entered into CODIS, the FBI's national DNA database, and hence were classified as "unknown." The discovery led to a significant change in the GBI lab's quality control procedures, including entering the anonymous DNA control samples into CODIS to avoid repeating this kind of error. Unfortunately, the material available for testing from the Thurmond case had been consumed in the process, leaving no option for retesting the specimen.*

The finding of this unknown male DNA had been one of the pillars of the defense's motion for a new trial. Jack Martin was livid. "If this shows how incompetent that lab is, then all their results, not only this case but in other cases, are suspect," he said. "It is incredibly suspicious that this would come up at the very last minute. Either the GBI crime lab is incredibly incompetent or there's been manipulation of the evidence." He called for a "full investigation" and postponement of the scheduled December 3rd hearing on motions for a new trial.[290] Though the defense's theories on the

---

* See footnote in chapter 43 for more information on the CODIS database. A detailed explanation of the discovery of this error was given by Stephanie Fowler, an assistant manager in the Forensic Biology section of the State Crime Laboratory at a February 26, 2014, hearing in Judge Jordan's court. There was a third DNA error as well, this one occurring in the GBI's Coastal Laboratory in Savannah. The basic problem appeared to be cross-contamination due to inadequate cleaning of utensils and/or equipment plus shared workspaces between technicians. Extensive changes were made in laboratory protocols to rectify these issues and prevent recurrences.

Thurmond DNA had now been destroyed, the discovery of unknown male DNA on the clothing of Gertrude Miller would still provide an opportunity to challenge the state's case. Significantly, that discovery had been made by the Virginia reference laboratory *after* the GBI lab had failed to find evidence of semen on Miller's clothes. Prosecutors, however, discounted the evidence, saying it was uncertain when Miller wore the clothes that were tested.

The hearing that had originally been scheduled for December 3, 2013, was moved to February 10, 2014, and then again to February 24th, each time at the defense's request. The week of February 24th through 28th saw daily hearings in the court of Judge Jordan, each lasting hours and many times revisiting evidential issues that had been addressed in earlier hearings. Jack Martin spoke for the defense. District Attorney Julia Slater, Assistant DA Don Kelly, Special Assistant DA Susan Boleyn, and Senior Assistant Attorney General Sabrina Graham represented the state. Carlton Gary's former attorney August "Bud" Siemon was the first to testify, saying in response to Jack Martin's questions that during Gary's trials and early appeals, he "was not given crucial evidence that would have cast doubt on Gary's guilt." On cross-examination by Susan Boleyn, however, Siemon's memory seemed to falter, often stating that he could not recall specific details of events such as receiving certain important documents.

Dr. Greg Hampikian, the defense's DNA and body-secretion expert, harshly criticized the GBI laboratory's procedures while at the same time attempting to explain why that facility was unable to detect semen on items of clothing from Gertrude Miller's attack. Sarah Shields, a senior DNA analyst for Bode Technology in Virginia, testified about recovering unknown male DNA from items of Miller's clothing. On cross-examination, she admitted that she could not, in fact, say that the DNA recovered from the clothing was from semen. It could have come from other types of cells. This admission, plus the uncertainty as to when Miller was wearing the garments and the possibility of outside contamination, cast some doubt on the defense's contention that this, too, like the discredited evidence from the Thurmond case, suggested the possibility of a second, unidentified rapist.

Edward J. Covington, a retired GBI agent who had worked with the Strangler Task Force in 1978, "said he never heard investigations had found any usable fingerprints" at the scene of the stranglings. Sabrina Graham countered his testimony by showing contemporaneous reports that police found latent fingerprints that matched with Gary's at the crime scenes of the Jackson, Thurmond, Scheible, and Woodruff murders. To Covington's contention that Gary's size 13 shoes did not match smaller shoeprints found at crime scenes, Graham referred to Gary's admissions to the police after his arrest that he "sometimes wore different size shoes, from size 9 to 11, to fool the police."[291]

Tuesday, the 25th, saw an even more contentious hearing than the day before. Most of the day was devoted to the issue of the bite mark found on Janet Cofer's breast. The first witness was James Dunnavant, the coroner who took over after Don Kilgore's death. He told of finding the missing bite mold and turning it over to the then-current district attorney. Next, Dr. Carlos Galbreath described making the mold from Ms. Cofer's breast, noting that the wound only showed the upper teeth, not the lower, and that one of the upper teeth was rotated and there was a gap between the teeth. Directly contradicting Galbreath, the defense called Dr. Thomas David, the forensic dentist who examined the mold at the request of prosecutors in 1984. As Gary had had dental work done on his upper teeth between the stranglings and his arrest, it was the district attorney's opinion at that time that no meaningful comparisons could be made with the bite mold. In this current hearing, Dr. David spoke of the bite mold showing lower teeth marks. Asked for his opinion, he said, "Mr. Gary is probably not the biter," but added by way of qualification, "I cannot absolutely exclude him, but I would say that he is probably excluded." The defense's next three witnesses, all of whom had known Gary prior to his arrest in the time frame the Strangler killings took place, testified that they had not observed a gap in his front teeth, or any broken teeth.

As his final witness of the day, Jack Martin called David Rose, the author of *The Big Eddy Club*, but acting this time in his role as investigator for Martin's law firm. Rather than testify, Rose produced a "standard foot measuring device" that he had obtained from the Payless shoe store in Columbus's Peachtree Mall. Over the objections of Sabrina Graham, he was allowed to measure Carlton Gary's foot, which, with his sock off, was size 13.5 and size 14 with the sock on. In contrast, the shoe sizes found at two of the Strangler's crime scenes were reported to be around size 9 or 10.

The hearings of Wednesday, February 26th, were devoted to often-arcane technical issues, including DNA evidence and blood group secretor status. John Wegel, the now-retired forensic serologist who had testified at Gary's trial in 1986, explained that Carlton Gary had blood type O and was a "secretor," that is, one who secreted markers in his body fluids that reflect his blood type. The importance of these findings had been largely supplanted by the use of DNA analysis, which was not available in the late 1970s at the time of the Strangler's murders. Based on the studies he performed on specimens obtained at that time, Wegel still contended that they did not exclude Gary as the killer. "Nothing has changed my mind on that conclusion," he said. The second part of the day focused on DNA testing and the systematic errors that led to the erroneous finding of the DNA of an unknown male in the specimen from the Thurmond case. Stephanie Fowler, the assistant manager of the crime lab's Forensic Biology Section, spoke frankly and at length about the discovery of the errors and the steps taken to prevent their happening in the future. She again affirmed that the initially reported Thurmond result was in error. Kristen Fripp, a DNA analyst at the Savannah division of the state crime lab, reviewed the data for the match between evidence found at the Dimenstien murder and Carlton Gary's genetic profile from the CODIS system. Statistically, and assuming that Gary did not have an identical twin, the chances of the DNA found being from someone other than Gary were one in ten billion.[†]

The next day's testimony shed light on the Marion Fisher murder case from Syracuse, New York. Evidence from the crime scene where her lifeless body was found raped and strangled on June 28, 1975, was discovered by cold case detectives in 2007 to match the DNA of Carlton Gary. Lieutenant Ronald Rockwood, at the time employed by the Criminal Investigations Division of the city of Syracuse, New York, was allowed to testify on behalf of the state over the strenuous objections of Jack Martin. Rockwell and another Syracuse police officer interviewed Gary in the Jackson, Georgia, prison in 2007 following the discovery. After advising him of his Miranda rights, Gary admitted familiarity with the Syracuse neighborhood and recalled talking with three ladies in a bar, one of whom was "a little intoxicated, that she had had a fight with her husband or her boyfriend or something like that." When shown a photo of Ms. Fisher, Gary said "it could be" her, but he wasn't sure. After talking for a while, "he said he and the lady went outside and went to the back parking lot and that they had sex on the hood of somebody's car." After that, "he said that the lady walked away and he went back in the bar." Her body was found the next morning some two and a half miles away. A towel at the crime scene

---

[†] In 2014, the human population of the entire Earth was estimated be 7.25 billion, allowing the witness to say with absolute certainty that Gary was the donor of the semen sample tested.

near Ms. Fisher's body was found to have Gary's DNA on it. Judge Jordan said he "[would] not consider Rockwood's testimony when deciding whether Gary gets a new trial."[292]

Next, Columbus police chief Ricky Boren, who, as a detective assigned to follow up on the Strangler case, was closely involved in Gary's arrest and the investigation that followed, testified as to the details of those events. In particular, he recounted the hours following the May 3, 1984, arrest when Gary spoke to him and other officers about the details of the Strangler's crimes while attempting to blame them on an accomplice.

As rebuttal for the earlier testimony stating that Carlton Gary did not have a gap between his teeth, the state called Annie Canady, the Muscogee School District's records management supervisor. Ms. Canady produced two school photos of Gary taken in 1960 and 1961 showing the gap between his front teeth. He would have been ten or eleven years of age at that time. As their final witness of the day, the state called Charles Rowe, now retired as Columbus's assistant chief of police. Rowe spoke at length, confirming and reinforcing the testimony of Chief Boren, especially regarding the statements made by Carlton Gary in the hours that followed his arrest.

The next day would hear testimony from retired Det. Sgt. Mike Sellers and former district attorney Bill Smith, both of whom played integral roles in Gary's arrest and conviction.

Chapter 48

More Than Five Years Later...

Friday, February 28th, marked the final day of testimony in Judge Frank Jordan's court. As succinctly described by reporter Tim Chitwood,

> After nine hours of sometimes contentious courtroom testimony Friday, convicted "Stocking Strangler" Carlton Gary's new-trial hearing finally ended at 7:00 P.M. Now defense attorneys and prosecutors await a transcript from five days of testimony on which to base their remaining motions and their written arguments. A decision from Superior Court Judge Frank Jordan Jr. likely will be weeks or possibly months away.
>
> Most of Friday's testimony came from former District Attorney Bill Smith, now a senior Superior Court judge, who prosecuted Gary in 1986. He recapped much of the evidence presented during the trial.[293]

Mike Sellers, the former Columbus police officer who initially made the connection that led to Carlton Gary's arrest, spoke first for the state. His testimony was frequently interrupted by objections from Jack Martin, who complained that his statements were already in the trial record. District Attorney Slater explained that the purpose of his testimony was to "aid the court" in understanding how Gary was originally identified as a suspect. Martin continued to object to Sellers's recounting Gary's confession of being involved in some of the Strangler's crimes, again saying "the evidence is already in the trial record."

Former district attorney Bill Smith's testimony followed that of Sellers and was—as described by Chitwood—contentious. The purpose of Smith's testimony was to tie together for the judge the evidence and sequence of events that gave a grand jury reasonable cause to indict Carlton Gary, and a jury sufficient proof to convict him of rape, burglary, and murder and sentence him to death. Slater's examination of Smith was interrupted by frequent objections from Jack Martin, and his cross-examination by Martin was at times confrontational. Martin questioned him at length about the Jerome Livas case, with the not-so-subtle implication that some of the evidence against Gary could have been fabricated.

During the hearing, author David Rose sat at the defense table with Jack Martin. At the end of Bill Smith's testimony, Slater addressed the judge:

> I want to place in the record that while we've been in court for [five days], that at the defense table they have had a copy of the book that's entitled The Big Eddy Club, and it's been passed back and forth. Mr. Rose would show a portion of it to Mr. Martin during the—while people were testifying it was referred to. It's been taken up to the lectern while cross-examination was done, parts of it have been read. We can see that in the courtroom, but I just want to make sure it's clear for the record that they have been using this book, passing it around the table and referring to it amongst themselves.

To that, Martin replied, "That's true. It's a handy way of getting to specifics about the case that are represented in the book, nothing more, nothing less." Rose's book appeared to have become a reference manual for the defense.

As his final witness of the hearing, Jack Martin called Gregory De-Clue, PhD, a Florida-based forensic psychologist. Dr. DeClue testified that in one study of 250 convicted criminals who were later freed by DNA testing, forty were later found to have given false confessions. With this background, he compared the statements given to police by Carlton Gary with those given by Jerome Livas. Although the circumstances were different—Livas had been shown crime scenes and was interrogated by one set of officers, then later taken back to the scenes by other officers to whom he gave a "confession"—the similarity was striking. DeClue's testimony was effectively countered, however, on cross-examination by Sabrina Graham, who elicited the fact that up to thirty of those forty incidences of false confession were given by individuals who were either juveniles, mentally ill, or mentally handicapped, as was the case with Livas.

At the end of the day, the attorneys for both sides agreed that further testimony and cross-examination were needed, but they also needed to review the transcripts of the week's testimony prior to another hearing. The date for that was left open pending completion of these documents. It would be nearly a full year before the hearings resumed, the delay attributed to the time it took to prepare the 1,343 pages of transcripts.

On February 5, 2015, the parties reassembled in Judge Jordan's court-room once again. It would be a short day. Carlton Gary was not feeling well, so only two witnesses testified, both for the defense, and both to follow up on testimony from the earlier hearings in February 2014. The first was Dr. Holland Maness, a forensic odontologist who had been brought in to testify about the grade school photos of Gary showing a gap between his front teeth that had been presented during the hearings a year earlier. She said such a finding was relatively common, occurring in about one in four children, but most were closed by adulthood. On cross-examination, she admitted that a rotated tooth, as had been seen in the bite mold, could cause the gap to persist. Next, Dr. Charles F. Fenton III, a podiatrist and attorney, testified on his examination of Carlton Gary's feet. In the hearings a year earlier, journalist David Rose, using a foot-size measuring device obtained from a local shoe store, demonstrated that Gary would wear a size 13½ shoe. Based on his findings, Fenton agreed with Rose's assessment of Gary's shoe size and stated that when he examined him, he could not force Gary's foot into a size-10 shoe. He had given a report to the defense lawyers that stated if he tried to wear a shoe of that size it "would be extremely uncomfortable and limit ambulation." On cross-examination, Sabrina Graham asked, "How uncomfortable would it be, would it be more uncomfortable to put your foot in a size shoe that's too small, or to be caught by police for raping and murdering a series of women?" To this, Fenton replied, "It would be more uncomfortable to be caught by the police than to put your feet in shoes that didn't fit."

The sole witness the second day of the hearings was former prosecutor Bill Smith. Following up on his testimony from a year earlier, Jack Martin questioned Smith primarily on the evidence tying Gary to the similar crimes for which he not been charged. Much of the exchanges related to topics and evidence that had been covered earlier and/or reviewed and upheld by other courts. Judge Jordan, the person responsible for issuing a decision on a new trial, listened, rarely intervening or asking questions.

The evidentiary hearings apparently completed, Julia Slater urged the court to proceed with speed in settling the pending issues in Gary's case. Pointing out that the case had been back in the Muscogee County Superior Court for more than five years, and that it had been two and a half years since the defense filed a motion for a new trial, she suggested a firm timeline for both defense and prosecution to submit their final briefs. After some discussion, Judge Jordan agreed to give the defense, the moving party in the matter, forty-five days after the transcript of the current hearing was available to submit its brief, followed by an equal period for the state to respond, then an additional thirty days for the defense to respond to the state's brief. By early December 2015, both sides had filed their final arguments. After a period of consideration of the testimony and evidence presented at the hearings, Judge Jordan would issue his decision on a new trial. Unless, of course, there were more delays.

Chapter 49

The Briefcase

On Saturday, January 9th, 2016, Robert Grubbs was cleaning out the attic of his in-laws' house, where he and his wife had lived for more than ten years. Grubbs had formerly been a correctional officer, serving as deputy sheriff and chaplain of the Muscogee County Sheriff's Office from 2008 to 2014. In 2005, he and his wife had moved in with her mother, Doris Miller Foxworth, who apparently was suffering from declining health due to cancer and Alzheimer's-type dementia. Ms. Foxworth had subsequently moved in with another daughter; the Grubbs were clearing out the house, planning to move out of state.

In the process of cleaning the attic, Mr. Grubbs discovered a black briefcase. Thinking it was similar to one that he once owned, he opened it to discover "investigative records of a very serious nature." On asking his wife if she knew anything about the briefcase, she said that her stepfather, Don Miller, had been a deputy in the Muscogee County Sheriff's Office, but he had retired in 1982 and died the next year. She knew that he had worked on the Strangler case and presumed the records in the briefcase were somehow connected to that investigation.

Later that afternoon, Grubbs happened to meet Chief Deputy John L. Fitzpatrick Jr. of the Muscogee County Sheriff's Office at the local Piggly Wiggly grocery store. Grubbs and Fitzpatrick had worked together and remained close friends. Grubbs said, "I described to him what I had found and asked him to take it off my hands." On Monday, January 15th, he met Fitzpatrick in a commercial parking lot near the airport and turned the briefcase over to him. In an affidavit, Grubbs stated, "I personally believe that the late Deputy Don Miller was holding the briefcase with his own records in it, in case he had to be called back to court for any reason, so he would have access to his own records as many in the field of law enforcement are instructed to do in Police Academy and according to the policies and procedures of their own departments."[294]

Chief Fitzpatrick sealed the briefcase and prepared a chain-of-custody form prior to turning it over to the Muscogee County Superior Court for further investigation. The news of the discovery made its way to Judge Jordan, who arranged in early February for both Jack Martin and District

Attorney Julia Slater to examine the documents together in the presence of Commander Steven Sikes, head of the Sheriff's Office Criminal Investigative Unit. The briefcase contained a variety of papers, notebooks, police reports, and photographs. Documents that the attorneys deemed relevant to the case were copied and distributed to both sides. "What ensued was a heated exchange over whether Gary's defense had ever seen the files," an allegation that supported the defense's narrative that the prosecution had actively hidden important documents from Gary's lawyers. By August 2016, an agreement was reached that the defense had, in fact, seen the documents, but during Gary's posttrial appeals years earlier.[295]

The one item of major interest to Jack Martin was a drawing of a black man dated October 31, 1977, and signed by Herman Boone, a self-taught amateur sketch artist and at the time an officer with the Columbus police. This image was created during the attempted hypnosis session of Ms. Gertrude Miller on that day. She was unhappy with it and said at the time it was not a satisfactory illustration of her rapist.* Though Carlton Gary was not formally charged with Miller's attack, her case was among the "similar crimes," and she identified him at trial in 1986. One of the defense's major efforts focused on discrediting her identification; this drawing, which did not especially resemble Gary, added credence to that line of attack on the state's case. On August 9, 2016, Martin filed a motion with Judge Jordan stating, "This suspect looks nothing like the defendant." He requested a hearing on this issue.

On the 12th and 13th of January 2017, the parties met once more in front of Judge Jordan to argue the admissibility of evidence found in the briefcase and to once again—hopefully for a final time—restate their positions on the still-pending motion for a new trial. Bud Siemon, now thirty years older than when he had defended Carlton Gary at trial in 1986, testified that he was aware of the briefcase drawing but had not been given a copy of it. The shirt that the individual in the drawing was wearing had designs of fruit on it, leading Siemon to comment, "Carlton wouldn't have worn something that looked like it came out of Goodwill. Carlton was very stylish." Don Kelly, speaking for the state, objected. He argued that the drawing was inadmissible because it was made when Ms. Miller was

---

* See chapter 8 for the details of this. A later drawing, done in early 1978 by Calvin Earl, was said to bear a closer resemblance to Miller's attacker.

under hypnosis.[†] Furthermore, Herman Boone, who made the drawing, and Stewart Wiggins, the hypnotist, were both deceased. There were no living witnesses to authenticate it. Judge Jordan ruled that because the state had consented to allow the defense to use the transcript of the hypnosis session to interrogate Ms. Miller in the 1986 trial, the sketch could be admitted as evidence. The remainder of the day was devoted the defense's efforts to reopen discussion of previously presented evidence of shoeprints found at the Strangler's crime scenes.

The entire day of the hearing on January 13th saw the final arguments of both sides on the defense's motion for a new trial. The position of the defense held that further discoveries since Gary's trial in 1986 had so weakened the evidence and testimony used to convict him that a new trial was necessary. Julia Slater, speaking for the state, reiterated the fact that these same issues had been heard on multiple occasions by all levels of the state and federal judiciary and had not been found sufficient to warrant a new trial. The so-called "new evidence" presented by the defense, had it been available or presented at the time of the original trial, would not have resulted in a different outcome. Judge Jordan said that he would consider all that had been presented before issuing his ruling.

Exactly a month after the hearings, on February 12, 2017, the cable crime channel Investigation Discovery aired an episode of "Vanity Fair Confidential" titled "Seeds of Doubt" featuring *Vanity Fair* contributing editor David Rose. In a well-illustrated overview of Columbus's Strangler killings, the case was briefly reviewed through Carlton Gary's conviction and sentencing, with emphasis on the failure of the court to provide funding to Gary's attorneys. A number of individuals who were involved or otherwise knowledgeable about the case were interviewed, including Billy Winn, Mike Sellers, Richard Hyatt, Jack Martin, William Fitzpatrick, Ron Rockwell, and Greg Hampikian. A bit more than halfway through the episode, Rose is introduced: "Year after year, a series of lawyers petition the court for a new trial. After ten years on death row, Carlton Gary's defense team finds a new ally, British investigative journalist David Rose." The narrator cites shoeprint evidence and the issue of the bite mold, suggesting these had been withheld from the defense. The Marion Fisher case from Syracuse, New York, is examined, with the comment that the findings implicating Gary were "unsubstantiated and have nothing to do with

---

[†] Evidence and testimony obtained from a witness under hypnosis cannot be admitted at trial under Georgia case law.

this Georgia case." Rose opined that the revelation of the DNA match in the Fisher case "helped to create the impression that [Carlton Gary] is a really bad guy." The episode ended with the statement that a judge would soon rule on Carlton Gary's petition for a new trial.[296]

Months passed without progress in the case. On June 27, 2017, prosecutors filed a one-page motion in the Superior Court of Muscogee County quoting a section of the Georgia code:

> In all counties with more than 100,000 inhabitants, it shall be the duty of the judge of the superior, state or city court, unless providentially hindered or unless counsel for the plaintiff and the defendant agree in writing to extend the time, to decide promptly, within 90 days after the same have been argued before him or submitted to him without argument, all motions for new trials, injunctions, demurrers and all other motions of any nature.[297]

What the motion did not say, but clearly implied by its reference, was a phase in the law from a paragraph that followed:

> If any judge repeatedly or persistently fails or refuses to decide the various motions, demurrers, and injunctions coming before him in the manner provided by such subsections, such conduct shall be grounds for impeachment and the penalty therefore shall be his removal from office.[298]

A signed editorial appeared nearly a month later in the *Ledger-Enquirer*. Calling any further delay unconscionable, the author pointed out,

> It has been forty years since the first of the rapes and stranglings of seven older Columbus women. Their families' wait for justice is well into its third generation now; it has been so long since these murders shook Columbus and the whole Chattahoochee Valley area that some of the victims' loved ones have lived out their lives, waiting futilely for justice, and passed on.[299]

Chapter 50

An Order and The End

On September 1, 2017, Judge Frank Jordan Jr. filed a fifty-page order in Muscogee County Superior Court under the weighty title of "Order on Petitioner's Extraordinary Motion for a New Trial or in the Alternative for a New Sentencing." Methodically and in detail, Jordan first reviewed the crimes for which Carlton Gary was indicted and the facts related to those crimes as well as other "similar transactions" in Georgia and New York with which Gary was not charged. He gave a detailed account of the procedural history of the case, including the three occasions on which the US Supreme Court ruled against Gary by refusing to review the rulings of lower state and federal courts. Jordan summarized the hearings held in his own court in February 2014, February 2015, and January 2017. He reviewed the evidence and testimony on which Gary's attorneys had based his appeal: the DNA testing, Gary's secretor status, the bite-mark mold, the fingerprints found at crime scenes, the composite sketch found in the briefcase, the shoeprint evidence, and Gary's confession given to police officers in the hours after his arrest. Jordan noted that the Georgia Supreme Court had already ruled against Gary on the claim that he was denied funds to pursue his defense.

In Georgia, motions for a new trial based on newly discovered evidence must meet certain well-established criteria derived from case law.[*] In a lengthy and well-documented legal analysis, Jordan demonstrated that Gary failed to satisfy these standards, and thus rejected the defense's motion for a new trial or alternative sentencing. It had been seven years and eight and one-half months, or more precisely 2,816 days, since the Georgia Supreme Court sent the case back to the Muscogee County Superior Court for DNA testing.

The reactions from the defense and prosecution were not unexpected. "We are very disappointed in the decision, but we definitely will have an appeal," Jack Martin said. District Attorney Julia Slater said she was pleased with Judge Jordan's ruling. "I think he made a sound legal decision

---

[*] The most frequently cited case is *Timberlake v. State*, 246 Ga. 488, 271 S.E.2d 792 (1980), in which the Georgia Supreme Court cited specific points that must be proven in order to warrant a new trial.

on the case. We will be moving on toward an execution."[300] On October 19th, seven weeks after releasing his decision, Judge Frank Jordan announced he would be retiring at the end of the year, cutting short his four-year elected term as Superior Court judge.

Barring a miracle, the time left before Gary's execution was now marked in weeks instead of years. On November 1st, Gary's defense team filed a ninety-page appeal to the Georgia Supreme Court, hoping to reverse Judge Jordan's ruling. "Had jurors in…Carlton Gary's 1986 trial seen the evidence his defense team since has uncovered, they likely either would have found him not guilty in the heinous serial killings of 1977 and 1978, or at least not sentenced him to death," the appeal stated.[301] "Cherry-picking a few questionable clues that cast doubt on Carlton Gary's guilt does not outweigh the overwhelming evidence proving he's the ritual serial killer that came to be known as the 'Stocking Strangler,'" prosecutors argued in an eighty-page response to the defense's appeal. "Defendant did not present a single claim during his extraordinary motion for a new trial proceeding that in any way diminished the credibility of his guilt," the filing stated.[302] At 4:00 P.M. on Friday afternoon, December 1st, the justices of the Georgia Supreme Court issued a unanimous decision rejecting Gary's appeal for a new trial or commuted sentence. The next step would be the remanding of the case to the Muscogee County Superior Court, where the judge would issue a death warrant designating a week during which Gary's execution was to take place.

On December 10th, Martin filed a motion for the Georgia Supreme Court to reconsider its decision. Referring to "newly discovered physical evidence," he said, "It is an abomination in the state of Georgia for us to be sending someone to be executed when it's obvious he did not get a fair trial." The prosecution filed its response five days later. Julia Slater, speaking for the state, said, "This verdict has been reviewed by no fewer than thirteen courts, none of whom have found any reason to reverse the conviction or the sentence."[303] On January 16th, the court rejected the motion for reconsideration. On February 23rd, Judge Frank Jordan Jr., now acting in the role of senior judge, signed Carlton Gary's death warrant specifying that he be executed in the seven-day period between March 15 and March 22, 2018. The Department of Corrections scheduled the sentence to be carried out at 7:00 P.M. on March 15, 2018.

In the meantime, Gary's lawyers filed a motion with the Muscogee County Superior Court on March 9th requesting a stay of execution while a petition for a fourth review of his case was pending before the US

Supreme Court. In a separate petition to the parole board, they wrote, "There is nothing more terrifying and horrible than for the state to take the life of an actually innocent citizen and this board stands as a bulwark against that calamity. Here, there is just too much doubt about Mr. Gary's guilt not known at the time of his trial to countenance his execution. We are not talking about questionable recanting witnesses who came forward long after trial, but hard physical evidence of innocence."[304] The pleadings now took on a note of despair. With an unintended bit of morbid banality, on March 13th, the Department of Corrections announced that Gary had declined to order a last meal and thus would be offered standard fare of grilled hamburger, hot dog, white beans, coleslaw, and a grape beverage.[305] On the same day, Superior Court judge Frank Jordan denied the petition for a stay of execution that had been filed four days earlier.

On March 14th, lawyers for the defense and prosecution presented their cases in a private meeting of the Georgia Board of Pardons and Paroles for three hours in the morning and an additional three and a half hours in the afternoon. If a majority of its five members agreed, the parole board had the option of commuting Gary's death sentence to one of life in prison, or alternatively, staying his execution for ninety days. Jack Martin, still focusing on "new evidence," brought with him Jack Pickel, one of the jurors who convicted Gary in his 1986 trial. Pickel "told the board he would not have voted to give Gary the death penalty had he seen the evidence available today, particularly a DNA test from the September 11, 1977, assault on Gertrude Miller." District Attorney Slater declined to say who the prosecution had presented as witnesses but noted "representatives from some of the victims' families were present." She expressed confidence that the board would uphold Gary's sentence. Contacted via email for his opinion, David Rose told the *Ledger-Enquirer*, "If Carlton is executed, it would represent a barbaric perversion of the course of justice," further referring to such an event as "judicial murder."[306] The board refused to alter Gary's sentence, allowing the scheduled execution to take place.

By the morning of the 15th, the scheduled day of execution, the US Supreme Court had not yet responded to Gary's petition for review. Another federal-level appeal with the US Eleventh Circuit Court of Appeals was pending at the same time. Near 7:00 P.M., the designated time for the execution, Gary was taken to the death house, a nondescript, white, concrete-block building on the campus of the Georgia Diagnostic Prison in Jackson. Inside were two larger rooms, the white-walled death chamber and an adjacent viewing area with rows of simple wooden benches arranged to provide witnesses a view of the execution through a line of four windows.

Around 9:00 P.M., word arrived that the Eleventh Circuit Court had rejected its appeal; defense attorneys immediately appealed that decision to the US Supreme Court as well. Around 10:00 P.M., word came that the high court had rejected both appeals. The prison warden addressed the witnesses via a microphone from the death chamber, reading the warrant signed by Judge Frank Jordan. He shut off the microphone and left the room. Gary was silent; he had declined the opportunity to make a final statement. A medical technician began the infusion of pentobarbital into Gary's veins. His "chest rose and fell rapidly, three or four times, then his lips fluttered, and then his mouth opened wide like a yawn and closed. Then his head drifted slightly to the left" as his respirations ceased. After a wait of a number of minutes, the warden and two physicians in white coats reentered the room. The physicians examined Gary, then nodded to the warden. He, in turn, announced the time of death—10:33 P.M.—and "proclaimed that the execution had been carried out under the law."[307]

Tim Chitwood, the *Ledger-Enquirer* reporter who had followed the Strangler case for several years and who was present for the execution, observed, "For those who believe that Gary is innocent—that his arrest, conviction and execution resulted from racism, conspiracies and cover-ups— the Stocking Strangler saga doesn't end with his last breath before a silent congregation in a cinderblock building. But it does end for the law enforcement officers who spent their career hunting him down." In a touch of irony, and with a nod to Gary's victims, Chitwood also observed, "The last thing the prison doctors did, after confirming Gary was dead, was leave his face covered with a sheet."[308]

Thoughts

The saga of Carlton Gary and the so-called "Stocking Strangler" is at once a horrific, bizarre, complicated, and fascinating tale that includes not only his crimes, but also issues of race, politics, police conduct, judicial integrity, as well as happenstance and unexpected turns in direction from beginning to end. After a sober and dispassionate review of the facts in the case, it is difficult to describe Gary as anything other than a career criminal and sociopathic murderer. During the thirty months of nonincarcerated freedom that Gary experienced between the murder and rape of Nellie Farmer in 1970 and his arrest in 1984, he is believed to have committed a total of at least nine murders as well as dozens of armed robberies, rapes, and burglaries. It is not unreasonable to speculate that there were likely other similar crimes that remain unsolved—for example, the attack on Essie Jones in Columbus's Ralston Towers in February 1979, or the earlier strangling murder of sixty-two-year-old Marion Brewer in New York in February 1970.[309]

The assertions that Gary's conviction and sentence were somehow based on conspiracy, or racism, or a simple desire to blame the Strangler's crimes on someone ring hollow when compared with the direct and circumstantial evidence that led to these outcomes. Allegations by naysayers aside, he received the full benefit of doubt and review in his appeals, which spanned the entire state and federal judicial systems multiple times. Gary's defenders, those who proclaimed his innocence, often based their reasoning on preconceived notions, including opposition to the death penalty or the belief that a person of color cannot be afforded a "fair trial" in the American South. There were yet others who were beguiled by Gary's con man persona and his oft-proclaimed statements denying culpability in the Strangler's crimes. Still others may have been motivated by simple distrust of the system or were pursuing self-promotion through their contrarian views.

When all is said and done, two facts remain: Carlton Gary was the instrument of untold fear, horror, and despair for his victims, their families, and the community at large. Carlton Gary was tried in a court of law and was put to death for his crimes.

Author's Note and Acknowledgments

The story of the Columbus Strangler is, without a doubt, the most complicated tale that I have ever attempted to put into words. Spanning in its entirety more than four decades, I estimate the written record, which includes transcripts and other court records, police reports, newspaper and magazine articles, as well as miscellaneous related documents, to be in excess of 15,000 pages. Sorting through these in both digital and print form while attempting to extract a cogent narrative from the seeming chaos was a monumental task. On top of this, there were hours spent interviewing those with firsthand knowledge of the case and viewing video recordings of the August 1986 trial. Over the years, various aspects of the Strangler case have been reported by print and broadcast journalists, as well as several books alleging alternative explanations for these murders. In writing this story, my goal was to present a factual and unbiased account of the crimes, the hunt for the killer, and the judicial proceedings that followed, keeping conjecture and editorial comment to a minimum. I believe the facts speak adequately for themselves.

Sources and quotes are documented with endnote citations except when the context of the material is stated and/or obvious, as in police reports and trial transcripts. Opinions and reactions were, for the most part, drawn from contemporary news articles. To assist the reader in keeping up with the details, a series of timelines have been included in an appendix.

A work of this complexity would not have been possible without the cooperation and assistance of many individuals. Billy Winn, a journalist and former member of the editorial staff of the *Ledger-Enquirer* newspapers, was kind enough to share his files of contemporary police reports and related documents collected during and after the Strangler's reign of terror in the late 1970s. Bill Smith, the district attorney who led the prosecution team following Gary's arrest and through his trial, shared his files and encyclopedic knowledge of the case during many hours of interviews, both in person and via telephone. His advice and input regarding legal issues was invaluable. Mike Sellers, the Columbus police officer who initially helped break the case and was integrally involved in Gary's arrest, shared his knowledge, insight, and extensive files on the case. After the arrest, Mike worked with the prosecution team during the pretrial period and was an important witness for the state during the trial. A word of special appreciation is due to Mike's wife, Sarah Sellers, for her comprehensive collection of newspaper clippings carefully preserved in scrapbooks, as well as digital copies of transcripts and similar files pertinent to the case. Richard Smith, the Columbus police officer who interviewed Carlton Gary in Greenville, South Carolina, in March 1979, shared police reports documenting that contact. Julia Slater, the district attorney for the Chattahoochee Judicial Circuit, allowed me to review evidence and files from the Strangler investigation and trial, and shared materials relating to the lengthy appeals process that followed. In addition to these individuals, Ricky Boren, Charlie Rowe, and Susan Boleyn discussed the case with me and provided insight and direction on several issues. Richard Hyatt and Tim Chitwood, who covered the Carlton Gary case for the *Ledger-Enquirer*, provided valuable insight into that aspect of the story.

A number of those mentioned above read the manuscript in partial or complete form and provided criticism and feedback. Other readers include Mark Shelnutt, Jessica Heldreth, Sarah C. Arnett, Rachel R. Mason, and Chix Miller. My assistant, Brandi Taylor, and others who work with me, including Deb Mantey, Penny Kent, and James and Sue Garrett, helped by providing me with the extensive free time I needed to complete this writing project. For this I am most grateful. Finally, I must thank my family and the good people at Mercer University Press for giving me the freedom, support, and opportunity to write this story.

William Rawlings
Sandersville, Georgia
July 1, 2021

Appendix

The story of Carlton Gary and the Stocking Strangler is a complex one. In order to assist the reader with the facts and the sequence of events, I have included three timelines: Carlton Gary 1950–1984; the 1977–1979 crimes in Columbus, Georgia; and Carlton Gary 1984 through 2018.

CARLTON GARY 1950–1984

This detailed timeline was prepared in November 1985 by Al Miller, one of the investigators for the prosecution team prior to Gary's trial. The original document is fourteen legal-sized pages in length, begins with Gary's birth in Columbus City Hospital in September 1950, and ends with his arrest in Albany, Georgia, in May 1984. Because of the size and complexity of this timeline, and because it speaks to who Carlton Gary was, while shedding light on his background and upbringing, rather than attempt to excerpt and summarize this document, I have chosen to make it available in its entirety online. It can be accessed at *https://www.williamrawlings.com/carltongarytimeline195084.html*. Readers who might wish to delve into Gary's upbringing, personality, and criminal history are encouraged to review it. Briefly, Gary was convicted of, or the prime suspect in, at least ten murders, twenty-two armed robberies, fourteen rapes, and twenty-one burglaries. It is not unreasonable to assume that he was associated with other crimes that remain unsolved.

CRIMES IN COLUMBUS, GEORGIA, ATTRIBUTED TO CARLTON GARY 1977–1979

On August 23, 1977, Carlton Gary escaped from the Onondaga County prison in Syracuse, New York, and returned to Columbus, Georgia. Prior to his arrest and incarceration in South Carolina on armed robbery charges approximately seventeen and a half months later, he is suspected of or known to have committed a number of crimes, including burglary, rape, armed robbery, and murder. This list refers only to crimes in the Columbus area that Gary admitted to or was strongly suspected of. Others, including several burglaries, are not noted. This list also excludes crimes committed elsewhere, for example in South Carolina, where Gary became known as the "Steak House Bandit." The dates given for murders are those when the body of the victim was found. In some cases, the actual time of the murder may have occurred prior to midnight the preceding day.

1977:

- September 11: Gertrude Miller, age 64, of 2703 Hood Street, is beaten, raped, and left for dead after being strangled. She survives and later identifies Gary as her attacker.

- September 16: Mary Willis "Ferne" Jackson, age 59, of 2505 17th Street, is raped and murdered by strangulation with a stocking.

- September 24: Jean Dimenstien, age 71, of 3027 21st Street, is raped and strangled with a stocking.

- October 8: The home of Callye East, age 75, and her sister Nellie Sanderson, age 78, at 1427 Eberhart Avenue, is burglarized. Among other items, a .22 caliber Ruger pistol that would later help lead to Gary's arrest is stolen.

- October 21: Florence Scheible, age 89, of 1941 Dimon Street, is raped and murdered by strangulation with a stocking.

- October 25: Martha Thurmond, age 70, of 2614 Marion Street, is raped and murdered by strangulation with a stocking.

- December 20: The home of Mr. and Mrs. William Swift at 1710 Buena Vista Road is burglarized.

- December 28: Kathleen Woodruff, age 74, of 1811 Buena Vista Road, is raped and murdered by strangulation with a scarf.

1978:

- January 1: The home of Mr. and Mrs. Abraham Illges, respectively age 85 and 75, at 2021 Brookside Drive is burglarized.

- February 11: The home of Mr. and Mrs. Abraham Illges at 2021 Brookside Drive is burglarized a second time. The burglar is frightened by an alarm that had been installed after the earlier burglary in January.

- February 11: Ruth Schwob, age 74, of 1800 Carter Avenue, is attacked, but the intruder is frightened away by a bedside panic alarm. She survives, and on arrival the police find her with a stocking wrapped around her neck.

- February 12: Mildred Borom, age 78, of 1612 Forest Avenue, is found raped and strangled with a curtain drawcord.

- April 20: Janet Cofer, age 61, of 3783 Steam Mill Road is raped and murdered by strangulation with a stocking.

- April 20: Gary robs the Burger King at 3520 Macon Road.

- May 14: Gary robs the Hungry Hunter at 1834 Midtown Drive.

- September 4: Gary robs the Western Sizzlin' restaurant at 4385 Victory Drive.

1979:

- February 15: Essie Jones, age 83, is attacked and raped in her apartment in Columbus's Ralston Towers. Gary was considered the likely suspect but was never charged.

- February 16: Gary is arrested following the robbery of a restaurant in South Carolina and would remain incarcerated until his escape from prison in March 1984.

Carlton Gary: March 1984 through March 2018

1984:

- March 15: Gary escapes from Goodman Correctional Institution in Greenville, South Carolina, where he had been serving a twenty-one-year sentence for armed robbery, with sixteen years of his sentence left to serve. He returns to Columbus, Georgia.

- April 3: Gary robs a Po' Folks restaurant in Phenix City, Alabama, and rapes a female employee there.

- April 16: Gary robs a Wendy's restaurant in Gainesville, Florida.

- April 18: Gary, using the alias of Michael Anthony David, is arrested in Columbus, Georgia, for possessing a small amount of marijuana but is released after posting a cash bond.

- April 19: Gary is tentatively identified as a suspect based on the recovery and tracing of the Ruger pistol that had been stolen in a burglary in October 1977.

- April 22: Gary robs a McDonald's restaurant in Montgomery, Alabama.

- April 28: Gary robs the County Seat Store in Gainesville, Florida.

- April 30: A copy of Gary's fingerprints arrive at the Columbus Police Department and are matched with a fingerprint from the Kathleen Woodruff crime scene.

- May 3: Gary is arrested in Albany, Georgia. That night, he is accompanied by police officers on a tour of crimes scenes in the Wynnton area of Columbus. He admits being at the scenes but alleges that another man committed the murders.

- May 4: Gary is indicted by a grand jury on three counts of rape, burglary, and murder. District Attorney Bill Smith announces that he will seek the death penalty if Gary is convicted.

- May 9: Judge John Land appoints attorneys William Kirby and Stephen Hyles to represent Gary.

- May 10: Gary is said to attempt suicide.

- August 28: Attorney August "Bud" Siemon takes over as Gary's lead defense counsel. Attorneys Bruce Harvey and Gary Parker join as co-counsels later in the fall.

1985:

- May: After a motion and hearing, Judge Land is recused based on questions of his objectivity. Judge E. Mullins Whisnant is assigned to the case. Within a matter of days, Whisnant recuses himself because he served as district attorney during some of the Strangler murders. The case is assigned to Judge Kenneth Followill.

- December 18: Parker withdraws as Gary's co-counsel. Harvey later withdraws.

- December 29: Gary's attempts at escape from jail are discovered. He is moved to another cell and security is increased.

1986:

- March 10: Gary's trial is to begin, but Gary refuses to come to court while his attorney, Siemon, alleges he is incompetent to stand trial. Judge Followill orders a psychological evaluation.

- March 24–28: Gary is sent to Central State Hospital in Milledgeville, Georgia, for evaluation of his competency. He refuses to cooperate with personnel there.

- April 21–28: Judge Followill holds a civil jury trial on Gary's competency. He is found competent to stand trial.

- June 9: A second attempt to try Gary on the charges of murder, rape, and robbery starts. Siemon files a motion for a change of venue on the seventh day of jury selection.

- June 18: Before evidence and witnesses are heard, Followill grants Siemon's motion for a change of venue without opposition from the State.

- July 2: Judge Followill announces that jury selection will take place in Griffin, Spalding County, Georgia, and that the jury from there will be brought to Columbus for the trial. Siemon attempts unsuccessfully to have Followill removed as judge.

- July 28–August 8: Jury selection for *State v. Carlton Gary.*

- August 8–27: Trial of Gary, beginning with hearings and motions, followed by testimony and presentation of evidence on August 11.

- August 26: After deliberating for approximately one hour, the jury finds Carlton Gary guilty on all charges.

- August 27: In the penalty phase of the trial, the jury hears appeals from both the defense and prosecution, and after deliberation, sentences Gary to death.

1986–1990:

- Gary's attorneys appeal his case in the state and federal courts system. After appropriate consideration, the appeals are rejected at each level, ending with the US Supreme Court declining to review the case in October 1990.

1991–1996:

- Gary's case is appealed in the state courts system with habeas corpus petitions. These were finally rejected by the Georgia Supreme Court in October 1996.

1997–2009:

- May 27, 1997: The US Supreme Court declines Gary's petition for a writ of certiorari.

- A series of appeals is filed in the federal courts system beginning with a habeas corpus petition filed in the US District Court for the Middle District of Georgia. Evidentiary hearings are held on several issues with rulings adverse to Gary. The US Supreme Court declines for the third time to review the case in November 2009, clearing the way for Gary's execution based on his 1986 conviction. The execution is scheduled for December 16, 2009.

- December 16, 2009: Less than four hours prior to Gary's scheduled execution, the Georgia Supreme Court remands the case to the Muscogee County Superior Court for the purpose of examining DNA evidence.

2010–2018:

- Between 2010 and 2017 a series of evidentiary hearings are held in the court of Superior Court Judge Frank Jordan Jr. in Columbus.

- July 9, 2012: Gary's attorneys file an Extraordinary Motion for a New Trial, alleging discovery of new evidence, among other issues.

- September 1, 2017: Judge Jordan denies Gary's petition for a new trial, again clearing the way for Gary's execution.

- February 23, 2018: Judge Jordan signs an execution warrant. The Georgia Department of Corrections schedules the execution for March 15, 2018.

- March 15, 2018: After exhausting all possible appeals, including those made to the Georgia Board of Pardons and Paroles and the US Supreme Court, Carlton Gary is executed by lethal injection.

Endnotes

[1] *Charleston (SC) News and Courier*, 5 February 1978. The title of the prologue is taken from the headline of the article.

[2] Andrew K. Frank, "The Rise and Fall of William McIntosh: Authority and Identity on the Early American Frontier," *The Georgia Historical Quarterly*, 86/1 (Spring 2002).

[3] Margaret B. Armistead, "Chief William McIntosh and the Indian Springs Treaties," *The Georgia Review*, 11/3 (Fall 1957): 315.

[4] www.georgiaencyclopedia.org/articles /counties-cities-neighborhoods/columbus. Accessed 1 October 2020.

[5] www.georgiaencyclopedia.org/articles /history-archaeology/thomas-brewer-1894-1956. Accessed 3 October 2020.

[6] Dallas (TX) Morning News, 19 February 1956.

[7] Charleston (SC) News and Courier, 20 February 1956.

[8] *Boston Daily Record,* 12 February 1957; *Oregonian* (Portland) 12 February 1957.

[9] Causey, Virginia E., *Red Clay, White Water & Blues: A History of Columbus Georgia.* Athens: University of Georgia Press, 2019, 177.

[10] See Causey, 226-230.

[11] Columbus (GA) Enquirer, 9 January 1976.

[12] Ibid., 23 August 1977.

[13] Columbus (GA) Ledger, 22 August 1977.

[14] Columbus (GA) Enquirer, 4 August 1977.

[15] Ibid., 13 September 1977.

[16] *Columbus (GA) Ledger,* 19 September 1977.

[17] Ibid.

[18] Ibid., 20 September 1977.

[19] Columbus (GA) Ledger-Enquirer, 18 September 1977.

[20] *Columbus (GA) Ledger,* 26 September 1977.

[21] *Columbus (GA) Enquirer,* 26 September 1977.

[22] *Columbus (GA) Ledger,* 26 September 1977.

[23] *Columbus (GA) Enquirer,* 26 September 1977.

[24] Ibid., 27 September 1977.

[25] *Columbus (GA) Ledger,* 27 September 1977.

[26] Ibid.

[27] *Columbus (GA) Ledger,* 29 September 1977.

[28] Ibid., 28 September 1977.

[29] *Columbus (GA) Enquirer,* 30 September 1977.

[30] *Columbus (GA) Ledger,* 27 September 1977.

[31] Columbus (GA) Ledger-Enquirer, 2 October 1977.

[32] Columbus Police Department Supplementary Report, 3 October 1977.

[33] Columbus (GA) Ledger, 4 October 1977.

[34] Columbus (GA) Enquirer, 4 October 1977.

[35] *Columbus (GA) Ledger*, 13 October 1977.

[36] Columbus (GA) Enquirer, 13 October 1977.

[37] Columbus (GA) Ledger-Enquirer, 15 October 1977.

[38] Columbus (GA) Enquirer, 18 October 1977.

[39] Statement of Paul G. Scheible to the Columbus Police Department, 22 October 1977.

[40] Columbus (GA) Ledger-Enquirer, 22 October 1977.

[41] Ibid.

[42] Official Report of Georgia State Crime Laboratory, Columbus Branch, in regard to Florence Scheible, 2 November 1977.

[43] Ibid., 25 October 1977.

[44] *Columbus (GA) Ledger*, 24 October 1977.

[45] *Brunswick (GA) News*, 27 October 1977.

[46] Columbus (GA) Enquirer, 26 October 1977.

[47] Ibid.

[48] *Columbus (GA) Ledger*, 26 October 1977.

[49] Columbus (GA) Enquirer, 26 October 1977.

[50] *Columbus (GA) Ledger*, 26 October 1977.

[51] Georgia State Crime Laboratory Official Report of evidence analysis of Thurman murder, 3 November 1977.

[52] Statement by Irene L. Darden to Columbus Police Department, 4 November 1977.

[53] *Columbus (GA) Ledger*, 26 October 1977.

[54] Ibid., 27 October 1977.

[55] Columbus (GA) Enquirer, 26 October 1977.

[56] Ibid., 28 October 1977.

[57] *Columbus (GA) Ledger*, 28 October 1977.

[58] Columbus (GA) Ledger-Enquirer, 6 November 1977.

[59] *Columbus (GA) Ledger*, 9 November 1977.

[60] Columbus (GA) Enquirer, 10 November 1977.

[61] *Columbus (GA) Ledger*, 18 November 1977.

[62] Columbus (GA) Ledger-Enquirer, 20 November 1977.

[63] Columbus Police Interoffice Memo, J. B. Hicks to All Persons of the Investigative Services, 25 October 1977.

[64] Columbus Police Interoffice Memo, R. A. Jones to Chief Curtis E. McClung, 28 October 1977.

[65] Columbus Police Detective Division Report, 29 October 1977.

[66] Columbus (GA) Ledger-Enquirer, 30 October 1977.

[67] Ibid., 27 November 1977.

[68] Columbus (GA) Ledger, 16 December 1977.

[69] Ibid., 22 December 1977.

[70] The date of this report, December 28, 1977, is ironic in that it summarized the status of the first four strangling cases and gave the impression that police were making progress in apprehending the Strangler. That very afternoon, the body of the fifth victim, Kathleen Woodruff, would be discovered strangulated and sexually assaulted in her home. One must make the assumption that the report would have been submitted on the morning of that day.

[71] Statement of Tommie Stevens to Columbus Police Department, 28 December 1977.

[72] *Mobile (AL) Register*, 30 December 1977.

[73] *Washington Post*, 30 December 1977.

[74] Columbus (GA) Enquirer, 29 December 1977.

[75] Ibid., 30 December 1977.

[76] *Columbus (GA) Ledger*, 29 December 1977.

[77] Columbus (GA) Enquirer, 29 December 1977.

[78] Ibid., 30 December 1977.

[79] Columbus (GA) Ledger-Enquirer, 1 January 1978.

[80] Ibid.

[81] Columbus (GA) Enquirer, 3 January 1978.

[82] *Brunswick (GA) News*, 2 January 1978.

[83] Columbus (GA) Enquirer, 6 January 1978.

[84] Columbus (GA) Ledger, 5 January 1978.

[85] "The Columbus Stocking Stranglings," a video production by the Brookstone School Young Historians (undated, but circa 2004–2005) offers several interviews of individuals who lived in Wynnton neighborhoods at the time, as well as with former district attorney, and later judge, William Smith.

[86] Columbus (GA) Ledger-Enquirer, 8 January 1978.

[87] Ibid., 5 February 1978.

[88] Report from Columbus police files, 18 January 1978.

[89] Ibid., 23 January 1978.

[90] *Columbus (GA) Ledger*, 23 January 1978.

[91] Columbus (GA) Ledger-Enquirer, 12 February 1978.

[92] Ibid.

[93] *Columbus (GA) Ledger*, 13 February 1978.

[94] Columbus (GA) Enquirer, 13 February 1978.

[95] *Marietta (GA) Journal*, 13 February 1978.

[96] Columbus (GA) Enquirer, 14 February 1978.

[97] Ibid., 13 February 1978.

[98] Ibid.

[99] *Columbus (GA) Ledger*, 14 February 1978.

[100] Columbus (GA) Enquirer, 13 February 1978.

[101] Ibid., 15 February 1978.

[102] Columbus (GA) Enquirer, 15 February 1978.

[103] *Columbus (GA) Ledger*, 15 February 1978.

[104] Ibid., 14 February 1978.

[105] Ibid., 16 February 1978.

[106] Ibid.

[107] *Columbus (GA) Ledger*, 22 February 1978.

[108] Columbus (GA) Enquirer, 23 February 1978.

[109] Ibid.

[110] *Columbus (GA) Ledger*, 27 February 1978.

[111] Columbus (GA) Enquirer, 28 February 1978.

[112] Ibid., 24 February 1978.

[113] Columbus (GA) Ledger-Enquirer, 26 February 1978.

[114] Ibid.

[115] Unless otherwise cited, the details and quotes in this chapter are from the trial transcript of *Georgia v. Hance*, held in Columbus, Georgia, in December 1978.

[116] Brunswick (GA) News, 1 April 1978.

[117] Columbus (GA) Enquirer, 21 April 1978.

[118] Ibid.

[119] Columbus (GA) Ledger, 20 April 1978.

[120] Brunswick (GA) News, 21 April 1978.

[121] Columbus (GA) Ledger, 21 April 1978

[122] Columbus (GA) Enquirer 21, April 1978.

[123] Marietta (GA) Journal, 1 June 1978.

[124] Ibid., 22 June 1978.

[125] Columbus (GA) Ledger, 20 July 1978.

[126] Ibid., 24 July 1978.

[127] Ibid., 27 July 1978.

[128] Columbus (GA) Enquirer, 28 July 1978.

[129] Columbus (GA) Ledger-Enquirer, 30 July 1978.

[130] *Columbus (GA) Enquirer*, 15 September 1978.

[131] The details of the assault on Mrs. Essie Jones are drawn from police reports of the incident.

[132] *Brunswick (GA) News*, 16 February 1979.

[133] Ibid., 18 April 1979.

[134] Ibid., 19 April 1979.

[135] Ibid.

[136] Ibid., 20 April 1979.

137 Columbus (GA) Ledger, 18 July 1980.

138 The details and quotes in this chapter are drawn from contemporary newspaper reports and interviews with former Columbus police officer Michael Sellers from January through May 2021.

139 Columbus (GA) Ledger-Enquirer, 5 May 1984.

140 Ibid.

141 Ibid.

142 Ibid.

143 Columbus (GA) Ledger, 4 May 1984.

144 Unless otherwise cited, the details and quotes in this chapter are drawn from interviews with Sgt. Mike Sellers and the August 1984 trial transcript of *Georgia v. Carlton Gary.*

145 Columbus (GA) Ledger, 4 May 1984.

146 Atlanta Constitution, 4 May 1984.

147 Columbus (GA) Ledger-Enquirer, 5 May 1984.

148 Ibid.

149 Atlanta Journal-Constitution, 5 May 1984.

150 Columbus (GA) Enquirer, 18 May 1984.

151 The details of Gary's arrest were drawn from testimony given in his August 1986 trial.

152 Ibid.

153 Columbus (GA) Enquirer, 18 May 1984.

154 Ibid., 11 May 1984.

155 Ibid.

156 Columbus (GA) Ledger, 16 May 1984.

157 Ibid., 18 May 1984.

158 Columbus (GA) Enquirer, 18 May 1984.

159 Ibid., 21 June 1984.

160 Ibid., 10 July 1984.

161 Columbus (GA) Ledger-Enquirer, 15 July 1984.

162 Columbus (GA) Enquirer, 18 July 1984.

163 Columbus (GA) Ledger-Enquirer, 15 July 1984.

164 Ibid.

165 Ibid.

166 Columbus (GA) Ledger, 29 August 1984.

167 Columbus (GA) Enquirer, 26 September 1984.

168 Columbus (GA) Ledger-Enquirer, 15 December 1984.

169 Ibid., 9 February 1985.

170 Columbus (GA) Ledger, 14 March 1985.

171 Ibid., 6 May 1985.

172 Columbus (GA) Enquirer, 22 May 1985.

[173] Ibid., 14 June 1985.

[174] Ibid., 21 June 1985.

[175] Columbus (GA) Ledger, 3 July 1985.

[176] Columbus (GA) Enquirer, 4 July 1985.

[177] Ibid., 8 October 1985.

[178] Ibid., 18 December 1985.

[179] Ibid., 19 December 1985.

[180] Atlanta Journal-Constitution, 1 January 1986.

[181] Columbus (GA) Ledger-Enquirer, 2 February 1986.

[182] Columbus (GA) Enquirer, 20 February 1986.

[183] Columbus (GA) Ledger, 24 February 1986.

[184] Columbus (GA) Enquirer, 27 February 1986.

[185] Ibid.

[186] Ibid., 10 March 1986.

[187] Columbus (GA) Ledger, 10 March 1986.

[188] Columbus (GA) Enquirer, 11 March 1986.

[189] Columbus (GA) Ledger, 11 March 1986.

[190] Atlanta Constitution, 11 March 1986.

[191] Columbus (GA) Enquirer, 25 March 1986.

[192] Columbus (GA) Ledger, 17 March 1986.

[193] Columbus (GA) Ledger-Enquirer, 13 April 1986.

[194] Ibid.

[195] Rose, David, *The Big Eddy Club* (New York: The New Press, 2007), 223.

[196] Columbus (GA) Ledger, 24 April 1986.

[197] Columbus (GA) Enquirer, 25 April 1986.

[198] Columbus (GA) Ledger, 24 April 1986.

[199] Columbus (GA) Ledger-Enquirer, 26 April 1986.

[200] Ibid., 27 April 1986.

[201] Columbus (GA) Enquirer, 29 April 1986.

[202] Ibid., 1 May 1986.

[203] Columbus (GA) Ledger, 10 June 1986.

[204] Columbus (GA) Enquirer, 13 June 1986.

[205] Ibid., 17 June 1986.

[206] Columbus (GA) Ledger, 19 June 1986.

[207] Columbus (GA) Enquirer, 19 June 1986.

[208] Ibid., 3 July 1986.

[209] Ibid., 8 July 1986.

[210] Ibid., 22 July 1986.

[211] Ibid., 25 July 1986.

[212] Columbus (GA) Enquirer, 29 July 1986.

[213] Columbus (GA) Ledger, 29 July 1986.

[214] Columbus (GA) Enquirer, 1 August 1986.

[215] Ibid., 5 August 1986.

[216] Columbus (GA) Ledger-Enquirer, 9 August 1986.

[217] Unless otherwise referenced, text in quotes is taken from trial transcripts.

[218] Columbus (GA) Enquirer, 21 August 1986.

[219] In counting the number of witnesses presented by the state, each separate testimony was counted as a single event. Some witnesses testified more than once, e.g., Dr. Joe Webber, the medical examiner who did autopsies on a number of the Strangler's victims.

[220] Columbus (GA) Enquirer, 26 August 1986.

[221] Ibid., 28 August 1986.

[222] Ibid., 29 August 1986.

[223] Columbus (GA) Enquirer, 29 August 1986.

[224] Ibid.

[225] Columbus (GA) Ledger, 27 August 1986.

[226] Ibid.

[227] Ibid., 28 August 1986.

[228] Ibid.

[229] Columbus (GA) Ledger-Enquirer, 31 August 1986.

[230] *Columbus (GA) Enquirer*, 9 September 1986.

[231] Ibid., 15 September 1986.

[232] Ibid., 4 September 1986.

[233] Ibid., 9 October 1986.

[234] Ibid., 12 November 1986.

[235] Columbus (GA) Ledger, 8 January 1987.

[236] Ibid., 22 January 1987.

[237] Columbus (GA) Enquirer, 27 March 1987.

[238] Columbus (GA) Ledger, 10 April 1987.

[239] Columbus (GA) Enquirer, 5 November 1987.

[240] Columbus (GA) Ledger-Enquirer, 7 November 1987.

[241] Columbus (GA) Enquirer, 13 November 1987.

[242] Ibid., 17 November 1987.

[243] Ibid., 6 January 1988.

[244] Ibid., 13 September 1989.

[245] Atlanta Journal-Constitution, 12 December 1993.

[246] Rose, *The Big Eddy Club* (2007 ed.), 298–300.

[247] From US Eleventh Circuit Court of Appeals, *Gary v. Hall*, decided 12 February 2009.

[248] Ibid.

[249] https://www.11alive.com/article/news/investigations/last-words-stocking-Strangler-talks-faith-innocence-and-truth-hours-before-execution/85-528753134 (Accessed 23 May 2021.)

[250] Rose, *The Big Eddy Club* (2007 ed.), 221.

[251] Atlanta Journal-Constitution, 13 May 2007.

[252] J. Mark Shelnutt, "The Rest of the Story" (lecture, St. Luke United Methodist Church, Columbus, GA, 22 August 2007).

[253] Ibid.

[254] Michael Sellers, interviewed by William Rawlings, Athens, Georgia, 21 May 2021.

[255] Syracuse (NY) Post-Standard, 30 June 1975.

[256] Ibid., 1 July 1975.

[257] https://www.syracuse.com/opinion/2018/12/da_fitzpatrick_1975_murder_marion_fisher_jack_fisher_seeking_justice_commentary.html (Accessed 16 May 2021.)

[258] Ibid.

[259] At times, Rose's publications have been questioned for their veracity. An example is the 2018 case of Sasha Wass, a British criminal attorney who was accused of legal malfeasance and "involvement in a criminal conspiracy" in an October 2016 "highly libelous article" written by Rose. The *Mail on Sunday* and the MailOnline "agreed to pay Ms. Wass substantial libel damages" and publish apologies in the paper (https://www.carter-ruck.com/wp-content/uploads/2020/04/WASS-Press_Release-120618.pdf, accessed 17 May 2021.) In 2017, Rose, writing for the *Daily Mail*, accused a British-born Pakistani man of acting as a "fixer" for pedophile cab drivers. A resulting lawsuit against Rose and the newspaper was settled for a large sum in favor of the accused man (https://www.thenews.com.pk/print/607316-david-rose-story-mail-loses-rs244m-defamation-case-to-pakistani-man, accessed 17 May 2021.) The interested reader is invited to further explore these cases and others via an internet search.

[260] Headline, *Macon (GA) Telegraph*, 4 December 2009.

[261] Columbus (GA) Ledger-Enquirer, 13 February 2009.

[262] Ibid., 1 December 2009.

[263] Atlanta Journal-Constitution, 8 December 2009.

[264] OCGA §5-5-41

[265] Columbus (GA) Ledger-Enquirer, 9 December 2009.

[266] Ibid., 11 December 2009.

[267] Ibid., 15 December 2009.

[268] Ibid., 16 December 2009.

[269] Ibid., 17 December 2009.

[270] Ibid.

[271] Columbus (GA) Ledger-Enquirer, 16 January 2010.

[272] Ibid., 22 March 2010.

[273] Ibid., 20 February 2010.

[274] Ibid., 23 February 2010.

[275] Ibid., 24 March 2010.

[276] Ibid., 14 December 2010.

[277] Ibid.

[278] Atlanta Journal-Constitution, 14 December 2010.

[279] Columbus (GA) Ledger-Enquirer, 15 December 2010.

[280] Ibid., 17 April 2011.

[281] Ibid., 20 April 2011.

[282] Ibid., 19 February 2011.

[283] Ibid., 21 December 2011.

[284] Atlanta Journal-Constitution, 7 March 2012.

[285] The digital version of article referenced was reviewed: https://www.dailymail.co.uk/news/article-2200236/Carlton-Gary-The-shocking-Death-Row-injustice-The-Stocking-Strangler.html (Accessed 12 September 2020.)

[286] Columbus (GA) Ledger-Enquirer, 21 November 2013.

[287] Ibid., 22 November 2013.

[288] Atlanta Journal-Constitution, 21 April 2011.

[289] Columbus (GA) Ledger-Enquirer, 5 January 2014.

[290] Ibid., 22 November 2013.

[291] From State's exhibit number 66, trial of *State v. Gary*, August 1986.

[292] Columbus (GA) Ledger-Enquirer, 28 February 2014.

[293] Ibid., 1 March 2014.

[294] Details and quotes are from an affidavit by Robert D. Grubbs, dated 13 January 2016.

[295] Columbus (GA) Ledger-Enquirer, 28 August 2016.

[296] "Seeds of Doubt," *Vanity Fair Confidential*, Season 3, Episode 4, originally aired 17 February 2017. (Accessed 5 June 2021. Video is available for purchase on Amazon Prime Video.)

[297] OCGA §15-6-21(b)

[298] OCGA §15-6-21(d)

[299] Columbus (GA) Ledger-Enquirer, 23 July 2017.

[300] Ibid., 2 September 2017.

[301] Ibid., 9 November 2017.

[302] Ibid., 15 November 2017.

[303] Atlanta Journal-Constitution, 6 January 2018.

[304] Columbus (GA) Ledger-Enquirer, 10 March 2018.

[305] Ibid., 14 March 2018.

[306] Ibid., 15 March 2018.

[307] Ibid., 17 March 2018.

[308] Ibid.

[309] Columbus (GA) Ledger-Enquirer, 15 July 1984.

Index